Studying for a Masters in T or Applied Linguistics

"This book will be extremely useful for students embarking on a TESOL or Applied Linguistics master's degree. It discusses areas and expectations which new students may not be familiar with and, importantly, gives sound advice on how to deal with them. I will be recommending it to my students!"
    Brian Paltridge, *Professor of TESOL, University of Sydney, Australia*

Studying for a Masters in TESOL or Applied Linguistics provides the definitive go-to text for all students studying an MA in TESOL or Applied Linguistics, as well as closely related degrees such as an MA in English Language Teaching. Written in a clear and user-friendly format and drawing on authentic and highly relevant source materials with the inclusion of practical tasks and answer keys for self-correction throughout, this book demystifies each stage of the MA TESOL/MA Applied Linguistics journey.

Covering practical programme components, such as lesson observation and teaching practice, this book helps the reader to develop the key skills required to successfully complete an MA including:

- How to effectively manage your time
- How to get the most out of your lectures
- How to develop effective reading skills
- How to become a better academic writer
- How to deal with various types of assessments
- How to deliver effective oral presentations

Guiding students step by step through the process of how to choose, research and then write a successful dissertation, this book closes with guidance and tips for students on how to proceed after completing an MA in TESOL/Applied Linguistics. This book is therefore essential reading for those contemplating or undertaking an MA in either of these areas.

Douglas E. Bell is currently Professor of Education at the University of Nottingham Ningbo China (UNNC) where he also directs and teaches on the MA TESOL. He has been involved in English and Modern Foreign Language teaching since the late 1980s and has a particular professional interest in TESOL, ESP and EAP.

Studying for a Masters in TESOL or Applied Linguistics
A Student Reference and Practical Guide

Douglas E. Bell

LONDON AND NEW YORK

Designed cover image: © Getty Images | jessicahyde

First published 2023
by Routledge
4 Park Square, Milton Park, Abingdon, Oxon OX14 4RN

and by Routledge
605 Third Avenue, New York, NY 10158

Routledge is an imprint of the Taylor & Francis Group, an informa business

© 2023 Douglas E. Bell

The right of Douglas E. Bell to be identified as author of this work has been asserted in accordance with sections 77 and 78 of the Copyright, Designs and Patents Act 1988.

All rights reserved. No part of this book may be reprinted or reproduced or utilised in any form or by any electronic, mechanical, or other means, now known or hereafter invented, including photocopying and recording, or in any information storage or retrieval system, without permission in writing from the publishers.

Trademark notice: Product or corporate names may be trademarks or registered trademarks, and are used only for identification and explanation without intent to infringe.

British Library Cataloguing-in-Publication Data
A catalogue record for this book is available from the British Library

Library of Congress Cataloging-in-Publication Data
Names: Bell, Douglas (Associate professor), author.
Title: Studying for a masters in TESOL or applied linguistics: a student reference and practical guide / Douglas E. Bell.
Description: Abingdon, Oxon; New York, NY: Routledge, 2023. | Includes bibliographical references and index. |
Identifiers: LCCN 2023004513 (print) | LCCN 2023004514 (ebook) |
Subjects: LCSH: English language—Study and teaching—Foreign speakers. | English language—Study and teaching (Higher) | Applied linguistics—Study and teaching (Higher)
Classification: LCC PE1128.A2 B438 2023 (print) |
LCC PE1128.A2 (ebook) | DDC 428.0071/1—dc23/eng/20230510
LC record available at https://lccn.loc.gov/2023004513
LC ebook record available at https://lccn.loc.gov/2023004514

ISBN: 978-1-032-21750-5 (hbk)
ISBN: 978-1-032-21749-9 (pbk)
ISBN: 978-1-003-26985-4 (ebk)

DOI: 10.4324/9781003269854

Typeset in Sabon
by codeMantra

Contents

Acknowledgements   x
Why This Book?   xi

1 Being an Effective Student in the Context of MA
TESOL/Applied Linguistics   1
    Introduction 1
  1.1 *What Should I Expect? What Will Others Expect of Me?* 1
  1.2 *Developing Effective Reading Strategies* 4
  1.3 *Planning Your Time* 12
  1.4 *Accessing Resources and Learning to Work Smart* 14
  1.5 *Identifying Sources of Support* 18
    Additional Resources for Further Reading 23
    Chapter References 23

2 Academic Speaking and Listening   27
    Introduction 27
  2.1 *Contexts Involving Academic Speaking* 27
    2.1.1 *Academic Speaking in Groups and Seminars* 29
    2.1.2 *Academic Speaking in Oral Presentations* 30
  2.2 *Contexts Involving Academic Listening* 40
    Additional Resources for Further Reading 47

3 Using Academic Sources   48
    Introduction 48
  3.1 *Why Do I Need Academic Sources?* 48
  3.2 *Plagiarism and How to Avoid It* 51
  3.3 *Avoiding Other Common Forms of Academic Misconduct* 52
  3.4 *Paraphrasing* 54

Contents

- 3.5 Making Citations 59
- 3.6 Direct Quotations 59
  - 3.6.1 A Few More Things to Be Aware Of and Pay Particular Attention To 63
- 3.7 Bringing It All Together 65
- 3.8 Compiling a Reference List or Bibliography 67
- 3.9 Different Academic Style Conventions 70
- Additional Resources for Further Reading 76
- Chapter References 76

4 Becoming a More Confident and Proficient Academic Writer 79
- Introduction 79
- 4.1 Fundamental Features of Effective Academic Writing 79
  - 4.1.1 The Importance of Clear Structuring 79
  - 4.1.2 Use of the First Person 81
  - 4.1.3 Hedging and the Avoidance of Sweeping Generalisations 81
  - 4.1.4 Use of Appropriate Academic Lexis 83
  - 4.1.5 Supporting All Claims with Evidence 85
- 4.2 Building a Coherent Academic Argument 85
- Additional Resources for Further Reading 92
- Chapter References 92

5 Dealing with Different Types of Written Coursework Assignments 93
- Introduction 93
- 5.1 Dealing with Academic Essays 93
  - 5.1.1 'Compare and Contrast' Type Essays 93
  - 5.1.2 'Discussing a Quotation' Type Essays 100
  - 5.1.3 'Critically Evaluate' Type Essays 103
- 5.2 Dealing with Linguistic Analysis Tasks 103
  - 5.2.1 Which Dimensions of a Text Should I Analyse? 104
  - 5.2.2 What Form Should a Textual Analysis Take? 107
- 5.3 Dealing with Reflective Writing Tasks 109
  - 5.3.1 The Difference between Description and Critical Reflection 110
- 5.4 Marking Criteria 112
- Additional Resources for Further Reading 118
- Chapter References 118

6 Teaching Observation and Practice   120
Introduction 120
- 6.1 The Relationship between Theory and Practice 120
- 6.2 Teaching Observation 123
  - 6.2.1 Observation Tools and Mechanisms 123
  - 6.2.2 The Observation Cycle 126
- 6.3 Lesson Planning 128
  - 6.3.1 Different Conceptualisations of Lessons 128
  - 6.3.2 Different 'Ingredients' in Lessons 130
  - 6.3.3 Approaches to Writing Lesson Plans 131
- 6.4 Teaching Practice 131
  - 6.4.1 Peer Micro-Teaching 133
  - 6.4.2 Team Teaching/Teaching Your Own Class 134
- 6.5 The Importance of Critical Reflection 134

Additional Resources for Further Reading 138
Chapter References 138

7 Planning Your Dissertation   140
Introduction 140
- 7.1 Choosing a Suitable Topic 140
  - 7.1.1 Where Do I Begin? 140
  - 7.1.2 How Should I Manage My Time? 151
- 7.2 Deciding on an Appropriate Research Paradigm 154
  - 7.2.1 Understanding Ontology and Epistemology 155
  - 7.2.2 Quantitative or Qualitative? 156
  - 7.2.3 Mixed Methods 157
- 7.3 Completing a Formal Proposal 158
- 7.4 What to Expect from Your Supervisor 160
  - 7.4.1 Some Tips for Getting the Most Out of the Supervisor-Supervisee Relationship 161

Additional Resources for Further Reading 170
Chapter References 170

8 Writing Up Your Dissertation Part I   172
Introduction 172
- 8.1 Dissertation Structure and Length 172
  - 8.1.1 Rhetorical Purpose 174
  - 8.1.2 The Importance of Effective Signposting 176
- 8.2 Writing Chapter 1: The Introduction 177

8.3 Writing Chapter 2: The Literature Review 183
8.4 Writing Chapter 3: The Methodology 192
    8.4.1 Quantitative Forms of Research Methodology 193
    8.4.2 Qualitative Forms of Research Methodology 193
    8.4.3 Approaches to Data Coding 197
    8.4.4 Ethical Considerations 199
    8.4.5 Reflexivity 200
    8.4.6 Some Closing Reminders 201
Additional Resources for Further Reading 208
Chapter References 208

9 Writing Up Your Dissertation Part II   211
Introduction 211
9.1 Writing Chapter 4: Results 211
    9.1.1 Presenting Quantitative Results 213
    9.1.2 Presenting Qualitative Results 215
9.2 Writing Chapter 5: Discussion 220
9.3 Writing Chapter 6: Conclusion 223
    9.3.1 A Note on Summarising 223
    9.3.2 Acknowledging Strengths and Limitations 225
    9.3.3 Recommendations for Future Action 227
9.4 Beginnings: Acknowledgements and Abstracts 229
9.5 Endings: Appendices 233
9.6 Final Considerations 235
9.7 Proofreading 239
Additional Resources for Further Reading 243
Chapter References 244

10 Life Beyond Your Masters   245
Introduction 245
10.1 Going on to Further Study 245
    10.1.1 Doing a PhD or an EdD 246
    10.1.2 Doing Other Qualifications 249
10.2 Going Back to Work 251
    10.2.1 Updating Your CV 251
    10.2.2 Jobs Using TESOL and Applied Linguistics 253
    10.2.3 The Traditional Job Search vs. the Creative Job Search 254
    10.2.4 Working in the Higher Education Sector 257

10.3 *Continuing Professional Development* 258
      10.3.1 *Publishing Your Dissertation* 258
      10.3.2 *Presenting at Conferences* 259
      10.3.3 *Finding Your Professional Niche* 260
10.4 *Closing Thoughts* 261
     Additional Resources for Further Reading 266
     Chapter References 266

A List of Common Journals for TESOL and Applied Linguistics   267
A List of Useful Professional Organisations   269
Index   271

Acknowledgements

Producing a book of this nature could never only be a sole effort and I would be remiss if I failed to acknowledge the various people whose generous support and expertise I have drawn upon along the way. To begin, I must give my grateful thanks to the editorial team at Routledge, first for accepting my initial proposal and agreeing for this book to go ahead, then for their ongoing support and guidance during the actual writing process. It was always reassuring to know that if ever I needed it, their help was only an email or phone call away.

Next, I must thank the many MA TESOL and Applied Linguistics students I have encountered during my career as an international educator. Teaching such students, talking to them about the daily academic challenges they face and being very closely involved in the production and assessment of their work have each played an important role in shaping the content of this book. Over two decades ago, when I first completed an MA of my own, a book like this basically did not exist and I can vividly remember what it felt like to be blindly feeling my way, learning what I was supposed to do via a very hit-and-miss process of trial and error, mostly error. It is my sincere hope that by having now written this book, the MA study journey for those who are kind enough to read it will be made significantly more transparent and also somewhat smoother.

Not surprisingly perhaps, my final thanks and heartfelt appreciation must go to my ever-patient and supportive wife and daughter. Committing myself to yet another extended writing project meant that most of the evenings and weekends over the past 12 months, which should have been spent with them, instead saw me locked away in my study, hunched over a computer. Now that this book is complete, I can only hope they will be happy with the outcome and agree with me that it was all worth it.

Douglas Bell, Ningbo China, 2023

Why This Book?

I have been involved in English Language Teaching now for nearly 36 years. For a significant chunk of that time, I have worked as a teacher trainer and educator on a wide range of certificate, diploma, undergraduate and postgraduate courses, representing an even wider range of international settings. Beyond the various roles I have held in my home country the UK, my career-based travels to date have taken me to locations as geographically diverse as Austria, Japan, Turkey, the United States, Australia and, for the past half-decade, the People's Republic of China. My involvement in postgraduate training programmes in several of these locations, most notably on courses such as MA TESOL and MA Applied Linguistics, has brought me into contact with students of many diverse ability levels and nationalities. While there have undoubtedly been many differences between these groups, one thing that all of these students have had in common are the challenges they have faced when first joining postgraduate-level study. This has been particularly true in the case of students studying their MAs in EMI environments while using English as a second or foreign language.

When trying to guide my Masters students and direct them to appropriate self-access material for their independent study, I have repeatedly been struck by the relative lack of books which deal directly with how to study for MA TESOL and MA Applied Linguistics. While there are quite a few *general* study guides out there now, I would contend that most of these tend to approach academic study as if it were a monolithic concept, with no clear distinctions being made between the demands of different academic disciplines, or what it means to study at the undergraduate or postgraduate levels. I have found that it can thus be quite difficult for students to make the necessary connections between the advice they are given in such books and the day-to-day practicalities which they then face in their own MA programmes. A further issue is that while most of the generic books on developing academic study skills are usually not short on offering their readers platitudes on what to do or what *not* to do, they are significantly much less forthcoming in providing any explicit guidance and practice in *how exactly* students should go about achieving this. In short, there is usually a very noticeable gap between theory and practice. To my own mind, simply *telling* someone that they should prepare well for something is actually of very limited use, unless there are also detailed explanations and some well-scaffolded practice activities to illustrate what exactly such preparation might consist of when viewed in more practical terms.

Conceptually, this book therefore sets out to be rather different.

I have tried to break down each stage and sub-stage of the MA TESOL or MA Applied Linguistics study journey from start to finish, with the intention of showing you exactly what you should expect. Each chapter deals with common elements of what you will most typically encounter during your Masters-level studies and you are encouraged to check your understanding of this material at each stage of the way by completing a series of independent tasks. Some suggested answers for many of these tasks are provided to allow for your self-assessment and a personal progress check, and at the end of each chapter, additional resources have also been suggested for your further reference and study.

Throughout this book, the topics and texts have all been drawn from authentic TESOL/Applied Linguistics materials and contexts. In designing things this way, my intention has been that this should then allow you to make relevant and hopefully highly transferable connections between the knowledge and skills you will develop in this book and the issues you will later, or concurrently, be studying on your MA. There is, of course, more than just one way to approach academic study and it goes without saying that individual MA TESOL/Applied Linguistics programmes may also differ from institution to institution. However, if you take the time to systematically work through the material and tasks presented in this book, I am confident that by the end, you will have a much better idea of what your MA TESOL/Applied Linguistics is likely to require of you and will thus be in a position to get more out of your studies and achieve higher grades.

Let your Masters journey commence ….

"A journey of a thousand li [a Chinese mile] starts beneath one's feet"

(Chinese saying allegedly taken from the Tao Te Ching manuscript circa 4–6 BC)

1 Being an Effective Student in the Context of MA TESOL/Applied Linguistics

Introduction

This opening chapter considers what it means to be an effective postgraduate student in TESOL/Applied Linguistics. It begins with a brief discussion of how such Masters' programmes are typically structured and delivered, which will give you a better idea of what to expect. It then introduces you to some specific self-study techniques, makes some recommendations about what constitutes successful time management and suggests some different avenues you can explore for academic and pastoral support. Throughout, this chapter encourages you to reflect critically on how to get the absolute most from your studies.

Additional resources for your further reading are listed on page 23.

1.1 What Should I Expect? What Will Others Expect of Me?

As a prospective or newly enrolled student on an MA TESOL/Applied Linguistics programme, you may only have a vague idea of what now lies ahead of you. This is *especially* likely to be the case if you are studying your Masters in a different country, in a second language or have joined an educational environment which is different to any that you have experienced before. It is therefore well worth you starting this book by thinking about what you should expect, as well as raising your critical awareness of what others are likely to expect of you.

Most British Masters' courses are built around a framework of 180 academic credits, which is then divided up into different taught modules. The size of individual modules will differ from institution to institution, but a very common model in the UK academic context is to have each individual taught module representing 20 credits. Under this configuration, in order to be awarded their Masters, students are required to successfully complete six taught modules (which together represent 120 credits) and then produce an independently written dissertation (normally weighted at 60 credits). I will be considering the dissertation stage of the Masters in quite some detail in Chapters 7, 8 and 9, but for now, let us remain focused on the taught module components.

If your Masters' programme requires you to complete six taught modules, then it is very likely that three of these will be considered 'core' and the remainder will be seen as 'electives'. As the name suggests, core modules deal with subject matter which the course designers have decided are essential to the study of an MA TESOL/Applied Linguistics, while the electives are intended to allow students some individual choice and to provide an opportunity for their specialisation in areas of particular interest.

As always, there are likely to be some slight variations from institution to institution, but if your Masters' programme has modules designated as 'core', then it is usually the case that these will need to be successfully passed in order to earn the final Master's degree. In some contexts, successful completion of core modules may even be designated as a stage 1 prerequisite before students are allowed to proceed to studying their electives. For this reason, most Masters' programmes which follow a core + elective model tend to cluster the delivery of their core modules in the first semester, as this then allows for such staging to take place. Under this type of degree structure, the first semester essentially becomes a qualifying round, which students must successfully pass in order to proceed.

In the case of the MA TESOL programme in my own institution, the first taught semester currently looks like this:

MA TESOL Core Module Structure

3 × core modules worth 20 credits each:

- Applied Linguistics for TESOL
- Developments in Language Teaching Methodology
- Research Methods in TESOL & Applied Linguistics

In deciding to structure the course in this way, my academic colleagues and I were in agreement that an understanding of different aspects of Applied Linguistics, approaches to language teaching methodology and an awareness of relevant research methods together constitute a fundamental professional knowledge base for TESOL. Other MA TESOL programmes may be configured slightly differently, but at some stage in their overall structure, I think all will be quite likely to cover aspects of these three key areas.

If you are a full-time student enrolled on a one-year Masters' degree which runs from September to September, you can expect to cover the first three modules in Semester 1, the next three modules in Semester 2, and then concurrently be working on your dissertation sometime between the early weeks of Semester 2 and the end of August. Although a full calendar year might seem like a very long time, you will soon discover that in practice, it passes extremely quickly. This means that developing good time management skills and learning how to get the optimum return on your study time becomes absolutely vital. I will be returning to consider the issue of effective time management skills in more detail in a later section.

Semester 1 modules are likely to run for anywhere from 10 to 15 consecutive weeks. The relationship between credits and contact teaching hours may differ from institution to institution, but 20 credit modules usually equate to three to four hours of taught classroom contact time each week. This means that if you are taking three modules at the same time, you can expect your weekly classroom contact time with lecturers to be in the region of 9–12 hours. Most of my own MA students initially find this very surprising, as they are much more used to an educational system in which taught classes account for 18–25 hours of their working week. However, two things must be kept in mind here. The first is that an MA TESOL/Applied Linguistics is a *postgraduate*, not an undergraduate qualification; postgraduate courses typically have much fewer taught hours. The second is that while 9–12 hours of classroom contact each week might *seem* very little, this time does not include all the necessary reading and background preparation which students are expected to do by themselves. If you are going to do your MA studies justice, then it is no exaggeration to say that those 9–12 hours will almost certainly need to be doubled or even trebled. If you are doing everything that you are *supposed* to be doing as a diligent postgraduate student, then consistently putting in *at least* a 24-hour study week should become the norm. Once you start working on your coursework assignments, it is also worth noting that this number of hours will undoubtedly increase.

A further point worth drawing your attention to is the style of teaching and classroom delivery. Having stated above that a 20-credit module typically equates to a classroom contact time of three to four hours each week, there can often be some variance in the way that these hours are then divided up. In some institutions, there will be a weekly one-hour or 90-minute lecture which *all* students attend, with the rest of the time then taken up by small group seminars. Other institutions may dispense with this large lecture + small seminar group format and simply deliver all of their postgraduate teaching as a series of three- to four-hour interactive input sessions. Much of this will come down to how many students are enrolled on your MA programme in the first place, and then logistical considerations around staff and room availability. In terms of preparing for the lecture and seminar content, I will be examining some of the finer details of what you should expect in Chapter 2.

Before I close this introductory section, one final point worth discussing here relates to what may be expected of you regarding attendance. Once again, institutions are likely to differ in their approaches to this. For some MA TESOL/Applied Linguistics programmes, maintaining regularly documented student attendance records is part of their course/institutional policy and penalties may be imposed if students are frequently absent without leave. In my own institution, for example, an electronic attendance register is formally taken at the beginning of each taught session, and over the course of a given semester, students must maintain an attendance profile of at least 80%. More than two consecutive absences without an accompanying justification usually trigger a warning letter from the School Senior Tutor. In situations like this, if the unexplained absences continue, the consequences might become more severe, and a student could even be asked to unenrol from the programme. Other institutions may take a more relaxed view of attendance, particularly as it is usually recognised that postgraduate students tend to be older than undergraduates and are likely to have other life commitments beyond their studies. That said, if you have decided to enrol on a full-time MA TESOL/Applied Linguistics programme and have made the necessary personal sacrifices which such a decision undoubtedly entails, then to my own mind, there should be very little point in you squandering the opportunity by not regularly attending the lectures and seminars. As I will be discussing throughout this chapter, having made the commitment to begin studying at the postgraduate level, you should now be fully applying yourself and trying to gain as much from the experience as you possibly can.

Check Your Understanding: Independent Task 1.1

A student enrols full-time on an MA TESOL programme. Her original plan was to stop working for the entire year of her studies, but when she gets her Semester 1 timetable, she is very surprised to see that she only has nine hours of classes: three hours on Monday afternoons, three hours on Tuesday mornings and three hours on Friday mornings. The student immediately goes back to the private language school she was working for and agrees to take on 12 hours of paid teaching with them. These hours are then spread over Wednesdays, Thursdays and Friday afternoons.

Has this student made a wise decision? If you were one of her tutors, what advice would you give her?

A suggested answer to this task has been provided on page 20.

1.2 Developing Effective Reading Strategies

When you begin an MA TESOL/Applied Linguistics, you are very likely to be given recommended reading lists for each of your modules. These are usually quite lengthy, and for the uninitiated, at first glance they can seem overwhelming. It is absolutely essential, therefore, that you quickly develop a set of effective reading strategies.

The first of these strategies comes in deciding which reading is essential and which is optional. Even the most diligent student in the world would be unlikely to have enough time to read absolutely *everything*, so you need to be able to prioritise. At the beginning, your course tutors may give you some help with this, highlighting on their reading lists what the most useful texts are and those which should be consulted first. However, you must not rely on this. It is far better that you learn to develop such critical awareness for yourself, as this will then stand you in good stead later, when you come to do your dissertation Literature Review (see Chapter 8).

When deciding what represents essential reading and what can safely be put aside for another time, much will depend on your reading purpose. Clearly there is a very big difference between perusing a series of journal articles as background reading for general interest, and scouring the literature for specific information to help you complete a written assignment.

When deciding how to prioritise your reading, you will need to keep some core principles in mind. One of the first things you must gauge is how *relevant* the work is to your interests and needs. In the case of journal articles, this is where abstracts play a vital role. Rather than straightaway reading an article from start to finish, you should begin by skimming the abstract, as this will provide you with a synopsis of the work in its entirety. Based on your understanding of this, you can then decide whether the article merits being read immediately, put aside for later or simply rejected. When it comes to books, you can go through a similar process by scanning the table of contents and then skimming individual chapters. In each case, the same principle applies: rather than reading everything word by word, you should be aiming to be much more discerning in your approach and trying to prioritise.

Another important criterion you can apply to books and articles is to look at their publication dates. As I will comment at different times in this book, as a general rule of thumb, when you are engaging with academic texts you should be drawing on sources *which are as recent as possible*. A common failing that I find in many of my own MA students' work is that they end up relying on texts which are massively out of date. In the case of our core module on Developments in Language Teaching Methodology, for example, it is not uncommon for me to find students citing academic sources they have found which date back to the 1950s and 1960s. In these cases, students may have been seduced by the apparent relevance of the article or book title, without considering the age of the text. To apply a medical analogy here, a treatise on how physicians should cure headaches from the early 1900s might well have been highly relevant and cutting edge in its day, but other than using it as an example from history, there would be very little point in you quoting from such a treatise in 2023. This is because things in medicine have obviously moved on, our understanding of the field has deepened and a lot has changed. This example has been deliberately over-stated to underline my point, but it is surprising how many students still manage to fall into this trap. When you are prioritising what to read, it is therefore essential that you take *both* the perceived relevance of the title and the publication dates into consideration.

Once you have chosen a given text and decided that you are going to read it, you then need to be strategic in the *manner* in which that reading is carried out. This becomes particularly important if English is not your first language. If you set out to read everything line by line and word by word (in the way that you might if you were reading a novel or magazine article for pleasure) you are not going to make very rapid progress. This is especially true if you are using English as a second language and find that you have to check the meaning of every other word in a dictionary. Under these conditions, the task of reading will soon become very laborious and highly de-motivating. Even for fluent native speakers of English, rather than approaching the reading of each text on a word by word basis, you should be training yourself to become proficient in skimming and scanning. How you apply these skills in practice will be dependent on your underlying purpose for reading. In the case of the texts mentioned below in Independent Task 1.2a, for example, if I decided to read the first named source on the list, the book chapter by my friend and colleague Professor Bob Adamson, I would be skimming and scanning to pull out the most salient points he makes on trends in language teaching methodology. Similarly, if I was reading the oft-cited article on the list by Prabhu (1990), my main objective would be to identify *why* he was arguing that there is no best method and then noting the evidence he had provided in support of this. In each of these cases, as the underlying purpose has been to gain a fuller picture of how approaches and attitudes to language teaching methodology have changed, it follows that the style of reading needs to keep those objectives firmly in mind from the outset. This then means that much of the text can be filtered out. If you are a purposeful reader, you will only need to concern yourself with certain aspects.

Check Your Understanding: Independent Task 1.2a

You have just enrolled on the module Developments in Language Teaching Methodology and have attended the first session. Your lecturer has distributed the introductory reading list below. Which of these 20 sources should you prioritise in your reading and why?

Adamson, B. (2004). Fashions in language teaching methodology. In A. Davies & C. Elder (Eds.) *The Handbook of Applied Linguistics* (pp. 605–622). Blackwell.

Arnold, J., Dörnyei, Z. & Pugliese, C. (2015). *The Principled Communicative Approach: Seven Criteria for Success*. Helbling Languages.

Bell, D.E. (2022). Methodology in EAP: Why is it largely still an overlooked issue? *Journal of English for Academic Purposes, 55*, https://doi.org/10.1016/j.jeap.2021.101073.

Bell, D.M. (2007). Do teachers think that methods are dead? *ELT Journal, 61*(2), 135–143.

Dalal, G. & Gulati, V. (Eds.) (2018). *Innovations in English Language Teaching in India: Trends in Language Pedagogy and Technology*. Lexington Books.

Flowerdew, J. (1993). Content-based language instruction in a tertiary setting. *English for Specific Purposes, 12*(2), 121–138.

Hall, G. (2011). *Exploring English Language Teaching. Language in Action*. Routledge.

Hanks, J. (2017). *Exploratory Practice in Language Teaching: Puzzling about Principles and Practices*. Palgrave Macmillan.

Kumaravadivelu, B. (2006a). TESOL methods: Changing tracks, challenging trends. *TESOL Quarterly, 40*(1), 59–81.

Kumaravadivelu, B. (2006b). *Understanding Language Teaching: From Method to Postmethod*. Lawrence Erlbaum.

Kumaravadivelu, B. (2001). Toward a postmethod pedagogy. *TESOL Quarterly, 35*(4), 537–560.

Lin, A. (2013). Towards paradigmatic change in TESOL methodologies: Building plurilingual pedagogies from the ground up. *TESOL Quarterly, 47*(3), 521–545.

Long, M.H. (2005). Methodological issues in learner needs analysis. In M.H. Long (Ed.) *Second Language Needs Analysis* (p. 99). Cambridge University Press.

Mazak, C.M. (2017). *Translanguaging in Higher Education: Beyond Monolingual Ideologies*. Channel View Publications.

McDonough, J. & Shaw, C. (1993). *Materials and Methods in ELT*. Blackwell.

Prabhu, N.S. (1990). There is no best method - Why? *TESOL Quarterly, 24*(2), 161–176.

Richards, J.C. & Rodgers, T.S. (2014). *Approaches and Methods in Language Teaching* (3rd ed.). Cambridge University Press.

Spiro, J. (2013). *Changing Methodologies in TESOL*. Edinburgh University Press.

Thornbury, S. (2017). *Scott Thornbury's 30 Language Teaching Methods*. Cambridge Handbooks for Language Teachers. Cambridge University Press.

Zulfikar, Z. (2018). Rethinking the use of L1 in the L2 classroom. *Englisia, 6*(1), 43–51.

A suggested answer to this task has been provided on page 20.

If English is not your first language, then becoming proficient in these skills is obviously going to be somewhat more challenging than if English is your mother tongue, but nonetheless, it is well worth you investing the time in their development. One of the core tenets of becoming an effective academic reader is that you need to be able to skim through an article or book chapter quite quickly and extract the main points. This is an ability which takes *practice*, and this goes back to my earlier point about the need for you to allow adequate time. In the downtime between your lectures and seminars, systematically training yourself to become proficient in these academy literacy skill areas should therefore be one of your key objectives.

In addition to developing the skill of skimming and scanning, in becoming an effective reader in academic contexts, you also need to devise strategies for keeping an accurate record of what you have read. Clearly, there would be very little point in you reading lots of books and articles, if you were then later unable to recall the content and apply it effectively to your studies. In this regard, mastering the art of note-taking and record keeping also becomes vital. There are many approaches to taking notes and you will need to find a system which works well for you (you can get some different ideas on this by consulting one of the many self-help books on academic skills development, so search in your university library catalogue to source some possible titles), but one specific information gathering technique I encourage my own students to develop is that of mind-mapping.

First popularised by the educationalist Tony Buzan in the 1970s, mind maps can be an extremely powerful note-taking technique which allow readers to capture and record key information in a highly accessible format, which then lends itself well to easy retrieval and comprehension later. I find that mind maps can be *particularly* suitable if you are trying to keep a record of a reading which covers many different aspects of a given topic area. For example, if you had been reading a piece of *academic research which had investigated the different reasons why students choose to invest in MA TESOL/Applied Linguistics qualifications, this information might then be represented in the mind map which is shown in the box below.

There are several points worth commenting on here. First of all, note how the mind-map format allows you to capture lots of different information at a glance. In terms of data processing, this makes it highly efficient. The mind map also lets you break down the information into relevant sets and sub-sets. Each of the four main headings, for example (the shaded bubbles), then branches off to include three sub-headings (the unshaded bubbles). Depending on the level of detail the mind-map creator wants to include,

---

* NB. These sources have been created here as an example only. The actual academic references in this case are not real.

Being an Effective Student in the Context of TESOL/Applied Linguistics 9

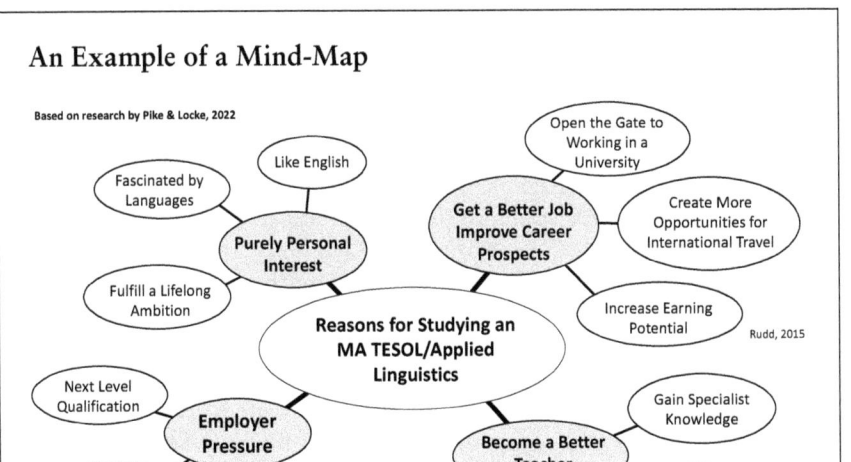

some of these sub-headings could then possibly be broken down even further. Finally, note how a record of the specific research studies mentioned by the authors Pike and Locke (though all completely fictitious in this case) have been listed next to the relevant points. This means that in total in this example, the findings of five different research studies have been successfully summarised and captured.

As I hope it will be apparent from the above, mind-mapping allows you to create a compact and easily accessible information summary. If you can become proficient in their creation and start to use mind maps regularly, you will soon build up a personal data bank to represent the extent of your academic reading throughout your MA studies. Such records will later become invaluable when you come to tackle your coursework assignments and need to access academic research information quickly and efficiently.

Check Your Understanding: Independent Task 1.2b

Based on the academic writing excerpt below, create a mind map titled 'Reasons for the Growth & Development of ESP/EAP'.

In surveying what the academic literature has had to say about the birth and early development of EAP, one immediate difficulty comes in distinguishing between the events that belong solely to the history of EAP, and those pertaining to the history of ESP more broadly. There is somewhat of a paradox here, in that while the majority of the early ESP work was university-based and therefore academic in nature, such activity was nonetheless labelled and categorised as being ESP rather than EAP, a blurring of the boundaries which has occasionally still persisted into the modern era (e.g. Hewings, 2001). In seeking to unpick the specifics of EAP's birth and early development, it is appropriate, therefore, to start with a history of ESP in general.

There is now strong agreement from the various writers who have commented on the birth and subsequent development of ESP (e.g. Mackay & Mountford, 1978; Hutchinson & Waters, 1987; Johns & Dudley-Evans, 1991; Robinson, 1991; Dudley-Evans & St John, 1998; Swales, 2000; Basturkmen, 2006; Hyland, 2006a; Belcher, 2009; Paltridge, 2011; Johns, 2013; Paltridge & Starfield, 2013) that its initial emergence took place during the 1960s and the early 1970s.

However, in understanding the specific conditions which would allow ESP's birth to occur, it is first necessary to go back almost two decades earlier, to the end of the Second World War in 1945. As a number of writers have commented (e.g. Hutchinson & Waters, 1987; Robinson, 1991; Flowerdew & Peacock, 2001; Starfield, 2013), the immediate post-war years witnessed a massive international expansion in terms of science, technology and economic activity. The expansion of these areas, in turn, created a demand for a common international language, a demand which would ultimately be met by English (Graddol, 1997; Flowerdew & Peacock, 2001).

Those commenting on this period (e.g. Kachru, 1985; Kennedy, 1987; Crystal, 1997; Graddol, 1997; McCrum, 2010) have suggested a range of factors as contributing to the emergence of English as the dominant world language, but all are in general agreement that the growth and ultimate hegemony of English around the world today can fundamentally be traced to the post-Second World War economic strength of those countries where English was spoken as the first language.

As a by-product of English assuming its role as the common international language, it is also generally agreed that the demand for training in English then generated a new type of English language learner. Students now needed access to the English language, not only for pleasure, aesthetic reasons or their personal fulfilment, but because competency in English was perceived to be the key with which they could access mainstream science, technology and commerce (Hutchinson & Waters, 1987; Starfield, 2013). Trade and other forms of international collaboration are much more likely to be successful, after all, if the supplier and customer are able to communicate using the same language (Graddol, 1997). Broadly speaking, it was in catering to these particular types of learning demands that the early development of ESP as a new branch of English Language Teaching initially took place (Hutchinson & Waters, 1987; Robinson, 1991; Dudley-Evans & St John, 1998).

In its very early stages, it is agreed that ESP was dominated by a particularly heavy focus on English for Science and Technology (EST). For most practitioners at that time, developments in EST were seen to be leading the way, and setting the trend for developments in ESP more broadly (Swales, 1985). As a number of writers have argued since (e.g. Coffey, 1984; Hutchinson & Waters, 1987; de Chazal, 2014), this dominance of EST in the early days of ESP probably owed much to the growth of oil industries in parts of the Middle East and in North Africa, which had together caused:

> a demand explosion... where could be found huge financial resources under national control, proliferating technological needs, an insufficiency of existing English-learning facilities and a degree of dependence upon expatriate expertise...
> (Coffey, 1984, p. 3)

However, by the 1970s, there were also some signs of steady growth in the numbers of students studying at English medium universities for whom English was not their first language (Hamp-Lyons, 2011b), and it was largely from *this* background, and in attempting to meet the sheer volume of *these* demands, that EAP gradually began to emerge as a more distinctive sub-branch of ESP (Flowerdew & Peacock, 2001; Hamp-Lyons, 2011b; de Chazel, 2014).

Further support for this argument has been provided by Kennedy (2001), who emphasises 'a strong link between the use of English in specialized domains (and hence EAP students who need to gain access to those domains)...' (p. 27). It may also be argued that the emergence and subsequent flowering of EAP was boosted by what de Chazel has termed 'the academicization of ESP' (2014), in other words, that with the increasing emphasis on professionalisation and specialisation, a growth in the demand for formal academic qualifications was created, which in turn resulted in greater numbers of students attending courses at universities. This has particularly held true for international students enrolling at universities whose medium of instruction is English (EMI). Indeed, the post-1960s boom in international students attending English medium universities has continued largely unabated to the present day, and can be seen as a significant factor in accelerating the expansion of EAP worldwide (Johns & Dudley-Evans, 1991; Flowerdew & Peacock, 2001; Hamp-Lyons, 2011b; de Chazal, 2014).

> Adapted from Bell, D.E. (2016). Practitioners, pedagogies, and professionalism in English for Academic Purposes (EAP): The development of a contested field. Unpublished PhD diss., University of Nottingham, UK.

A suggested answer to this task has been provided on page 22.

1.3 Planning Your Time

As I stated earlier in this chapter, being able to manage your time well is a vital skill for postgraduate students. Although you may think that an academic year is quite an extended period, in reality, it soon flashes by and if you are not paying close attention your MA experience will be over almost before you know it. *From Day 1* of your studies, therefore, you need to be thinking about how to get the most out of the limited time available to you. This means that you need to become acutely aware of both time and project management.

One of the key hallmarks of effective time and project management is the ability to identify goals and staging posts. Large tasks should always be broken down into smaller more achievable tasks and then matched with appropriate completion milestones. When setting these milestones, it is often a good idea to start by looking at the desired end point and then work backwards. In the case of Semester 1, for example, if you are enrolled on three different modules, then this most likely means that you will have three different sets of assessments. These may be coursework based, or they may take the form of end-of-semester exams. In either case, however, you should look at the date when these are scheduled to take place and then work backwards from those points to establish a completion timeline and start setting yourself appropriate goals.

If I use the 2022 first semester of my own institution's MA TESOL as an example, where 100% of the Semester 1 assessment is currently coursework based, this process might look something like the timeline shown in the box below.

As this schedule illustrates, every week of the first semester is fully accounted for in terms of the preparatory self-study which should be going on behind the scenes. There are a few specific aspects of this worth commenting on. Beyond the creation of a timeline and the setting of specific milestones, another key component of effective time management involves the ability to multi-task and keep several plates spinning at the same time. When you have multiple commitments and deadlines to meet, it is vital

An Example of a Coursework Completion Schedule

Module	Applied Linguistics for TESOL	Developments in Language Teaching Methodology	Research Methods in TESOL & Applied Linguistics
Assessment	4000 word essay **due on Dec 13**	4000 word essay **due on Dec 14**	Oral presentation **on Dec 12** 3000 word essay **on Dec 19**
w/c Dec 12	Final checks - submit essay on Dec 13	Final checks - submit essay on Dec 14	Deliver oral presentation on Dec 12. Do final checks then submit essay on Dec 19
w/c Dec 5	Refine and polish draft of essay	Refine and polish draft of essay	Refine oral presentation Complete draft of essay
w/c Nov 28	Complete draft of essay	Refine and polish draft of essay	Draft oral presentation
w/c Nov 21	Work on writing essay	Complete draft of essay	Work on oral presentation
w/c Nov 14	Work on writing essay	Work on writing essay	Work on writing essay
w/c Nov 7	Work on writing essay	Work on writing essay	Work on writing essay
w/c Oct 31	Work on writing essay	Work on writing essay	Work on writing essay
w/c Oct 24	Work on writing essay	Work on writing essay	Work on writing essay
w/c Oct 17	Draft essay framework	Draft essay framework	Draft essay framework
w/c Oct 10	Gather core literature	Gather core literature	Gather core literature
w/c Oct 3	Gather core literature	Gather core literature	Gather core literature
w/c Sept 26	Choose which essay	Choose which essay	Choose which essay

that you are able to do this. You will rarely have the luxury of dealing with tasks in a linear fashion and completing one before you start another. It is far more common to find yourself having to work on a number of projects *simultaneously*. This is readily apparent from the schedule above, where the preparatory work on the assessments for all three modules needs to be continuing apace. This is somewhat extra complicated by the fact that the Research Methods module has two separate pieces of coursework assessment rather than just one. If (as some of my students sometimes misguidedly do) a writer decided to work on each individual module assessment one at a time, and only progress from one to the other when the first had been completed, it would be very difficult indeed, if not downright impossible, to get everything completed in the time available. The lesson here should now be clear: learn to multi-task and build this dimension into all of your time management considerations.

Another point worth commenting on above is the time allocated to background reading. As I discussed in the previous section, one of the major drains on your time as a postgraduate student will be the process of accessing and then digesting the relevant academic literature. Once you have decided which coursework essays you are going to attempt (most MA programmes will give you some choice in this matter) your next step should be gathering together the relevant sources. In the timeline above, I have suggested the allocation of at least two full weeks for this process, but this is a very conservative estimate and more time might be needed, especially if you are finding it difficult to locate and access the resources you require (see section 1.4 below). I will be suggesting some step-by-step approaches to dealing with written coursework requirements in more detail in Chapter 3.

One final point before I close this section, and something that I will also be returning to in Chapter 3, concerns the highly cyclical nature of academic writing. In the proposed timeline above, you can see that a drafting and editing process has been built in for the different coursework assignments under each module – this is very important. From my experience as an MA programme director, far too many students neglect this feature and approach their coursework writing in an overly linear fashion, typically working right up to the wire and then submitting their essays without even giving them one cursory proofreading. This is NOT the recommended way to do things. If you want to produce good quality work and be awarded high grades, you must recognise from the outset that effective academic writing is always highly recursive in nature and will involve you in an extended process of drafting, re-drafting and polishing. Adequate time needs to be allowed for this, so when you map out your goals and target completion mileposts, do try to make sure that this factor has been properly accounted for.

1.4 Accessing Resources and Learning to Work Smart

Some years ago now, one of my MA students came to me in a tearful panic saying that although she had spent days and days looking, there were no relevant books for her assignments in the library. I expressed some healthy scepticism over this claim and asked her to explain to me how exactly she had been searching. It turned out that she had (a) only been looking for hard copy books and (b) not using the library catalogue very effectively even for that. From what she went on to relate, it transpired that most of her days of fruitless searching had actually been based on randomly perusing the bookshelves in the hope that she might happen upon something relevant and useful. Needless to say, taking such an approach was not very effective, nor was it an example of working 'smart'. It was clear that this student needed to become significantly more aware of how to access academic resources properly. I would like to think that she was an extreme and random case, but on the evidence of what I continue to witness at universities, I suspect that the academic literacy weaknesses she shared with me are sadly much more commonplace than academics like myself might ideally wish for or suppose. As with all the other skills I have highlighted in this chapter, learning how to access academic resources effectively and efficiently is a key ability which all postgraduate students rapidly need to master.

The first thing you need to be aware of when accessing academic sources is that in this day and age, most of the material you will need to find is likely to be stored online. The days of card indexes and large folders containing backdated hard copies of academic journals are now long gone and most university libraries nowadays have as many (if not significantly more) of their resources located in cyberspace as they do with resources stored as physical hard copies. This means that instead of just relying on what you manage to find on the library shelves, you must become proficient at using online databases and repositories. In the case of MA TESOL/Applied Linguistics students, the starting point for this comes in recognising which electronic resources are likely to be the most useful for your needs. As part of their module reading lists, most lecturers will highlight specific recommended journals but for your reference, a list of the most common ones used in TESOL/Applied Linguistics has been provided on page 267.

Knowing which journals you should regularly be accessing is obviously a very important first step, but this knowledge alone will not be very much help to you, if you are then unable to use academic search engines proficiently. Before I close this section, it is therefore worth me reviewing a few key points. In the numbered steps and examples which follow, I will be basing my advice on several of the most common electronic journals you are likely to be accessing, e.g., the *ELT Journal*, the *Journal of English for Academic Purposes* and *Applied Linguistics*. However, remember that the same broad principles will apply to *any* academic journals you might wish to access.

1. Locate the journal homepage using your institutional log-in

    Most universities offering degrees in TESOL and Applied Linguistics will include full-text subscriptions to journals such as the *ELTJ*, *Journal of English for Academic Purposes* and *Applied Linguistics* as part of their normal services. This means that you will be able to navigate to those journal homepages directly by typing the journal name into your university library online catalogue and then clicking on whatever access links come up.

    Note that if you try to access such journals simply by searching independently online, while you will still get into their homepages, you will almost certainly not then have the same full-text access rights as you would by going through your institutional subscription. This is why it is always best to start your journal searches from your institution's online library catalogue.

2. **Once you land on the journal homepage, decide how you are going to search**

   If you know in advance what you are looking for, typing the article name into the search engine should immediately locate it for you. Note also that the Advanced Search option on the top right allows you to search the entire journal database by authors, titles, volumes and years of publication.

   As an experiment, go into the journal homepage for Applied Linguistics and try to find this article from 1980 by John Mch Sinclair:
   Some implications of discourse analysis for ESP methodology
   At the start of most literature searches though, rather than looking for a specific article, you may just be browsing more generally to see what articles are available on a given topic. With this kind of general approach in mind, as another experiment, try typing the key words **Communicative Approach** into the *ELTJ* homepage search function and see what comes up.

   Whenever you do a literature search, it is always worth bearing in mind that different ways of searching will generate different sets of results. If you were searching to see what had been published on methodology and pedagogy, for example, typing those words into a journal search engine as is would get you a certain number of hits. However, carrying out your search by putting speech marks around the key words would get you a very different set of results.

   As an experiment to show you how this works, now go into the homepage for the *Journal of English for Academic Purposes (JEAP)* and compare the results you get from carrying out the following two searches:
   a. methodology in EAP
   b. "methodology in EAP"
   When I recently did these searches myself, search method (a) generated a total of 445 results, representing all of the articles which had been broadly categorised as covering methodological matters up to that time. Search method (b) on the other hand located only seven articles. This search method (putting the keywords in speech marks) is known as a **Boolean Search** and as you can see from the results, it is much more precise. The seven articles which this search uncovered are all the works in the journal database which *explicitly* link the keywords methodology in EAP together. When you are trying to find very specific material, knowing the difference between a Boolean and non-Boolean keyword search should therefore definitely form an important part of your academic literacy toolkit.

3. **When you locate an article you want to read, download it to your computer**

   Clicking on the title of an article you want to read usually takes you directly to it. When the article opens, the first thing you will see is the abstract. As I have already advised in this chapter, you should quickly skim through this to see if the article is worth reading in more detail. If you decide that it is, then depending on your institution's access rights, you have the option of either reading it on the screen there and then, or downloading it as a PDF file, which you can keep and access later.

If you are trying to gather together a *range* of texts (for example, as preparatory background reading for a coursework assignment as I have suggested above) then I would suggest that the most time-efficient approach would be to save the file for later and keep on searching.

On this note, a very quick way to gather lots of literature in a short time is to find what you think is the most recent and relevant article on your subject and then scroll to the end and look at the bibliography of sources. You would then choose a small selection of the texts listed there and go through the same search and download process again. By following this 'leap frog' approach a few times with different articles, you can very soon build up an extremely useful and relevant bank of academic sources.

Check Your Understanding: Independent Task 1.4

Go into your university online library catalogue and practice searching for the following seven texts. If the institutional access rights allow you to do so, download each article as a PDF and save it to a clearly labelled folder on your computer.

Belcher, D. (2006). English for specific purposes: Teaching for perceived needs and imagined futures in the worlds of work, study and everyday life. *TESOL Quarterly, 40*(1), 133–156.

Bell, D.E. (2021). Accounting for the troubled status of English language teachers in Higher Education. *Teaching in Higher Education*, 1–16. https://doi.org/10.1080/13562517.2021.1935848.

Coxhead, A. (2000) A new academic word list. *TESOL Quarterly, 34*, 213–238.

Ellesworth, E. (1989). Why doesn't this feel empowering? Working through the repressive myths of critical pedagogy. *Harvard Educational Review, 59*(3), 297–325.

Ferguson, G. & Donno, S. (2003). One-month teacher training courses: Time for a change? *ELT Journal 57*(1), 26–33.

Fox, J., Cheng, L. & Zumbo, B.D. (2014). Do they make a difference? The impact of English language programs on second language students in Canadian universities. *TESOL Quarterly, 48*(1), 57–85.

Fulcher, G. (2004). Deluded by artifices: The common European framework and harmonization. *Language Assessment Quarterly, 1*(4), 253–266.

1.5 Identifying Sources of Support

We are now approaching the end of this first chapter, but before I close, it is worth me saying a little about different sources of support and how you should access them. Indeed, if there was just one piece of advice I could give to newly enrolled students, whether undergraduate or postgraduate, it would be that they should never underestimate how many sources of help and support are available to them. Most modern universities offer students an extremely rich environment in this regard and part of becoming an effective member of the university community involves knowing where you should go if you need help.

Broadly speaking, university support services fall into two broad categories: academic and pastoral. Although there may sometimes be a degree of overlap between the two, there are usually services (and people) explicitly engaged with one or the other.

In the case of academic support, after enrolling at the university you may be assigned a personal tutor. This person will usually be an academic member of staff in your school or faculty and may even be one of your own MA lecturers. Personal tutors are responsible for the welfare of the students in their care and you may be invited to meetings with them once or twice each semester. These meetings are an opportunity for you to talk in private about any issues you may be facing and get some advice. Although the primary remit of personal tutors is general academic support, they may also fulfil a pastoral function and may be willing to discuss issues you are facing outside of your studies. If they themselves are unable to solve your problems directly, they will almost certainly be able to direct you to someone else at the university who can, so they can be a very valuable resource and should probably be your first port of call.

Other forms of academic support are typically provided by Student Services, the Library or, if English is not your first language, the English Language Centre. In each of these cases, workshops may be offered on different aspects of academic literacy development. In my own institution, for example, the Centre for English Language Education (CELE) offers courses and clinics each semester focusing on issues such as academic citing and referencing, summarising and paraphrasing, using research databases and giving effective oral presentations. This support is offered to students free of charge and is intended to make them more effective in their studies. As a newly enrolled MA TESOL/Applied Linguistics student, you should definitely avail yourself of all such opportunities and get as much academic help and support as you can.

When it comes to pastoral support, most universities again offer a range of services. Beyond the personal tutor system I have described above, students can book appointments with university counsellors and other professional advisers. Such services are once again free of charge and can provide you with the opportunity to get confidential help. As with my advice on academic support, I encourage my students to fully utilize all the pastoral facilities that are available to them. There is never any need for you to feel alone at university; there will always be somebody who can help if you take the time to source what services are available.

As a final piece of advice before I close this chapter, what should you do if you find that despite your best efforts to follow all the steps I outline in this book, you are still unable to submit your assignments by the stated deadlines? In this scenario, you will most likely need to be drawing on what is called Extenuating Circumstances, usually known in university-speak as EC for short. All universities recognise that there are sometimes good reasons why students are unable to meet their deadlines. It may be that they have faced an illness, or suffered some recent bad news such as a family bereavement. In these cases, the EC system allows you to apply for coursework extensions and even resubmissions, just as long as you can present evidence that your studies have been negatively impacted by unforeseen events. As soon as you enrol as an MA TESOL/Applied Linguistics student, make sure that you fully familiarise yourself with the EC policies and procedures at your university. At the end of the day, all academic institutions want their students to succeed. As I hope to have shown in this chapter, one of the key skills in becoming an effective postgraduate student is about making the most of all the opportunities that are available to you.

Check Your Understanding: Independent Task 1.5

A student enrols on an MA TESOL/Applied Linguistics. For the opening weeks of the first semester, things seem to be going well, but then he finds that he just can't keep up with the required amount of reading. English is not his first language, and although he got a good grade in IELTS (7.0 overall with 6.5 in reading), the texts he now has to access are much longer than anything he has had to tackle before, with lots of unknown words and phrases. Indeed, he has found that whenever he tries to read something, he seems to spend most of his time with one hand on a dictionary.

The student is becoming more and more depressed about his academic performance and is even starting to question whether he should just drop out of university altogether. These thoughts only add to his stress, however, as he knows all too well that his family clubbed together to pay for his tuition fees and are expecting him to return home with a Master's and secure a good job. If he goes back to his family empty-handed, the loss of face would be unbearable.

What should this student do?

A suggested answer to this task has been provided on page 22.

Suggested Answers to Independent Tasks

Task 1.1

This student has almost certainly not made a very wise decision. She has evidently interpreted the taught hours shown in her weekly timetable as if these are representing the *only* study she will be required to do. In reality, of course, her weekly MA TESOL studies will require *at least double* this amount of time. The student also seems not to have realised that her 12 hours of teaching will involve her in preparation and marking. This will be an extra commitment which will then further take time away from her Masters. If I were this student's personal tutor, I would therefore be seriously advising her to reconsider her decision. If she was to insist on working, then at the very least, I would be recommending her to significantly reduce the number of contact hours.

Task 1.2a

As you are at the very beginning of the module, your top priority here should be to get as familiar with the general topic as you can. This means that your early reading needs to be broad in scope and not too specialised in its focus. The main purpose at this point is simply to gather useful background information.

With that criterion in mind, you should probably approach the following three texts *first*:

- Richards, J.C. & Rodgers, T.S. (2014). *Approaches and Methods in Language Teaching* (3rd ed.). Cambridge University Press.
- Spiro, J. (2013). *Changing Methodologies in TESOL*. Edinburgh University Press.
- Thornbury, S. (2017). *Scott Thornbury's 30 Language Teaching Methods*. Cambridge Handbooks for Language Teachers. Cambridge University Press.

Although it is not immediately apparent from the title, the text by Graham Hall also includes some very useful discussion of methodologies, so this would also be worth consulting:

- Hall, G. (2011). *Exploring English Language Teaching. Language in Action*. Routledge.

In principle, the book by McDonough and Shaw might also be useful, although compared to the other texts it is perhaps now a little dated. This would arguably move it a little further down your priority list:

- McDonough, J. & Shaw, C. (1993). *Materials and Methods in ELT*. Blackwell.

Once you have gained a good general understanding of ELT methodologies and their historical development, your reading can start to explore more critical angles. Based on this criterion, you should probably **then** look at:

- Adamson, B. (2004). Fashions in language teaching methodology. In A. Davies & C. Elder (Eds.) *The Handbook of Applied Linguistics* (pp. 605–622). Blackwell.
- Bell, D.M. (2007). Do teachers think that methods are dead? *ELT Journal, 61*(2), 135–143.
- Kumaravadivelu, B. (2001). Toward a postmethod pedagogy. *TESOL Quarterly, 35*(4), 537–560.
- Kumaravadivelu, B. (2006a). TESOL methods: Changing tracks, challenging trends. *TESOL Quarterly, 40*(1), 59–81.
- Kumaravadivelu, B. (2006b). *Understanding Language Teaching: From Method to Postmethod*. Lawrence Erlbaum.
- Lin, A. (2013). Towards paradigmatic change in TESOL methodologies: Building plurilingual pedagogies from the ground up. *TESOL Quarterly, 47*(3), 521–545.
- Prabhu, N.S. (1990). There is no best method - Why? *TESOL Quarterly, 24*(2), 161–176.
- Zulfikar, Z. (2018). Rethinking the use of L1 in the L2 classroom. *Englisia, 6*(1), 43–51.

Based on your reading up to this point, you should have developed a good understanding of the main issues in language teaching methodology and be aware of what some of the key criticisms have been. This means that you are now ready to start looking into more specific areas.

Depending on your personal interests, the following four texts might now be worth exploring:

- Arnold, J., Dörnyei, Z. & Pugliese, C. (2015). *The Principled Communicative Approach: Seven Criteria for Success*. Helbling Languages.
- Dalal, G. & Gulati, V. (Eds.) (2018). *Innovations in English Language Teaching in India: Trends in Language Pedagogy and Technology*. Lexington Books.
- Hanks, J. (2017). *Exploratory Practice in Language Teaching: Puzzling about Principles and Practices*. Palgrave Macmillan.

- Mazak, C.M. (2017). *Translanguaging in Higher Education: Beyond Monolingual Ideologies*. Channel View Publications.

The remaining three texts from the module reading list each deals with methodological concerns in highly specialised areas of ELT. As such, they should probably be approached *last, if at all*:

- Bell, D.E. (2022). Methodology in EAP: Why is it largely still an overlooked issue? *Journal of English for Academic Purposes, 55*, https://doi.org/10.1016/j.jeap.2021.101073.
- Flowerdew, J. (1993). Content-based language instruction in a tertiary setting. *English for Specific Purposes, 12*(2), 121–138.
- Long, M.H. (2005). Methodological issues in learner needs analysis. In M.H. Long (Ed.) *Second Language Needs Analysis* (p. 99). Cambridge University Press.

Task 1.2b

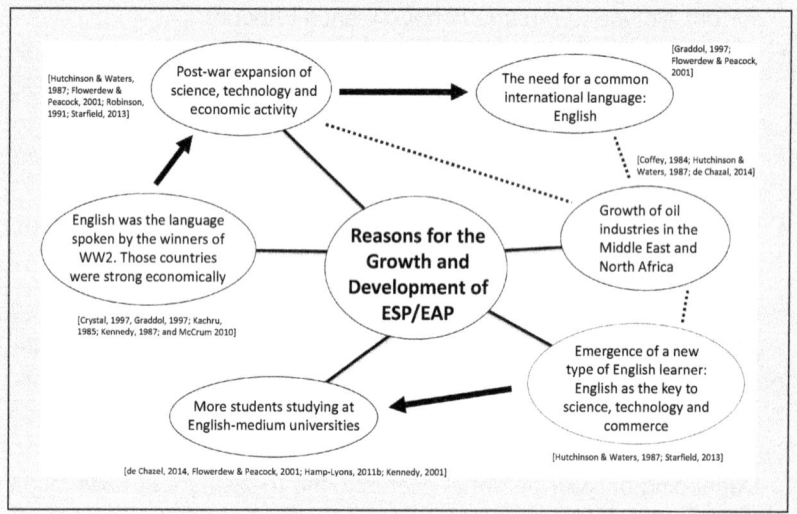

Task 1.5

The first thing this student needs to do is to recognise that help and support are available. In the first instance, it would be useful for him to schedule an appointment with his personal tutor so that he can get some friendly advice and a more objective perspective on things. It is quite normal for students transitioning to postgraduate-level study to notice a few dips compared to their usual performance, especially if English is not their first language and they have not had any previous experience of studying in an EMI environment. However, they must not let this completely destroy their confidence. In this particular case, one of the things that the student's personal tutor might advise would be for him to enrol on an adjunct EAP course with the English Language Centre. This would provide him with strategies to improve his reading skills. The personal tutor might also help the student to create a Self-Study Action Plan. This would allow the student to break his learning down into more manageable chunks. If the student is feeling so depressed that he feels unable to study at all, then it would be worth booking an appointment with a member of the University Counselling Service. It would also be a very good idea to look into the possibility of submitting EC applications to cover any forthcoming coursework or other forms of assessment.

Additional Resources for Further Reading

Burns, T. & Sinfield, S. (2022). *Essential Study Skills: The Complete Guide to Success at University* (5th ed.). Sage.

Buzan, T. & Buzan, B. (2010). *The Mind Map Book. Unlock Your Creativity, Boost Your Memory, Change Your Life*. Pearson.

Davies, M. (2011). *Study Skills for International Postgraduates*. Palgrave MacMillan.

Zwier, L.J. (2010). *Mastering Academic Reading*. University of Michigan Press.

Chapter References

Adamson, B. (2004). Fashions in language teaching methodology. In A. Davies & C. Elder (Eds.) *The Handbook of Applied Linguistics* (pp. 605–622). Blackwell.

Arnold, J., Dörnyei, Z. & Pugliese, C. (2015). *The Principled Communicative Approach: Seven Criteria for Success*. Helbling Languages.

Basturkmen, H. (2006) *Ideas and Options in English for Specific Purposes*. Lawrence Erlbaum.

Bell, D.E. (2016). Practitioners, pedagogies, and professionalism in English for Academic Purposes (EAP): The development of a contested field. Unpublished PhD diss., University of Nottingham, UK.

Bell, D.E. (2021). Accounting for the troubled status of English language teachers in Higher Education. *Teaching in Higher Education*, 1-16 https://doi.org/10.1080/13562517.2021.1935848.

Bell, D.E. (2022). Methodology in EAP: Why is it largely still an overlooked issue? *Journal of English for Academic Purposes, 55,* https://doi.org/10.1016/j.jeap.2021.101073.

Bell, D.M. (2007). Do teachers think that methods are dead? *ELT Journal, 61*(2), 135–143.

Belcher, D.D. (Ed.) (2009). *English for Specific Purposes in Theory and Practice.* University of Michigan Press.

Belcher, D. (2006). English for specific purposes: Teaching for perceived needs and imagined futures in the worlds of work, study and everyday life. *TESOL Quarterly, 40*(1), 133–156.

Coffey, B. (1984). ESP- English for specific purposes [State of the art article]. *Language Teaching: The International Abstracting Journal for Language Teachers and Applied Linguists, 17,* 2–16.

Coxhead, A. (2000). A new academic word list. *TESOL Quarterly, 34,* 213–238.

Crystal, D. (1997). *English as a Global Language.* Cambridge University Press.

Dalal, G. & Gulati, V. (Eds.) (2018). *Innovations in English Language Teaching in India: Trends in Language Pedagogy and Technology.* Lexington Books.

De Chazal, E. (2014). *English for Academic Purposes.* Oxford University Press.

Dudley-Evans, T. & St-John, M. (1998). *Developments in English for Specific Purposes: A Multi-Disciplinary Approach.* Cambridge University Press.

Ellesworth, E. (1989). Why doesn't this feel empowering? Working through the repressive myths of critical pedagogy. *Harvard Educational Review, 59*(3), 297–325.

Ferguson, G. & Donno, S. (2003). One-month teacher training courses: Time for a change? *ELT Journal, 57*(1), 26–33.

Flowerdew, J. (1993). Content-based language instruction in a tertiary setting. *English for Specific Purposes, 12*(2), 121–138.

Flowerdew, J. & Peacock, M. (2001). *Research Perspectives on English for Academic Purposes.* Cambridge University Press.

Fox, J., Cheng, L. & Zumbo, B.D. (2014). Do they make a difference? The impact of English language programs on second language students in Canadian universities. *TESOL Quarterly, 48*(1), 57–85.

Fulcher, G. (2004). Deluded by artifices: The common European framework and harmonization. *Language Assessment Quarterly, 1*(4), 253–266.

Graddol, D. (1997). *The Future of English.* The British Council.

Hall, G. (2011). *Exploring English Language Teaching. Language in Action.* Routledge.

Hamp-Lyons, L. (2011). English for academic purposes. In E. Hinkel (Ed.), *Handbook of Research in Second Language Teaching and Learning,* Vol 2 (pp. 89–105). Routledge.

Hanks, J. (2017). *Exploratory Practice in Language Teaching: Puzzling about Principles and Practices.* Palgrave Macmillan.

Hewings, M. (2001). *A History of ESP through English for Specific Purposes.* Retrieved from: http://www.esp-world.info/Articles_3/Hewings_paper.htm

Hutchinson, T. & Waters, A. (1987) *English for Specific Purposes. A Learning-Centred Approach.* Cambridge University Press.

Hyland, K. (2006). English for specific purposes: Some influences and impacts. In J. Cummins & C. Davison (Eds.) *International Handbook of English Language Teaching,* (pp. 379–390). Springer International Handbooks.

Johns, A.M. (2013). The history of english for specific purposes research. In B. Paltridge & S. Starfield (Eds.) *The Handbook of English for Specific Purposes*. Wiley-Blackwell.

Johns, A.M. & Dudley-Evans, T. (1991). English for Specific Purposes: International in Scope, Specific in Purpose. *TESOL Quarterly, 25*(2), 297–314.

Kachru, B.B. (1985). Standards, codification and sociolinguistic realism: The English language in a global context. In R. Quirk & H. Widdowson (Eds.) *English in the World: Teaching and Learning the Languages and Literatures*. (pp. 11–30). Cambridge University Press.

Kennedy, C. (1987). Innovating for a Change. *ELT Journal, 41*(3), 163–170.

Kennedy, C. (2001). Language use, language planning and EAP. In J. Flowerdew, & M. Peacock (Eds.) *Research Perspectives on English for Academic Purposes* (pp. 25–41). Cambridge University Press.

Kumaravadivelu, B. (2001). Toward a postmethod pedagogy. *TESOL Quarterly, 35*(4), 537–560.

Kumaravadivelu, B. (2006a). TESOL methods: Changing tracks, challenging trends. *TESOL Quarterly, 40*(1), 59–81.

Kumaravadivelu, B. (2006b). *Understanding Language Teaching: From Method to Postmethod*. Lawrence Erlbaum.

Mackay, R. & Mountford, A.J. (1978) *English for Specific Purposes*. Longman.

McCrum, R. (2010). Globish: *How the English Language Became the World's Language*. W.W. Norton & Company.

Lin, A. (2013). Towards paradigmatic change in TESOL methodologies: Building plurilingual pedagogies from the ground up. *TESOL Quarterly, 47*(3), 521–545.

Long, M.H. (2005). Methodological issues in learner needs analysis. In M.H. Long (Ed.) *Second Language Needs Analysis* (p. 99). Cambridge University Press.

Mazak, C.M. (2017). *Translanguaging in Higher Education: Beyond Monolingual Ideologies*. Channel View Publications.

McDonough, J. & Shaw, C. (1993). *Materials and Methods in ELT*. Blackwell.

Paltridge, B. (Ed.) (2011). *New Directions in English for Specific Purposes Research*. University of Michigan Press.

Paltridge, B. & Starfield, S. (Eds.) (2013). *The Handbook of English for Specific Purposes*. Wiley-Blackwell.

Prabhu, N.S. (1990). There is no best method - Why? *TESOL Quarterly, 24*(2), 161–176.

Richards, J.C. & Rodgers, T.S. (2014). *Approaches and Methods in Language Teaching* (3rd ed.). Cambridge University Press.

Robinson, P. (1991). *ESP Today: a Practitioner's Guide*. Prentice Hall.

Sinclair, J.M. (1980). Some implications of discourse analysis for ESP methodology. *Applied Linguistics, 1*(3), 253–261. https://doi-org.ezproxy.nottingham.edu.cn/10.1093/applin/I.3.253.

Spiro, J. (2013). *Changing Methodologies in TESOL*. Edinburgh University Press.

Starfield, S. (2013). The historical development of languages for specific purposes. In C.A. Chapelle (Ed.) *The Encyclopaedia of Applied Linguistics*. Oxford: Wiley-Blackwell.

Swales, J.M. (1985). *Episodes in ESP*. Prentice Hall International.

Swales, J.M. (2000). Languages for specific purposes. *Annual Review of Applied Linguistics, 20*, 59–76.

Thornbury, S. (2017). *Scott Thornbury's 30 Language Teaching Methods.* Cambridge Handbooks for Language Teachers. Cambridge University Press.

Zulfikar, Z. (2018). Rethinking the use of L1 in the L2 classroom. *Englisia, 6*(1), 43–51.

2 Academic Speaking and Listening

Introduction

This chapter examines the nature of academic speaking and listening on an MA TESOL/Applied Linguistics and highlights some of the different contexts you are likely to find yourself in. It begins by discussing spoken interactions with academic staff and makes some suggestions for how you should most effectively approach these. It then considers the nature of oral interactions involved in group work and peer learning before focusing in some detail on the specific academic skill of how to give effective oral presentations. The second half of the chapter turns its attention to academic listening and provides you with some tips on how to get the most from your lectures and seminars.

Additional resources for your further reading are listed on page 47.

2.1 Contexts Involving Academic Speaking

The first academic speaking context you are likely to encounter involves knowing how you should address your lecturers. As with all human interactions, there are some right ways and wrong ways to go about doing this, although the expected social 'rules' are rarely ever directly stated. However, as a new postgraduate student wanting to make a good impression, it is definitely worth you becoming aware of a few etiquette-related do's and don'ts.

The first issue you will need to consider are appropriate levels of formality and informality. In most British universities nowadays, the general pattern is for academic staff to lean towards informality, and the majority of academics will therefore ask their students to address them by their first name or a variant thereof. I usually tell all my own postgraduate students, for example, to simply call me 'Doug'. However, you should not automatically assume that such informality will always be the case. Some academics may prefer to keep more of a social distance and will expect to be addressed as doctor or professor. A point worth noting here is that if you *do* address members of academic staff with such titles, then they need to be used together with their surnames and *not* their first names, i.e., if somebody

DOI: 10.4324/9781003269854-2

decides to engage with me formally, then they should address me as Professor Bell, NOT Professor Douglas or Professor Doug. Similarly, to avoid the potential of inadvertently giving offence, you need to develop some sensitivity to what different academic titles mean. Almost all academics in the university will have completed a doctorate, which then gives them the professional right to be addressed as 'Doctor', but out of that pool, not all of them will be full professors and they should not therefore be addressed as such. Within traditional UK higher educational contexts, the typical academic hierarchy goes from Teaching Fellow (the most junior member of staff) to Assistant Professor (lecturer/senior lecturer), through to Associate Professor (senior lecturer/principal lecturer), and then finally full Professor (the most senior academic rank). Unless you have been invited to use their first names, this means that all Teaching Fellows, Assistant Professors and Associate Professors should be formally addressed using the title 'Dr', while full professors should be addressed as 'Professor'. Getting these points of academic etiquette wrong is not going to be a hanging offence and most academics are not hugely sensitive about such issues, but calling someone 'Mrs' when they should be addressed as 'Dr', or calling someone 'Dr' when they should be addressed as 'Professor' is certainly not going to win you their admiration or respect. Pay close attention to the professional titles that academic staff use in their online profiles or e-signatures and use these as the basis for your interactions with them unless you are told to do otherwise.

Although it is technically a written not an oral mode of communication, at this juncture it is also worth me saying a little about the effective use of email. All the 'rules' I have described above obviously apply to email writing too, and you do need to become sensitive to these issues when you write to academic staff. Opening your messages with salutations such as 'Hey Dude' or 'Yo!' and then closing them with love and kisses is *definitely not* appropriate, and while most academics these days are more likely to just laugh than formally take you to task for such social transgressions, you are still not going to be making a very favourable impression. As a rule of thumb, until you are invited to be informal in your interactions with academic staff, it is always safer for you to err on the side of formality. This means that when writing an email to someone you have never met, or who you do not yet know very well, your opening salutation should either be 'Dear Dr X' or 'Dear Professor Y'.

Beyond you meeting these expected levels of basic politeness, your interactions with academic staff should usually be fairly straightforward and you are likely to find that you will develop a close working relationship with your tutors. Compared to most undergraduate courses, MA TESOL/Applied Linguistics programmes are typically quite small, which means that the staff-student ratio can be very favourable, and you will have the opportunity to receive a lot of individual attention. This will be particularly true if you share the same professional academic interests as your tutors and such crossovers can lead to some fruitful collaborations. I will be returning to this topic of student-staff interaction and how to get the most out of it in Chapter 7, when I discuss what you should expect from your dissertation supervisor.

2.1.1 Academic Speaking in Groups and Seminars

Aside from your interactions with academic staff, your time on an MA TESOL/Applied Linguistics programme is naturally also going to involve you in oral communication with your classmates. One of the key features of a so-called Western education is the heavy emphasis that is usually placed on peer work and learning in small groups. Indeed, many of your assessments may well turn out to be group-based and this can come as a surprise if you are from an educational system which is based more on measuring individual performance in tests and exams. This tendency for Western academia to lean towards group work and peer-based learning is deeply rooted in social constructivist beliefs about education and ideas on what are generally considered to be the most effective approaches for building skills and knowledge. Over the years, many of my own students have commented on how surprised they were to see MA TESOL classes taking such a student-centred approach, as they had initially expected everything to be much more teacher-led. If this sounds like you, then you should be prepared to make some adaptations when you start your postgraduate studies. It is worth raising your awareness of this from the outset.

The most typical form that peer learning tends to take on MA TESOL/Applied Linguistics programme comes in small group discussions, when you may be asked to share your opinions on a particular point or issue with the people sitting next to you. To get the most out of such sessions, it goes without saying that all participants need to be willing to get involved and freely share their thoughts. If you have been asked to discuss your experiences of learning a foreign language, for example, and then critically relate these to what the theories have typically said about Second Language Acquisition, clearly there would be very little to be gained if everyone just sat there in silence and refused to talk. Part of becoming an effective student and getting the most out of your MA TESOL/Applied Linguistics comes in recognising this need for you to openly share your opinions and experiences and be willing to learn from the opinions and experiences of others. Students enrolled on Masters' programmes typically come from a wide range of backgrounds and many of your classmates are likely to be practising teachers or applied linguists already; some may even have professional experience and expertise in areas that you yourself are aspiring towards. If they are conducted in the way that they are intended, this means that group work discussions can represent an excellent opportunity for you to widen your awareness, deepen your professional knowledge and build useful ties for the future.

Check Your Understanding: Independent Task 2.1a

You have just started the first taught module of your MA TESOL/Applied Linguistics and you are taking part in a seminar. The course tutor has divided the class into groups of four and you have been asked to discuss the extent to which a critical awareness of one's first language can help with learning subsequent languages. The tutor has allocated a maximum of 15 minutes for this task and has asked for one person in each group to act as a scribe and make a note of all the different ideas that are discussed. These points will then later be shared in an open discussion with the class as a whole.

In your group, the other three members seem very unwilling to get involved. Nobody is volunteering to be the scribe and two people have just started playing with their phones. The other person is studiously avoiding all eye contact and just looking down at her feet.

What should you do?

A suggested answer to this task has been provided on page 44.

2.1.2 Academic Speaking in Oral Presentations

Aside from seminar discussions, another very common form of academic speaking on MA TESOL/Applied Linguistics programmes is that found in oral presentations. These can take a variety of different forms. Some may be highly informal and will only involve you in speaking for a couple of minutes; others may constitute part of a formal assessment and may require you to prepare PowerPoint slides and speak for up to half an hour. Some presentations will be individual affairs in which you will have sole responsibility for your work; others will represent a collaborative effort in which you may be teamed up with another three or four of your classmates and each of you will be expected to deliver a specific part. However, whichever format they take, *all* varieties of academic oral presentations will have certain core features in common. It is therefore well worth familiarising yourself with these, so that you know what to expect and can prepare yourself accordingly.

Perhaps the first thing to be said about oral presentations is that unlike a spontaneous conversation, they are artificially constructed speech events; as such, they follow a highly contrived and predictable structure. When you are preparing to give an academic oral presentation, this dimension actually works to your advantage because it means that you will largely know in advance what is expected of you. Structuring an oral presentation well is literally half of the battle, so it is definitely worth you paying some attention to this aspect from the outset. Seven different stages in the rhetorical structure of a typical informative academic presentation are outlined below:

Academic Speaking and Listening 31

Different Stages in an Oral Presentation

① GREETING & INTRODUCTION: The presenter greets the audience and tells them his/her name.
② PRESENTATION OVERVIEW: The presenter announces the title of the presentation and provides a brief synopsis of how it will be structured.
③ LEAD-IN: The presenter signals that a discussion of the presentation content is about to begin.
④ BODY: The presenter goes through each of the points in turn that were mentioned in the overview.
⑤ CLOSING: The presenter signals that the presentation is about to close.
⑥ OPPORTUNITY FOR QUESTIONS: The presenter opens the floor to questions from the audience.
⑦ ENDING: The presenter thanks the audience for their attention and signals that the presentation is now at an end.

Check Your Understanding: Independent Task 2.1b

Match the oral presentation excerpts below with their appropriate stages in the overall rhetorical structure.

a. This basically brings us to the end of my presentation today.
b. For the next 25 minutes or so, I'm going to talk about the ways in which Schema Theory can be applied to the teaching of reading.
c. Does anybody have any questions?
d. So let's get started then with a few definitions of what Schema Theory actually is.
e. My presentation will be in three main parts. I'll start by sharing some of the ways in which Schema Theory has been defined and conceptualised by researchers. Next, I'll look at....
f. Good afternoon everyone. As you know, my name is Tony Zhang. I'm very happy to be speaking here today.
g. If there are no more questions, I'll finish my presentation here. Thanks very much for listening.

h. There are various ways in which Schema Theory can be applied while teaching. One activity I often use with my own students is to give them a story in which they have to make predictions about what they think will happen at different stages. The story is designed in such a way that the most obvious predictions actually turn out to be wrong. This usually comes as a big surprise to the students and can be used to raise their awareness of how Schema Theory operates instantly and subconsciously.

A suggested answer to this task has been provided on page 44.

When you first start planning an academic oral presentation, as with a written coursework essay you will need to decide how you are going to select and organise your material. If you can, try to structure your presentations so that they do not go beyond a maximum of four parts. This stops the presentation content from becoming too unwieldy and will force you to break your information down into appropriate themes and sub-themes. In the case of Independent Task 2.1b, for example, the presenter might have decided to structure the presentation body as follows: some definitions of Schema Theory and the different ways in which it has been conceptualised, some landmark research studies which have investigated Schema Theory, some practical examples of Schema Theory in action and, finally, some ways in which Schema Theory can be incorporated into reading instruction. In a 25-minute presentation, following a structure like this would result in the presenter talking for around four to five minutes per section of the body with a few minutes then left over for questions.

You should also keep in mind that as with a written coursework essay, effective oral presentations need to make frequent use of signposting language. I will be discussing the role and key features of *written* signposting in more detail in Chapters 4 and 8, but in the case of oral presentations, spoken signposting is needed at very specific stages. In Stage 2, for example, when the presenter explains what the talk will be about and how many parts it will be in, effective use of signposting becomes critical. Stage 3, the lead-in, is also an example of oral signposting, as are the opening statements in Stages 5, 6 and 7. Within Stage 4, the presentation body, presenters will also need to be able to use signposting language in signalling to their audience when they are transitioning from one section to another. When effective use of such signposting language is absent, oral presentations can become disjointed and difficult for listeners to follow, so it is vital that you have a store of appropriate phrases that you can draw on.

Look at some different examples of such phrases in the box below. In each case, the content has been taken from a TESOL/Applied Linguistics presentation about the work of Stephen Krashen:

Some Useful Phrases for Oral Presentations

In my presentation today, I'm going to talk about the work of Stephen Krashen. I've divided this content into three main parts.

I'll start by looking at the distinction which Krashen has made between Language Acquisition and Language Learning, and as part of this, I'll be focusing on his now famous Monitor hypothesis and the concept of i+ 1.

Next, I'll discuss how Krashen has contributed to deepening our understanding of language learner motivation with his Affective Filter hypothesis.

Let's get started then with the important distinction that Krashen has drawn between acquiring a second language and deliberately trying to learn it.

This brings us to the final part of my presentation and Krashen's claim that we acquire items in a second language in a predictable order.

I think this leads quite nicely to my second point today which is to do with the role our emotions play in learning and Krashen's concept of the Affective Filter.

Finally today, I'll say a little about Krashen's Natural Order hypothesis and his claim that L2 acquisition follows a predictable sequence.

OK, I think I've reached the end of my presentation. Thank you very much for your attention. If anyone has any questions, I'll do my best to answer them.

When you apply signposting language to provide an outline of your presentation, always try to vary the action verbs that you use and don't just keep saying the same thing, i.e., rather than saying, I'll *talk about* X, then I'll *talk about* Y, then I'll *talk about* Z, you can create a much better stylistic effect by being more discerning in your verb choices and drawing on different lexis, e.g., I'll *talk about* X, then I'll *focus on* Y and to finish off, I'll *discuss* Z. Similarly, when you are signposting the oral presentation structure, you also need to become sensitive to your use of verb tenses. You basically have four options here. You can either use the **Future Simple**, as in 'I'll talk about', **Going to**, as in 'I'm going to examine', the **Future Continuous**, as in 'I'll be discussing', or the **First Conditional**, as in 'I'd like to focus on'. All of these are acceptable ways to signpost your intentions in an oral presentation, so choose whichever style you feel most comfortable with and then practice delivering your presentation openings until you can do so smoothly and with confidence.

The academic presentation style and structure I have considered up to now represents a basic foundation which will serve you well in most situations

> **Two Alternative Ways of Opening an Oral Presentation**
>
> Good morning everyone. As you know, my name is Simon Carter. It's a great pleasure for me to be speaking here today.
>
> Now, before I start my presentation, I'd like to ask you a quick question. How many of you in the room speak more than one language? Can you raise your hand?
>
> Good afternoon. As I think you all know, my name is Yue Zhang and I'm majoring in Applied Linguistics with TESOL.
>
> In my presentation today, I'm going to be talking about affective factors and the role these can play in language learning.
>
> Before I start though, I have a small task for you. Can you please change where you're currently sitting and go to sit next to someone you think you'd like to work with. I'll tell you why in a moment...

and contexts. As you gain in confidence though, you may decide to experiment with other modes of delivery. If you want to give your presentation a little more impact, then you might consider using a slightly different way of opening. Rather than simply stating your presentation topic directly, for example, you could get your audience's attention more forcefully by asking them an opening question, or giving them a task.

Look at how these two techniques might work in each of the examples shown in the box above.

Choosing slightly quirky, offbeat approaches to opening an oral presentation like these can help to make your talk stand out from the rest. The only limitation here is your own creativity and there are in fact lots of different possibilities. Beyond questions and tasks, some presenters choose to create more impact by showing their audience engaging images or sharing surprising facts. All of these techniques can be used to good effect, but of course in order for them to work well they need to be a good match with the style and temperament of the presenter. If you are a shy and introverted person, it might be safer to play it safe at first and just stick with the standard oral presentation format I described at the beginning. For more adventurous personality types though, sometimes varying this framework can help you to make your presentations more memorable.

Almost all presentations nowadays are likely to involve the use of slides based on software such as PowerPoint. There can be little doubt that such technology allows for the creation of highly professional work in terms of a presentation's visual appearance; when it comes to the actual delivery

Check Your Understanding: Independent Task 2.1c

If you are currently enrolled on an MA TESOL/Applied Linguistics, choose an oral presentation topic which would be relevant to one of the modules on your course and draft an opening in which you either (a) follow the basic approach or (b) have a go at something more adventurous. If you are not yet a Masters' student, choose a general topic which you think is relevant to TESOL/Applied Linguistics and do the same.

Practice delivering your chosen opening and, if possible, record yourself doing so.

though, do be aware that an over-reliance on PowerPoint can *detract* from the overall performance rather than enhance it. It is therefore well worth spending some time on learning how to use PowerPoint for maximum effect and reviewing a few do's and don'ts around its application.

One of the most common weaknesses I find in my own MA students' use of PowerPoint is that they often try to cram too much information onto their slides. In order for them to look effective and achieve their desired purpose, PowerPoint slides need to use white space well and to have been designed using appropriate formatting in terms of colours, bullet points and font sizes. With the exception of academic quotations or citations, more of which below, remember that the text on a PowerPoint slide should generally only serve as a structural aide-memoire for the speaker; it is not meant to be a carbon-copy of everything which the speaker says. Dense passages of text are therefore best avoided and should be replaced by short bullet-point statements with adequate spacing included between each line.

A further issue to be aware of when designing PowerPoint slides is your choice of font. It is very easy to become seduced by the huge array of available font types but the best advice here is to keep things clear and simple. Mixing together elaborate font types may make your presentation content difficult to read, so it is better to stick with just one or two. Calibri and Arial can be good choices in this regard, as the style of their lettering is clear and easy on the eye.

Once you have designed the general layout and structure of each slide, it is then worth thinking about whether you want to use animations. Hiding different parts of each slide's content and only having them appear mouse-click by mouse-click can be a very good way of focusing the audience's attention. If you show everything on the screen in one go and then start reading through that information point by point, chances are that the audience will already be reading ahead of you and not really be paying much attention to what you are saying. It is better to be more strategic in the information that you share and only reveal each bullet point when you are ready to talk about it.

One of the cardinal sins of using PowerPoint, of course, is when speakers end up reading everything verbatim from their slides, in which case their presentation becomes little more than a read-aloud exercise. If you do this in an assessed oral presentation, you will definitely lose a lot of marks and you may even be given a fail grade. As I have described above, the content of your slides should only be serving as a presentation memory aid, it should not be a word-for-word list of absolutely everything that you say. This means that when you are presenting, you should only be glancing at your slides and orally rephrasing whatever is written there; your main attention should always be on your audience. I will be discussing some of the finer details of this in a subsequent section below.

A final point you should be aware of when designing the PowerPoint slides for an academic presentation is that you will be expected to list academic sources and citations as supporting evidence for all your claims, similar to what you would typically do in an academic essay. This aspect is arguably one of the things which make academic oral presentations different to presentations in other contexts. Aside from the citations being listed on individual slides, any academic sources you have consulted for your presentation should also then appear on a slide at the end in the form of a full references list. However, as with an academic essay, this list should *only* include the material you have already made references to; do not be tempted to pad things out by adding additional sources. In an assessed oral presentation, the markers will be wise to tricks like this and if you do so, it will almost certainly cost you marks.

Check Your Understanding: Independent Task 2.1d

Look at the oral presentation PowerPoint slide represented in the box below. Identify what you think are any weaknesses and try to improve them. A suggested answer to this task has been provided on page 45.

The Work of Stephen Krashen

- Stephen Krashen has made several significant contributions to the field of ELT, particularly in deepening our understanding of Second Language Acquisition. One of his most famous claims is the distinction he makes between acquisition and learning.
- Krashen sees these as separate processes, claiming that items which are formally learned cannot be converted into language that is acquired. As far as Krashen is concerned, only acquired language can initiate spontaneous language use. Language that has been formally learned acts as a Monitor and fulfils an editing and checking role.

Once you have decided on the content of an oral presentation and have created your PowerPoint slides, your next consideration will be aspects of the presentation delivery. Even the best designed PowerPoint presentation in the world will fall flat and lose marks if the presenter is unable to deliver the actual talk well. This means that you need to pay attention to how you are going to speak. Oral presentations can be a cause of major stress in this regard, especially if English is not your first language. Few people genuinely enjoy standing up to speak in front of a crowd, especially if they know their performance is being assessed. However, with some awareness of the main things to watch out for and adequate prior preparation, there is no reason why anyone cannot deliver a presentation well.

One of the first things you should think about when it comes to oral presentation delivery is the sound and volume of your voice. Although the audience will be getting *some* of the information from your slides, at the end of the day, it is how you convey the presentation content by using your voice which will make or break the audience's overall impression. This means that you will need to enunciate your words clearly, using correct pronunciation and with the appropriate application of stress and intonation. Although it is not classed as a tonal language in the same way as say Chinese or a few other Asian languages, English does nonetheless rely on tonal variations when conveying different meanings and emotions and good presenters are well aware of this fact. Delivering your presentation in a flat monotone is unlikely to impress anyone or win you high marks. You therefore need to be aware of when your voice should rise and when it should fall, and also which words in a sentence should be stressed or unstressed. If English is not your first language, it might be worth you consulting some reference works on this, as the rules around English intonation patterns may be different to what you expect. In one of my earlier publications (Bell, 2014 – see page 47) I provide some guidance and practice exercises on English stress and intonation in academic presentations for non-native English speakers. This textbook also comes with an accompanying audio CD and DVD, so you can listen to some model answers and learn from the features they exemplify.

Another point to keep in mind when you are presenting is that you will also need to speak with sufficient volume. You certainly don't want to be shouting at your audience, but you also don't want to be whispering to them either. You always need to make sure that you are speaking at an appropriate pace with effective use of pausing. A very common problem that I frequently witness in oral presentations is that feeling nervous tends to make people start to speak quickly and they begin to gabble. Try not to do this. Rehearse your presentation a few times before the day of formal delivery and on each of those practice occasions, check that you are speaking clearly and at an appropriate speed. If you can, enlist the help of a friend and either audio- or video-record yourself and then critically reflect together on the strengths and weaknesses of your performance. If you pay adequate attention to improving and polishing aspects of your delivery, it can really make all the difference between a mediocre grade and a high grade or, in some cases, even a pass and a fail.

In addition to the effective use of your voice, another extremely important feature of oral presentation delivery is your use of eye contact. Resist the temptation to just read from your slides and force yourself to maintain regular eye contact with your listeners. A further point worth mentioning here is that as far as possible, you should aim to be equal in your gaze and try to include *everybody* in the audience. I often encounter students who are happy to maintain steely eye contact with me their teacher, but then completely neglect to look at anybody else in the room. This is wrong. When you are delivering an oral presentation, try to shift your gaze around the audience and strive for an equal balance of eye contact so that everyone present feels fully included.

Before I bring this part of the chapter to a close, I would like to consider one more aspect of oral presentations and that is the question and answer session, which as we have seen usually takes place towards the end. This is potentially the trickiest part of the entire presentation because it is the area over which the presenter arguably has the least control. As I have suggested in this chapter, other parts of a presentation can be fully prepared for in advance and carefully rehearsed, but when it comes to questions from the audience, much less is certain. However, this is not to suggest that the situation is *entirely* out of the presenter's control and there are still a few things that you can (and should) be aware of.

One very important point here is the absolute necessity for presenters to *own* their presentation content. If you have been presenting on a given topic, then it should go without saying that you need to know what you have been talking about. However, from my experience of grading MA student oral presentations, I must say that this dimension is not always quite as evident as it should be. I was assessing a student's oral presentation with an academic colleague quite recently, for example, the topic of which was quantitative and qualitative approaches to research design in TESOL/Applied Linguistics. The student in question had been asked to select two different articles from a research journal, one of which took a quantitative approach and the other which was qualitative, and then talk for 20 minutes on how these approaches were different. When discussing the research in the quantitative article, the student mentioned that several statistical tests for reliability had been applied by the article authors, such as ANOVA and Cronbach. I wanted to check that she knew what these were and how they operated, so in my questions at the end, I asked her to explain in more detail. The result was complete bafflement. Although she had freely been using the terms ANOVA and Cronbach in her presentation, it soon became painfully apparent that this student actually had no idea what these were, how they operated or why they had been chosen; she was simply parroting terms with no real understanding. The situation then worsened when my colleague asked her a follow-up question about one of the other points she had been discussing. Once again, the result was an embarrassing silence. The lesson here should be clear: always make sure that you are fully on top of your presentation content because it is quite likely in the Q&A session that you may be asked to elaborate and provide further details. Indeed, when you are preparing an oral presentation, with a little bit of foresight, you should be able to second-guess what the most likely questions from the audience will be. All of this goes back to the need for adequate prior planning though, which I would hope this chapter has now made abundantly clear.

Perhaps the last thing to be said about the Q&A section of oral presentations is that there is no shame in you not being able to answer a question if you genuinely do not know. This is not the same thing as the example I gave above. There is a very big difference between not knowing the answer to something you should have checked and being asked a question which you have genuinely not considered. In these situations, the best approach is simply to admit that you do not know. You can always offer to find out the answer after the presentation finishes and get back to the person later. This would be an acceptable compromise and, in most cases, you would not lose any marks for responding like this.

Check Your Understanding: Independent Task 2.1e

In one of the earlier sections above, I discussed the importance of varying your stress and intonation when delivering an oral presentation and not talking in a monotone.

There are some phonological rules in English which govern whether a speaker's intonation should be rising, falling or falling-rising based on the position of particular words.

Read presentation excerpts (i)–(vi) aloud and in each case, try to decide what the most appropriate intonation pattern should be for the word(s) highlighted in bold and why you think this is.

  i. That brings us to the end of my presentation **today**.
 ii. What about **Schema Theory?**
iii. L1 transfer often results in lexical errors in English, but it can't account for everything, **can it?** Evidently learners make mistakes for other reasons too.
 iv. Future advances in studies of the brain **may** help to shed more light on why some words are so easily remembered and others so easily forgotten.

> v. Three typical such dichotomies are **teacher-centred vs. learner-centred, inductive vs. deductive** and **use of L1 vs. avoidance of L1**.
> vi. It has often been said that non-correction of learners' errors leads to fossilisation, but **does it really?** Some recent research indicates that ...
>
> A suggested answer to this task has been provided on page 45.

2.2 Contexts Involving Academic Listening

When it comes to formal academic listening, the most common context you are likely to encounter as an MA TESOL/Applied Linguistics student will be lectures. As I discussed in the previous chapter, whether these are delivered as interactive sessions, or in the more traditional large-scale format, for the period that you are enrolled on the MA, lectures will constitute a key component of your weekly learning experience. It is important therefore that you have some awareness of what to expect and can start to prepare yourself accordingly.

In the first taught week of a given module, it is common practice for lecturers to share with their students an overview of the lecture topics for each week of the semester. This allows everyone to see what is coming and to plan ahead. In the current age of virtual learning environments (VLEs) such as Moodle and Blackboard, some lecturers will assign their students pre-lecture readings and other preparatory tasks. You should always do your best to complete these before attending the lecture, as they will have been designed to provide you with important background information and get you thinking about key concepts. This then means that you are not approaching the lecture content 'cold'. Paying attention to this pre-listening stage can become very important in academic listening, especially if English is not your mother tongue, as it allows you to become familiar with the core concepts and lexis. Having such background knowledge can then massively assist with your overall comprehension when you attend the lecture and are forced to process aural input on the spot.

It is also worth remembering that similar to oral presentations, academic lectures are an artificially contrived (as opposed to spontaneously constructed) speech act. This means that they can be expected to follow a predictable rhetorical structure. From an academic listening perspective, one immediate outcome (and benefit) of this is that you can make several educated guesses about the kinds of language you are likely to encounter. Textbooks on academic listening often draw attention to this dimension when they highlight the role played by discourse markers. Although there are several different categories of discourse markers commonly found in academic lectures – more of which below – all of them usually function as a means of signposting a speaker's intentions. I have already highlighted the importance of signposting language earlier in this chapter during my

Check Your Understanding: Independent Task 2.2a

Discourse markers in academic lectures can often be grouped under specific categories. *Structural markers*, as the name suggests, are used to signal different stages in the lecture structure; *markers of importance*, however, are used when speakers want to draw their listeners' attention to specific or noteworthy features of the lecture content.

Look at academic lecture excerpts (i)–(vi) and decide which category of discourse marker each of the parts highlighted in bold represents.

  i. Now, when we're talking about all these different methodologies, you've **got to keep in mind that** we can't really say that one is necessarily better than another. That would be too simplistic. All language teaching methodologies have their relative strengths and weaknesses.
 ii. **This brings us onto the second point** I want to cover this morning which is…
iii. **Let's get started then by looking at** what Chomsky said about behaviourism.
 iv. **And the main thing to note here is that** we make these predictions instantly; we're not even aware of doing it.
  v. **The final thing I'd like us to consider** today is …
 vi. **One of the most important differences** between GTM and strong versions of CLT is the way that each approaches classroom use of the L1.

A suggested answer to this task has been provided on page 46.

---

discussion of oral presentations, and the same principles now apply to academic lectures. If you know which signposting phrases to expect and can recognise when such markers are being used, it will help with your overall listening comprehension.

Being able to process and understand the content of academic lectures is obviously a very important skill that you will need to work on and refine, but of equal importance is the ability to keep detailed and accurate records of what you hear. In this regard, developing effective note-taking skills and having an efficient personal filing system become vital. Although there has been a tendency in recent years for note-taking to be seen as a somewhat passé and outdated academic skill (the typical argument here runs that students can now take photographs of lecture slides using their phones and lecturers will in any case upload their slides to Moodle or other VLE platforms which makes lecture notes unnecessary) there is still much to be gained by learning how to do this well. Even if lecturers *do* post their PowerPoint slides online, at best these will still only represent a skeleton of what was covered; they will not capture the full richness and detail of the lecture. When you later come to work on your coursework assignments, you will almost certainly need to draw on some of the content which was covered orally in your lectures. Memory alone is usually not very reliable for this, especially if you are thinking back to an event which happened some weeks or even months ago, so you will obviously have the best chance of recollecting what happened if you have kept accurate records of what each lecture contained. It follows, therefore, that effective note-taking still has an important role to play and you should aim to make it part of your academic toolkit.

There are many possible ways of taking notes from lectures and you are encouraged to investigate and experiment with these by sourcing some self-help books from your university library. Some potentially useful texts for this have been listed for your reference on page 47. However, no matter which approach to note-taking you ultimately decide to follow, the underlying core principles will always remain the same: all methods will involve you in using a system of written shorthand to allow for the capture and recording of information accurately and efficiently. In the downtime between your lectures, practice listening to different types of academic speaking and taking notes – if your university has an English Language Centre, they are likely to have a bank of such academic listening material which you can access directly or borrow. The more proficient you can become at listening and note-taking, the more effective you will be in your studies.

Check Your Understanding: Independent Task 2.2b

How might you go about making notes on the following lecture excerpts?

i. "The Grammar Translation Method of language teaching was particularly prevalent in Germany during the 1800s. It thus later became known as 'The Prussian Method'. As the name suggests, Grammar Translation Methodology bases itself on a detailed analysis of grammatical rules. At all times, the learners' native language is used as the medium for instruction and there is a heavy reliance on bilingual vocabulary lists, with learners encouraged to translate directly from one language to another. Not surprisingly perhaps, the main focus in Grammar Translation is on teaching learners to read and write in the target language and as a result, little attention is paid to developing their oral fluency. Learners are taught rules about language deductively and the main emphasis is on the accurate reproduction of these rules when manipulating language."

ii. "The Natural Method of language teaching–which was also known as The Direct Method and then The Berlitz Method after it was adopted by the famous chain of language schools– was largely based on the principles of how it was then believed children learn their first language. The emphasis was therefore primarily on developing the learners' spoken ability. Under the pedagogic approaches advocated by this method, it was believed that translation from one language to another should be avoided and all of the teaching was supposed to be carried out in the target language, NOT the learners' L1. A further core tenet of this method was that it was believed that grammar should be taught inductively and that language should always be contextualized."

A suggested answer to this task has been provided on page 46.

Before closing this chapter, a final point I would like to make about note-taking from lectures is that not too long after each lecture has finished, you should go over your notes and make sure that everything is legible and that it all makes sense. There would obviously be very little point in you taking notes if you were to find that they are incomprehensible when you come to revisit them a few weeks or months later.

Some lecturers advise their students to write up their lecture notes each evening so that they turn into a fully comprehensive written record. If you have sufficient time to do this then by all means do so, as such a system is clearly going to offer you the optimal clarity. I can still remember one of my classmates when I was an MA student. Her lecture notes were always neatly typed up and she was the envy of us all, especially during the end-of-semester examination period when most of us were struggling to remember what had been said in lectures and discovering the unfortunate gaps in our note-taking techniques.

In the ideal world, we would probably all aspire to be students as diligent as my former classmate. In reality, though, most of us are rarely so perfect. My own perspective on this is that you do not necessarily need to have a week-by-week series of typed up notes in pristine condition; you do, however, need to have sets of notes which are fit for purpose and which will work well *for you*. As with all other aspects of academic literacy and self-study, with sufficient experimentation and practice, you should be able to find your own happy medium.

Suggested Answers to Independent Tasks

Task 2.1a

If you were to find yourself in this situation, you should take some agency and lead from the front. For example, you yourself could volunteer to be the group scribe. You could then encourage your group mates to share their opinions by asking them questions and guiding the discussion directly. If they were still refusing to cooperate, then by this point it should have become obvious to the course tutor that there is a problem in the grouping and he/she would be likely to intervene. The *worst* thing you could do would be to do nothing.

Task 2.1b

a. This basically brings us to the end of my presentation today. **[STAGE 5: CLOSING]**
b. For the next 25 minutes or so, I'm going to talk about the ways in which Schema Theory can be applied to the teaching of reading. **[STAGE 2: PRESENTATION OVERVIEW]**
c. Does anybody have any questions? **[STAGE 6: OPPORTUNITY FOR QUESTIONS]**
d. So let's get started then with a few definitions of what Schema Theory actually is. **[STAGE 3: LEAD-IN]**
e. My presentation will be in three main parts. I'll start by sharing some of the ways in which Schema Theory has been defined and conceptualised by researchers. Next, I'll look at.... **[STAGE 2: PRESENTATION OVERVIEW]**
f. Good afternoon everyone. As you know, my name is Tony Yamamoto. I'm very happy to be speaking here today. **[STAGE 1: GREETING & INTRODUCTION]**
g. If there are no more questions, I'll finish my presentation here. Thanks very much for listening. **[STAGE 7: ENDING]**
h. There are various ways in which Schema Theory can be applied while teaching. One activity I often use with my own students is to give them a story in which they have to make predictions about what they think will happen at different stages. The story is designed in such a way that the most obvious predictions actually turn out to be wrong. This usually comes as a big surprise to the students and can be used to raise their awareness of how Schema Theory operates instantly and subconsciously. **[STAGE 4: BODY]**

Task 2.1d

There were several weaknesses worth commenting on in the original PPT, e.g., overly dense text, a poor choice of font (both for the PPT title and the body) and inadequate use of white space. These problems have been rectified in the example PPT below.

The Work of Stephen Krashen

- Several significant contributions to Second Language Acquisition.
- Makes a distinction between acquisition and formal learning. Only acquired language can initiate spontaneous language use.
- Formally learned items cannot be converted into language that is acquired.
- Formally learned language acts as a Monitor for editing and checking.

Task 2.1e

i. That brings us to the end of my presentation today. [**Falling intonation. Reason: to indicate that something is finishing**]
ii. What about Schema Theory? [**Rising intonation. Reason: to indicate a question**]
iii. L1 transfer often results in lexical errors in English, but it can't account for everything, can it? Evidently learners make mistakes for other reasons too. [**Falling intonation. Reason: to indicate a tag question when the speaker is sure of something**]
iv. Future advances in studies of the brain may help to shed more light on why some words are so easily remembered and others so easily forgotten. [**Rising-Falling intonation. Reason: to indicate uncertainty**]
v. Three typical such dichotomies are teacher-centred vs. learner-centred, inductive vs. deductive and use of L1 vs. avoidance of L1. [**The first two bolded items should be spoken with rising intonation, the final bolded item with falling intonation. Reason: when giving a list, the intonation rises on the first few items then falls on the last**]

46   *Academic Speaking and Listening*

vi. It has often been said that non-correction of learners' errors leads to fossilisation, but does it really? Some recent research indicates that ... [**Rising intonation. Reason: to indicate a question**]

Task 2.2a

i. Now, when we're talking about all these different methodologies, you've **got to keep in mind that** we can't really say that one is necessarily better than another. That would be too simplistic. All language teaching methodologies have their relative strengths and weaknesses. [*Marker of Importance*]
ii. **This brings us onto the second point** I want to cover this morning which is ... [*Marker of Structure*]
iii. **Let's get started then by looking at** what Chomsky said about behaviourism. [*Marker of Structure*]
iv. **And the main thing to note here is that** we make these predictions instantly; we're not even aware of doing it. [*Marker of Importance*]
v. **The final thing I'd like us to consider** today is... [*Marker of Structure*]
vi. **One of the most important differences** between GTM and strong versions of CLT is the way that each approaches classroom use of the L1. [*Marker of Importance*]

Task 2.2b

Various answers are possible here. Note-taking is usually a highly individual activity and everyone will approach things slightly differently. The suggested answers for (i) and (ii) represent two *possible* sets of notes.

i. GTM orig. v. common in Germany 1800s → 'The Prussian Method'. GTM = analysis of rules. L1 used when teaching; bilingual vocab lists also common; learners translate L1 and L2. Main focus = reading/writing; not speaking. Pedagogy = deductive. Learners expected to learn/reproduce rules accurately.
ii. Nat Method = Direct Method = Berlitz Method. All same. Based on how children develop their L1. Main focus = speaking. Should avoid all translation; teach using the L2 not the L1. Teach grammar inductively. Always contextualise language.

Additional Resources for Further Reading

Bell, D.E. (2014). *Passport to Academic Presentations* (2nd ed.). Garnet Education.

Dunkel, P. (2005). *Advanced Listening Comprehension: Developing Aural and Notetaking Skills*. Thomson Heinle.

Hemmert, A. & O'Connell, G. (1998). *Communicating on Campus: Skills for Academic Speaking*. Alta Book Center Publishers.

Lim, P.L., & Smalzer, W. (2005). *Noteworthy: Listening and Notetaking Skills*. Thomson Heinle.

McCormack, J. & Watkins, S. (2012). *English for Academic Study: Speaking*. Garnet Education.

Salehzadeh, J. (2006). *Academic Listening Strategies: A Guide to Understanding Lectures*. University of Michigan Press.

3 Using Academic Sources

Introduction

This chapter aims to provide you with the knowledge and skills for how to use and correctly cite academic sources in your writing. It opens by briefly discussing why you need to draw on academic sources in the first place, considers where those sources should come from and offers some practical criteria for their selection. It then looks at plagiarism and other common forms of academic misconduct and makes several suggestions for how such problems can best be avoided. The chapter next examines the nuts and bolts of paraphrasing, citations and direct quotations, and provides you with detailed guidance and practice tasks on how to apply each of these skills when incorporating other authors' ideas. It closes with some advice and practice tasks on how you should go about compiling a reference list or bibliography and also provides a brief overview of some different academic style conventions.

Additional resources for your further reading are listed on page 76.

3.1 Why Do I Need Academic Sources?

For anyone already familiar with a Western educational environment, the above question probably seems redundant. Most people coming from this kind of background are likely to take it for granted that one of the key hallmarks of academic writing is that we are expected to make reference to the work of others. For students coming from other educational systems, however, this is not always the case. In these instances, the answer to the above question may not be as obvious as it might first seem. It is therefore worth briefly discussing here *why* academic sources are seen as being important. It is also worth considering what is meant by the term academic sources, where such sources are to be found and which criteria should be applied when sources are being selected.

As one of my own MA lecturers once told me long ago, when we join a university and start researching and writing in academia, our work is building on an existing tradition. In effect, this means that we are joining an extended academic family. We show our respect for this fact by acknowledging what has gone before and by demonstrating how our own work fits into that bigger picture.

> If I have been able to see further than others, it was because I stood on the shoulders of giants.
> Quote attributed to Sir Isaac Newton
> Source: https://www.forbes.com/quotes/8663

An MA TESOL/Applied Linguistics student writing on an aspect of Second Language Acquisition, for example, thus not only needs to be able to give their own opinions, but also demonstrate that they know which opinions others have expressed about the same topic. Closely linked with this, using academic sources often covers a slightly different function, in that the cited material may serve as supporting evidence for the writer's own arguments and points. In the case of final dissertations and theses, which usually require students to have completed original primary research (see Chapters 7–9), there will also be the added expectation that the students' own work will be contributing to and extending the wider pool of academic knowledge. For all of these reasons, drawing on academic sources is seen as a necessary and integral component of effective academic writing in Western educational contexts.

Viewed in more pragmatic terms, another reason why lecturers expect to see references to academic sources in their students' writing is because in the process of them doing so, students are providing their course tutors with evidence that they have carried out some reading around the subject. On this point, a question I am very commonly asked by many of my own Masters' students is 'how many sources should my essay include?' In answering this query, I am afraid there is no magic number. Based on discussions with their tutors, students will need to develop their own sense of what is and is not sufficient in doing a given topic justice.

In a typical 4,000-word academic essay at the MA level though, I myself would generally expect to see somewhere between 20 and 30 sources listed in the reference list at the end. However, the final number may be more or less than this, depending on the subject and the exact nature of the essay task. Needless to say, other lecturers' requirements may well differ. The advice I usually give to my own students is that rather than worrying about identifying a definitive *number* per se, they would be better advised to focus their energies on making sure that all the academic sources they *do* use are always as ***relevant*** and, ideally, as ***recent*** as possible. In this regard, quality is definitely a much more important criterion than quantity.

50   *Using Academic Sources*

On the subject of quality though, a very common problem I encounter is that students often end up drawing on academic sources which are simply too dated, or the claims of which have since been comprehensively disproved. While there is no definitive cut-off point on how old a source should be before it may no longer be used, students should certainly become sensitive to publication dates and always ask themselves if a given source is the most relevant and timely for inclusion. In an essay discussing the merits and defects of different approaches to teaching grammar, for example, there would be very little point in using claims from an article written in the 1930s and then positioning those claims as if they were the latest cutting-edge pedagogy. Common sense should tell us that much has changed in our collective thinking since then and academic writers do need to be sensitive to this fact. Conversely though, a student might well decide to cite an early academic text as a means of comparison and to make an argument for how the field has moved forward. In this case, drawing on a dated source would be perfectly legitimate. It must also be said that some early texts in Applied Linguistics/TESOL are now recognised as seminal works of their genre. In these cases, so long as they are being used wisely, and with a clearly explained rationale, their mention in a modern essay would not in itself seem odd.

With regard to the matter of which sources are appropriate though, students *do* need to be very discerning about the materials which they consult. Clearly, relying on a source such as Wikipedia is never going to be seen as academically acceptable, but there are other cases which are much less clear-cut. The internet, for example, is now awash with articles and papers and, in some cases, even bogus academic journals. When coming across such materials, students naturally need to be cautious and exercise their critical judgement. As a rule of thumb, it is always safest to stick with material from academic books and well-established international journals, as one can then be confident that anything which is published there will have been through a rigorous process of peer review. This does not necessarily mean that what has been written is 'The Absolute Truth' and not open to any criticism, but it does usually mean that some recognised checks and balances for ensuring academic credibility have been applied. Most lecturers suggest reading lists and recommend target journals for their students as a matter of course, but an indicative selection of potentially useful academic journals for TESOL/Applied Linguistics has been provided on page 267.

When considering whether or not to include an academic source, it can be useful to learn and apply the following **3R Formula** as a quick test:

R1: Is the source **Relevant**?
R2: Is the source **Recent**?
R3: Is the source **Reliable**?

Check Your Understanding: Independent Task 3.1

A student is writing an essay which asks for a critical evaluation of current approaches to learner error correction. The student has found sources (a)–(e). Are all of these equally acceptable for use, or are some better than others? If you think that any are *not* acceptable for this essay, then why not?

a. Mackey, A., Park, H.I. & Tagarelli, K.M. (2016). Errors, corrective feedback and repair. In G. Hall (Ed.) *The Routledge Handbook of English Language Teaching* (pp. 499–512). Routledge.
b. Russell, J. & Spada, N. (2006). The effectiveness of corrective feedback for the acquisition of L2 grammar. A meta-analysis of the research. In J.M. Norris & L. Ortega (Eds.) *Synthesizing Research on Language Learning and Teaching* (pp. 133–164). John Benjamins.
c. Canagarajah, A.S. (1996). Appropriate methodology and social context. *ELT Journal, 50*(1), 80–82.
d. Li, S. (2014). Oral corrective feedback. *ELT Journal, 68*(2), 196–198.
e. Pollock, E. (2012). Feedback and correction. *English Teaching Professional, 83,* 51.

Some suggested answers to the task can be found on page 71.

If your answer to each of these R questions is 'Yes', then the source will probably be suitable for inclusion. If you find yourself saying 'No' at any stage, then you might be better off looking for something else.

As with so many things in life though, much of what I have written above ultimately comes down to you applying your own common sense and personal judgement. However, if you are in any doubt about the legitimacy, appropriateness or relevance of a given academic source, then naturally it is always best to seek your MA course tutors' advice.

3.2 Plagiarism and How to Avoid It

Plagiarism, in the narrowest sense of the term, describes the act of taking what someone else has written and then passing it off as if it were entirely your own work, with the original author unacknowledged. In most Western universities, plagiarism is seen as a major breach of academic conduct and may therefore attract a broad spread of penalties ranging from reduction of grades, through to the requirement for a complete re-submission, sometimes even as far as expulsion from the university. It is therefore **essential** that all students familiarise themselves with what constitutes plagiarism and know how to avoid it.

The first, and arguably most obvious, piece of advice is quite simply that you should NEVER EVER directly use another person's writing and pretend that it is your own. As most universities now operate automated plagiarism detection software such as Turnitin, and all student written submissions are usually fed through such software as a matter of course, if you *do* lift what somebody else has written and try to pass it off as your own work, whether by accident or design, then it is extremely likely that you will be found out.

While a detailed discussion of all the reasons why students *wilfully* decide to engage in plagiarism is far beyond the scope of this chapter, it must be said that in a great many cases, it seems that students often end up doing so due to panic about impending deadlines and the inability to cope. The best way to avoid finding yourself in this situation is to develop effective time management skills from the outset of your studies (see Chapter 1) and to learn how to plan ahead.

As plagiarism relates to writing, the next piece of advice is that you will need to invest time and effort in becoming a better and more confident academic writer. One of the key components of this means mastering the skills of paraphrasing, citation and quotation. Later in this chapter, we will be looking at each of these areas in detail. You are strongly recommended to spend as much time as possible working through the practice tasks for these topics until you are confident that you know exactly how each works when producing effective academic writing. Do each task at least a couple of times and check your writing with the answers provided, paying attention to the areas that you feel less confident about and trying to learn from the model texts. Remember: there are no shortcuts to becoming a better academic writer; you will need to invest considerable time and effort. However, if you start by applying the right principles, and genuinely want to improve, then the more academic writing you do, the better you will become.

3.3 Avoiding Other Common Forms of Academic Misconduct

Although plagiarism probably accounts for the lion's share of academic misconduct cases in universities, there are several other academic offences, which students may intentionally, or sometimes unintentionally, end up committing:

Cheating in exams: This can take a variety of forms. It might mean looking at somebody else's work or taking pre-prepared answer notes into the exam room. It might also simply mean not adequately following the exam invigilator or proctor's instructions, e.g., talking with the person next to you; using a dictionary or calculator when you were advised not to do so; not switching off your mobile phone.

How to Avoid: Keep your eyes on your own work at all times. Never try to take any notes or other material into an exam room. Always do <u>exactly</u> what the exam invigilator or proctor tells you to do.

Collusion: This refers to working in partnership with somebody else. For example, you might decide to work on an essay task with one of your classmates and share the load. If this then resulted in you submitting a piece of work which was basically the same as your classmate's submission, then you would be guilty of collusion.

How to Avoid: Make sure that your work is always your own. Do not share your essays with your classmates or ask to see theirs.

Paying someone else to do the work for you: This might mean using a commercial writing service, sometimes known as an 'essay mill'. In recent years, the internet has been filled with websites offering students the option of having their work professionally produced, usually for a high fee.

How to Avoid: As above, make sure that your work is always your own. Do not be tempted to pay someone else to do the work on your behalf. Your tutors are likely to be familiar with your style of writing and will be able to recognise any work which doesn't appear to be your own.

Submitting the same piece of work for more than one assignment: This is known as 'double-dipping' or 'self-plagiarism'. According to academic regulations, you cannot receive a grade for the same piece of work twice, even if your work was submitted in a different year and on a different course.

How to Avoid: Deal with each assignment separately and do not be tempted to take shortcuts by re-using any previously submitted work in a different context.

Check Your Understanding: Independent Task 3.3

A boyfriend and a girlfriend are studying at the same university and on the same MA TESOL course. To save themselves some time, they decide that they will work together on one of the coursework essay assignments. The girl agrees to write the introduction and conclusion parts of an essay, while the boy focuses on preparing the detail in the body. They produce their essays well ahead of time and submit them to their tutor, expecting that they will get good grades.

They are then very surprised a couple of weeks later when they receive an email from the university asking them to attend an academic misconduct hearing with their tutor and the MA TESOL course director.

If you were a fellow student on the course, what advice could you have given to these students? Have they done anything wrong?

A suggested answer to the task can be found on page 72.

54 Using Academic Sources

These examples above are some of the most common forms of academic misconduct, but there are also others. The best advice is to read your course handbook very carefully and make sure that you are always following the rules.

3.4 Paraphrasing

When used in the context of academic writing, paraphrasing can be defined as the act of reproducing what someone else has written, but then putting it into your own words. In doing this, however, there are three cardinal rules:

- You must not use exactly the same language as the original.
- You must not retain the original structure but then simply replace several key words with synonyms (this is called 'Patchwriting' – see below).
- You must not change, or in any way distort, the original meaning of what has been written.

> **Check Your Understanding: Independent Task 3.4a**
>
> A student is writing an essay comparing First and Second Language Acquisition. In their discussion of the former, they have decided to draw on some of the early work by Noam Chomsky. From reading one of Chomsky's seminal articles – Chomsky, N. (1959). A review of B.F. Skinner's verbal behaviour. *Language, 35*(1), 26–58 – they discover that in those early days of cognitivism, Chomsky had postulated the following:
>
>> There is some part of the mind-brain dedicated specifically to language. Just as there is a part dedicated to vision, there is a language faculty. It's like an organ.
>
> The student decides to paraphrase this information and comes up with six possible drafts. These are listed under (a)–(f) below.
> Which of these paraphrases (if any) of what Chomsky originally wrote are acceptable/unacceptable? Why?
> Some suggested answers to the task can be found on page 72.
>
> a. According to Chomsky (1959), there is some part of the mind-brain dedicated specifically to language, just as there is a part dedicated to vision. It's like an organ.
> b. According to Chomsky (1959), in the same way that there is a part of the brain that deals with vision, there is also a part that deals specifically with language.

c. According to Chomsky (1959), different parts of the brain deal with different functions, for example, language and vision.
d. According to Chomsky (1959), the part of the brain that deals with language is like an organ.
e. According to Chomsky (1959), both language and vision are processed by the brain.
f. According to Chomsky (1959), there is a portion of the human brain committed especially to language, just like there is a portion committed to seeing. This functions as an organ.

As I have described above, some students tend to approach paraphrasing as if it is simply a matter of changing a few words here and there and applying some synonyms. Authors commenting on some of the difficulties and problems with student academic writing have described this process as 'patchwriting' (e.g., see Pecorari, 2003). While there can be no doubt that some skilful student patch writers probably do 'get away with it', just as some of those who blatantly plagiarise also sometimes still manage to slip under the detection net, the practice is a poor and rather unethical approach to academic writing. In its worst guises, it may be seen as a weaker form of academic misconduct.

The best way to avoid patchwriting is to stop thinking of the paraphrasing process as being nothing more than a mechanical matter of finding synonyms or trying to make things look cosmetically different. Instead, when teaching yourself to paraphrase, it can be helpful to break the process down into a series of steps.

I often advise my own students to do the following:

1. First of all, ask yourself what exactly the author is trying to say. What main point(s) is he/she making? To help you to do this, identify any key parts of the text.
2. Try to represent these main ideas in a shorthand form using notes or equations. If English is not your first language, you can also complete this step by writing in your mother tongue.
3. Try to create a new sentence or paragraph in English using your own words, and *only by looking at and expanding what you wrote down in note form or in your own language,* i.e. at this stage, it is best to put the original text to one side for a moment.
4. Compare your new version with the original text and check that you have preserved the main meaning(s). Have you inadvertently distorted or misrepresented anything? Does what you have written still make sense? If English is not your first language, is what you have written grammatically and semantically accurate?

56 *Using Academic Sources*

> **Paraphrasing from an Academic Text**
>
> Jackson, D.O. & Burch, A.R. (2017). Complementary theoretical perspectives on task-based classroom realities. *TESOL Quarterly, 51*(3), 493–506.
>
> Research serves multiple roles in fostering educational practice. To begin, there are good reasons to consult research for pedagogic insights.... And yet, one can ask precisely how theoretically motivated research makes itself relevant to actual classroom practices.

Let us look at an example of how this step-by-step paraphrasing process might work with a real piece of academic text. The box above contains an excerpt from an article which originally appeared in the journal *TESOL Quarterly* in 2017.

STEP 1: Identify the main points/key parts of the text (it can help to underline or highlight these)

<u>Research</u> serves <u>multiple roles in</u> fostering <u>educational practice</u>. To begin, there are <u>good reasons to consult research for pedagogic insights</u>... And yet, one can ask <u>precisely how theoretically motivated research</u> makes itself <u>relevant to actual classroom practices</u>.

STEP 2: Represent these main points in a shorthand note form

Research = helpful in various ways for educ. practice. Useful to look at research for understanding pedagogy. BUT... Theoretical research – classroom: how to link?

STEP 3: Expand your notes to create a new piece of writing using your own words

As Jackson and Burch (2017) have pointed out, when it comes to educational practice, research can be helpful in several ways. However, while it can be useful to look at research as a means of understanding pedagogy, the question remains of how exactly theoretical research should be linked with what happens in the classroom.

STEP 4: Compare your new writing with the original

In this case, the new piece of writing, though structured and worded differently, has stayed faithful to the points expressed in the original. There has been no distortion of meaning and the original authors have been properly acknowledged in the citation.

Check Your Understanding: Independent Task 3.4b

Have a go at paraphrasing the academic text below by going through the four steps. Pecorari, D. & Petrić, B. (2014). Plagiarism in second-language writing. *Language Teaching, 47*(3), 269–302.

Plagiarism has long been used as a umbrella term covering various types of unacceptable behaviour, some of which, but not all, refer to textual activity. Poor referencing, inadequate paraphrase and inaccurate citation are sometimes placed in the same category as commissioning a paper from a commercial service and submitting another student's paper as one's own.

A suggested answer to the task can be found on page 72.

In the different examples of paraphrasing provided so far, you have probably noticed that the writer first introduced the academic source with a reporting phrase:

According to Chomsky (1959) …
As Jackson and Burch (2017) *have pointed out,* …

There are a variety of such reporting phrases in English which can be used to introduce an academic source. As a writer, your decision on which phrase to select will largely depend on the relationship between your own opinion and the information you are presenting. Some reporting phrases are **NEUTRAL** in tone, which means that it is impossible to tell the writer's own stance; others carry a connotation of **AGREEMENT**; others still may appear to cast **DOUBT** or suggest **DISAGREEMENT**, while a final category may suggest to the reader that there is **EMPIRICAL EVIDENCE**.

Check Your Understanding: Independent Task 3.4c

There are 13 different examples of reporting verbs below.

Write an **N** next to the phrase if you think it is **NEUTRAL**
Write an **A** next to the phrase if you think it suggests **AGREEMENT**
Write a **D** next to the phrase if you think it casts **DOUBT** or shows **DISAGREEMENT**
Write an **E** next to the phrase if you think it shows there is **EMPIRICAL EVIDENCE**

58 *Using Academic Sources*

> According to....   As ... has/have pointed out,   ...argues that
>
> Research by ... suggests that   As ... see/sees it,
>
> ... claims/has claimed that   ...has/have demonstrated that
>
> ... proposes that   ...defines X as   ...advocates   ... found that
>
> The results of x's study show/showed that
>
> ... suggests/has suggested that
>
> Some suggested answers to the task can be found on page 72.

Now look at some examples of these phrases in action. The academic sources cited here are all real, highly relevant to studies in TESOL/Applied Linguistics, and have been listed in full for your further reading on pages 76–78:

a. According to Chomsky (1959), the human competency for learning our first language is innate.
b. As Jackson and Burch (2017) have pointed out, research can help to inform educational practice.
c. Pecorari (2008) argues that intertextuality is a core component of all discourse.
d. Research by Wenger (1998) suggests that learning is socially constructed.
e. As Kumaravadivelu (2001) sees it, English language teaching has moved beyond its earlier preoccupations with methodology into what he has termed the post-method era.
f. Swales (2019) claims that a common failing of some of the published work on genre is that the writers often fail to make clear connections with classroom pedagogy.
g. Abasi and Graves (2008) have demonstrated that not every case of student plagiarism can be attributed to deliberate deception.
h. Hutchinson and Waters (1987) propose that taking an overly narrow view of target situation needs can be counter-productive when teaching ESP. They argue that there should instead be more of a focus on how learners prefer to learn.
i. Hamp-Lyons (2011) defines EAP as belonging to the field of Education, although she also acknowledges its close relationship with ESP.
j. Ding (2016) advocates EAP practitioners' engagement in continuing professional development as a means of them enhancing their personal agency.
k. Bell (2021a) found that having his MA TESOL students take part in a structured debate activity helped them to make stronger connections

between what the theories on Communicative Language Teaching claim and how this methodological approach might operate in practice.
l. The results of Lowton's study (2020) show that the number of private provider partnerships with UK universities has continued to increase.
m. Bell (2021b) has suggested that Bourdieu's construct of capital can be a very useful tool when trying to account for some of the challenges relating to EAP practitioners' professional status.

Check Your Understanding: Independent Task 3.4d

Choose four of the above sentences and re-write them using a different reporting phrase each time in order to change the connotation.
Some suggested answers to the task can be found on page 73.

3.5 Making Citations

In each of the examples provided so far, the method of providing the academic source has been what Swales (1990) has termed 'integral citation'. This means that the name of the author(s) appears first. As Pecorari (2003) has discussed, following this form of citation can serve to make the academic source appear more prominent and enhance its authority.

Swales (1990) has also described an alternative method for presenting academic sources, which he terms 'non-integral citation' or 'parenthetical citation' (Swales, 2014). In this format, the name of the author(s) appears at the *end* of a statement, either in parenthesis or as a footnote.

Compare the following:

Bell (2021c) claims that using poetry in the ELT classroom can help to stimulate learners' capacity for critical thinking. [**integral citation**]

It has been claimed that using poetry in the ELT classroom can help to stimulate learners' capacity for critical thinking (Bell 2021c). [**non-integral or parenthetical citation**]

As an MA TESOL/Applied Linguistics student, it is highly likely that you will find yourself using both forms of citation in your academic writing. However, these differences in practice are not always so arbitrary. Different academic disciplines and different discourse communities may show a marked preference for one style or the other.

3.6 Direct Quotations

Although paraphrasing others' ideas is probably the more frequently used skill when referencing academic sources, writers may also sometimes prefer to quote from a source text directly. Depending on the specific academic conventions being followed (see Section 3.9) there are often slightly different rules and expectations governing how quotations should be applied, but it is useful to be familiar with some broad principles. These are outlined below.

> Short quotations i.e., when the material being quoted represents just a line or two, should usually be indicated with speech marks and incorporated as part of the main body of writing, preceded by the author's surname, with the source publication date in parenthesis. The page number appears in parenthesis at the end of the quotation.

In the box below, there is an excerpt from an Applied Linguistics essay examining some of the reasons why English has become such a dominant world language. The writer is arguing that trade and other forms of international business have played a key role in this process.

Look at how the writer incorporates a short quotation from a book by David Graddol to emphasise this point.

Example of how to Incorporate a Short Quotation

As Graddol (1997) has pointed out, "Trade and other forms of international collaboration are more likely to be successful if suppliers and customers can communicate using the same language" (p. 320) and there can be little doubt that such business arrangements have helped to expand the international footprint of English.

> Source text: Graddol, D. (1997). *The Future of English*. The British Council.

Check Your Understanding: Independent Task 3.5

Gather together a small selection of articles from journals representing very different academic disciplines, for example, Education; Psychology; Medicine; Economics; Linguistics; Engineering; Plant Biology etc.

Do you notice any differences between the specific disciplinary citation practices?

Some suggested answers to the task can be found on page 73.

Check Your Understanding: Independent Task 3.6a

You are writing an essay about the relative usefulness and relevance of MA TESOL programmes for pre-service and in-service teachers. Use a short quotation from the source text reproduced below to make an argument that in-service teachers clearly start their studies with several advantages over pre-service teachers. You should list the page number for your quotation as page 9.

A suggested answer to the task can be found on page 74.

Source text: Bell, D.E. (2021a). Linking theory with practice. *Modern English Teacher, 30*(3), 9–14.

The benefits of only starting a Masters' programme after a certain level of practical experience and expertise has already been achieved are obvious. Such teachers have stood in front of a class of students and have taught the subject. They will therefore already be familiar with things such as lesson planning, ELT materials and classroom management and thus have a practice-based contextual peg on which concepts that are more theoretical can later be hung.

Longer quotations i.e., when the material being quoted goes beyond just a couple of lines, should usually be *set apart from the main body of writing* by using a colon, appropriate spacing and indenting. When using such longer quotations, there is no need to use speech marks. The author's surname, the source publication date and the page number(s) should appear at the end in parenthesis below the quotation.

In the box below the writer is continuing to discuss the different factors responsible for the rise and dominance of English. Look at how a slightly longer quotation is now used, this time from a book by David Crystal, and how it is being positioned as evidence for the role played by technology.

Another interesting point about the proliferation of English is made by Crystal (1997) in his discussion of the effects of new technology:

Although it was predicted by some that the rise of the internet might challenge the position of English as the dominant world lingua franca, it now seems abundantly clear that this has not

> been the case. If anything, the Internet, and other forms of social media have both increased and enhanced the use of English worldwide.
>
> (Crystal, 1997, p. 150)
>
> As the global reach of the internet becomes ever wider, it seems fair to predict that the role it plays in helping to expose more and more people to English will only continue.
>
> Source text: Crystal, D. (1997). *English as a Global Language*. Cambridge University Press.

Check Your Understanding: Independent Task 3.6b

Later in the same essay about the usefulness of MA TESOL programmes for pre-service and in-service teachers, you want to make the point that if such programmes *lack* an observed and assessed practice teaching component, then pre-service teachers are likely to struggle in making the necessary links between theory and practice. One possible consequence of this is that students may graduate from their MA TESOL without being able to see the relevance of what they studied.

Use a longer quotation this time from the text reproduced below to bolster and act as supporting evidence for these claims. If you use a quotation from lines 1–7, list the page number as page 9. If you use a quotation from lines 8–13, you should list the page number as page 10.

> Source text: Bell, D.E. (2021a). Linking theory with practice. *Modern English Teacher, 30*(3), 9–14.

A suggested answer to this task can be found on page 75.

For those joining an MA TESOL programme as the first real step in their ELT career, the situation is clearly quite different. With little or no prior teaching experience, such individuals typically face a very steep learning curve, in which they not only have to get to grips with what can often seem quite abstract theories and paradigms, but then also link these with strategies for classroom practice. This problem is often then compounded by the fact that many MA TESOL programmes do not include a practical teaching component, nor necessarily encourage their students to make explicit links between what

Using Academic Sources 63

the ELT research says and how this might then translate into what happens in the classroom.

From my personal involvement in the delivery of MA TESOL programmes, often with quite experienced students, a very common complaint from participants is that even after having successfully passed their Masters, they sometimes fail to see the practical relevance of what they covered on the course, or apply this learning to their daily lived-in realities. In its extreme form, this is analogous to the English language learners who perform well in discrete-point grammar tests and can achieve high examination results, but then struggle to communicate when they find themselves in an English-speaking environment.

3.6.1 A Few More Things to Be Aware Of and Pay Particular Attention To

When you quote, the material that you are quoting must be directly relevant to the point you are making.

This probably sounds obvious, but over the years, I have seen *many* examples of student quotations when there is not a very clear logical or semantic match between the point that is being argued and the quotation that is being offered as supporting evidence. The link(s) between your point and the accompanying quotation must always make sense.

Look at the example below of a *poorly* chosen student quotation using the text from Independent Task 3.6a:

> It can be useful for teachers to get work experience before they start their MA. As Bell (2021a) argues, "concepts that are more theoretical can later be hung" (p. 9). Pre-service teachers do not understand this.

In the above case, the link between work experience and concepts that are more theoretical does not make sense. It is also not clear why these concepts can later be hung – whatever that means – or why pre-service teachers do not understand this.

When you quote, the text that forms the quotation itself must align well grammatically and stylistically with both the preceding and following sections of your own writing.

This one is potentially a little trickier, especially if you are not a native speaker of English. When you quote, you must always ensure that there is a good 'fit' between the quotation and your own writing. This becomes especially important when you use longer quotations. The sentence stub which introduces the longer quotation and ends in a colon must match well grammatically and stylistically with the writing that comes before and after.

Look at this example of a longer student quotation which *doesn't* fit very well grammatically. It has been taken from the text in Independent Task 3.6b:

> As Bell (2021a) has discussed, when pre-service teachers join MA TESOL programmes, they can encounter some difficulties:
>
> > fact that many MA TESOL programmes do not include a practical teaching component, nor necessarily encourage their students to make explicit links between what the ELT research says and how this might then translate into what happens in the classroom.
> >
> > (p. 9)

In the above case, although the preceding sentence ending in a colon is fine, there is a poor grammatical 'run-on' with the part of the text being quoted. If the student had started the quotation section from 'many', the writing would have made much better grammatical sense.

When you quote from a section of text, it is not necessary to include absolutely everything in your quotation, especially if you think that there are some redundant parts. Alternatively, you may sometimes need to add a word or two of your own to make the meaning clear. As long as the grammar of the writing is not negatively impacted, such omissions and additions are perfectly acceptable.

You can hide any redundant areas by using three dots like this … to show that some text is missing.

You should indicate any words that you have added yourself by enclosing them in square brackets like this [ ].

Look at this example of a quotation when the writer has omitted some of the wording used in the text from Independent Task 3.6b:

> Common sense dictates that someone joining an MA TESOL with prior teaching experience is going to be more familiar with practical teaching issues than someone joining such a course with no background knowledge or experience of teaching at all. As Bell (2021a) rightly points out, those with prior teaching experience will already

> be familiar with "lesson planning, ELT materials and classroom management... and thus have a practice-based contextual peg on which concepts that are more theoretical can later be hung" (p. 9). This finding has important ramifications for MA TESOL student recruitment and for who should and should not be allowed to join such programmes.

Now look at this example of a slightly longer quotation when the writer has added three words of his/her own to the text from Independent Task 3.6b:

> Few would deny that someone starting an MA TESOL with prior teaching experience is going to be much more familiar with practical teaching issues than someone joining such a course with no background knowledge or experience of teaching at all. As Bell (2021a) points out:
>
>> [Experienced teachers will] have stood in front of a class of students and have taught the subject. They will therefore already be familiar with things like lesson planning, ELT materials and classroom management and thus have a practice-based contextual peg on which concepts that are more theoretical can later be hung.
>> (p. 9)
>
> All of the above suggests that taking students onto an MA TESOL programme when they have no grounding in the field may in fact serve to put them at a disadvantage.

3.7 Bringing It All Together

In the material that has been covered up to now, paraphrasing, citation, and using direct quotations have each been presented as discrete items. In the real world, of course, students need to be able to use all three of these skills confidently and fluently. In an extended piece of academic writing, it would not be unusual to find writers employing a judicious mix of paraphrasing, integral and non-integral citations, as well as short and long direct quotations. Being able to apply and interweave these different writing techniques effectively is one of the hallmarks of being a good academic writer.

Check Your Understanding: Independent Task 3.7

You are writing an essay in which you want to discuss the historical development of English for Academic Purposes (EAP). One of the arguments you are trying to make is that EAP has now broken away from its early beginnings as a sub-field of ESP and has become a more fully recognised form of English Language Teaching in its own right.

Use a mix of paraphrasing, citation and direct quotation from the text excerpt below (you can choose whether to use a short or long quotation format) to create a coherent piece of academic writing. If you quote anything from the first four lines, list the page number as page 161. Any quotations from lines 5–15 should be referenced as page 162.

Source text: Bell, D.E. (2018). The practice of EAP in Australia: A rose by any other name? In L.T. Wong & W.L.H. Wong (Eds) *Teaching and Learning English for Academic Purposes. Current Research and Practices* (pp. 161–177). Nova Science Publishers Inc.

Few would deny that since its formal emergence in the early 1970s, the field of English for Academic Purposes (EAP) has enjoyed a period of significant expansion. Not surprisingly perhaps, one of the economic outcomes of this steady growth is that EAP now represents a multi-million-dollar industry worldwide.

From a disciplinary perspective, it might also be said that compared to the early days of its existence when EAP was emerging as a science and technology-dominated sub-field of English for Specific Purposes (ESP), the discipline as we know it today has considerably widened its scope and more explicitly marked out its boundaries. In so doing, EAP has evidently gained a much stronger sense of its professional identity. For example, while scholarly outputs dealing with EAP would once have appeared in the *ESP Journal*, they are now much more likely to be found in the pages of EAP's own dedicated journal, the *Journal of English for Academic Purposes (JEAP)*.

In keeping with a developmental trajectory which appears to be common to new and emerging disciplines, EAP has also started to coin its own meta-language, as evidenced by the use of EAP-specific terminology such as English for General Academic Purposes (EGAP) and English for Specific Academic Purposes (ESAP).

A suggested answer to the task can be found on page 75.

3.8 Compiling a Reference List or Bibliography

At the end of most pieces of written academic work, you will usually be required to provide a reference list or bibliography listing all the sources that you consulted. Although some people use these terms interchangeably, technically speaking, a reference list should only include the sources which you have directly cited in the body of your writing; a bibliography, on the other hand, would include sources which you perhaps consulted, but then didn't directly cite. As always, check with your course tutors exactly what they require from you when submitting written work.

Depending on the specific academic style that you follow, there are some slightly different conventions governing how exactly each reference should be listed (see Section 3.9) but as a general rule of thumb, your sources should always be listed in *ascending* alphabetical order, and you should always be *consistent* in whichever style you use.

As the whole purpose of providing a reference list or bibliography is to allow the reader to be able to access the same sources that you did, you must be sure to provide sufficient information for them to do so, i.e., the author's name; the year of publication; the title of the publication; and finally, an indication of what kind of publication it was; for example, a book, a chapter in an edited collection, a journal article, an unpublished source such as an MA dissertation or a doctoral thesis, or a conference paper. Nowadays, it is also quite common to see references to academic material on websites and blogs.

Look at some examples of these different source listings below:

A BOOK
Crystal, D. (1997). *English as a Global Language.* Cambridge University Press.

A SINGLE CHAPTER IN AN EDITED COLLECTION
Bell, D.E. (2018). The practice of EAP in Australia: A rose by any other name? In L.T. Wong & W.L.H. Wong (Eds) *Teaching and Learning English for Academic Purposes. Current Research and Practices* (pp. 161–177). Nova Science Publishers Inc.

A JOURNAL ARTICLE
Bell, D.E. (2021a). Linking theory with practice. *Modern English Teacher, 30*(3), 9–14.

AN UNPUBLISHED SOURCE
Lowton, R. (2020). The (T)EAP of the iceberg: The role of qualifications in teaching English for academic purposes. MA TESOL diss., University of Nottingham Ningbo China.

A CONFERENCE PAPER
Bell, D.E. (2021b). *Using poetry as a means of promoting creativity and criticality in ELT.* Paper delivered at the 24-hour MATSDA International Language Learning Conference. Kuala Lumpur: Universiti Sains Malaysia.

A WEBSITE
BALEAP. (2008). *Competency Framework for Teachers of English for Academic Purposes*. Retrieved from: https://www.baleap.org/wp-content/uploads/2016/04/teap-competency-framework.pdf.

A BLOG
Alexander, O. (2009). *Understanding EAP Context. Teaching English Blog*. Retrieved from: http://www.teachingenglish.org.uk/blogs/olwyn-alexander/understanding-eap-context.

If the above seven sources had been cited in an academic essay and were then compiled as a reference list at the end, it might look like this:

References

Alexander, O. (2009). *Understanding EAP Context-Teaching English Blog*. Retrieved from: http://www.teachingenglish.org.uk/blogs/olwyn-alexander/understanding-eap-context.

BALEAP. (2008). *Competency Framework for Teachers of English for Academic Purposes*. Retrieved from: https://www.baleap.org/wp-content/uploads/2016/04/teap-competency-framework.pdf.

Bell, D.E. (2018). The practice of EAP in Australia: A rose by any other name? In L.T. Wong & W.L.H. Wong (Eds.) *Teaching and Learning English for Academic Purposes. Current Research and Practices* (pp. 161–177). Nova Science Publishers Inc.

Bell, D.E. (2021a). Linking theory with practice. *Modern English Teacher, 30*(3), 9–14.

Bell, D.E. (2021b). *Using poetry as a means of promoting creativity and criticality in ELT*. Paper delivered at the 24-hour MATSDA International Language Learning Conference. Kuala Lumpur: Universiti Sains Malaysia.

Crystal, D. (1997). *English as a Global Language*. Cambridge University Press.

Lowton, R. (2020). The (T)EAP of the iceberg: The role of qualifications in teaching English for academic purposes. MA TESOL diss., University of Nottingham Ningbo China.

Note from the above that if you use two sources by the same author in the same year, then in both the main body of your writing and in the final reference list, you will need to differentiate between them. This is usually done by adding small case letters after the publication date, i.e., (2021a, 2021b), as in the publication listings by Bell above.

Also note from the above the stylistic differences in the way that different publication types have been listed. These conventions allow the reader to see immediately whether a given source is a book, an article, a conference paper etc.

Software packages such as EndNote, Zotero and Mendeley can help to compile academic reference lists for you automatically. However, while these tools can be useful in saving the writer time, as with all automated services, they can sometimes inadvertently cause formatting errors. For this reason, I always advise my own students first to become proficient at compiling their reference lists *manually* and not to rely on automated software. This gives them much greater control of their own work; it also means that they will develop a better understanding of the underlying academic principles.

As with all other aspects of academic writing, the more you practice compiling reference lists, the better you will become.

Check Your Understanding: Independent Task 3.8

There are four different sources detailed below. Format these correctly and then put them into a reference list, so that they would be acceptable when presented at the end of an academic essay.

(It should be obvious that in this case, the 'academic' sources are, of course, all entirely fictitious.)

(a)
BOOK TITLE: The wonderful world of cheese
AUTHOR: Charles Cheddar
PUBLICATION YEAR: 1998
PUBLISHER: The Dairy Press

(b)
JOURNAL TITLE: Modern Cheese Lover
VOLUME, EDITION AND PAGE NUMBERS: 65(3), 22–36
ARTICLE TITLE: Is port always the best match?
AUTHORS: Veronica Stilton and Marjorie Gouda
PUBLICATION YEAR: 2015

(c)
BOOK TITLE: Cheese, cheese, and more cheese: a definitive guide
BOOK EDITORS: Christou Halloumi and Georgios Feta
PUBLISHER: The Gourmet Press
PUBLICATION YEAR: 2009
BOOK CHAPTER TITLE: The many many uses of mozzarella
CHAPTER AUTHOR: Luigi Scamorza
PAGE NUMBERS: 221–240

(d)
WEBSITE: http://www.gourmetadventurer.com/blogs/andy-emmental/crackers-matter
AUTHOR: Andy Emmental
DATE: 2021
BLOG TITLE: Now we've got the cheese, what about the crackers?
A suggested answer to the task can be found on page 76.

3.9 Different Academic Style Conventions

As I have already mentioned, there are several different academic style conventions currently in worldwide common use. As an MA TESOL/Applied Linguistics student, the ones that you will probably most commonly encounter are:

- Harvard
- APA
- MLA

In most cases, your lecturers will tell you which academic style conventions they prefer, and you should follow their instructions very carefully on this. Guidance on academic style requirements is also typically provided in course material such as module handbooks and student conduct guides. As a postgraduate student, remember that it is *your responsibility* to familiarise yourself with such content, so that you know exactly what is expected of you and you can present your academic work in an appropriate manner.

Whichever academic style conventions you decide to follow, the cardinal rule is that you must be consistent, i.e., you should choose one style and then stick with it. Do NOT mix different conventions together.

The following websites provide further useful guidance on each style:

HARVARD STYLE:
https://www.imperial.ac.uk/media/imperial-college/administration-and-support-services/library/public/harvard.pdf
APA STYLE:
https://apastyle.apa.org/
MLA STYLE:
https://owl.purdue.edu/owl/research_and_citation/mla_style/mla_formatting_and_style_guide/mla_formatting_and_style_guide.html

Suggested Answers to Independent Tasks

Task 3.1

In terms of their academic credibility, each of these sources is generally fine. All of them are well-established, bona fide publishing outlets for scholarly work in the field of English Language Teaching/Applied Linguistics although in the case of source (e), the magazine *English*

Teaching Professional, some might argue that the publication is aimed more at classroom practitioners than academic researchers. For an essay of this nature, however, this should not necessarily be an issue.

Some of the publication dates are worthy of more critical consideration, however. The essay task asks for an evaluation of *current* approaches to error correction, so sources that are already over a decade old such as source (b) may now seem rather dated. Although this source provides a meta-analysis of the research up to 2006, one might expect there to have been further developments between this time and 2022. When marking the essay, some lecturers might therefore draw some negative attention to this.

Depending on how it has been used, probably the weakest source here is the article by Canagarajah from 1996. Although this author is certainly very highly respected and the source of the article itself, *English Language Teaching Journal*, is also beyond question, aside from the fact that the article is already over two decades old, a more worrisome issue is that the content and focus of this particular piece has very little to do with error correction. It *may* be that the writer was trying to make the point that social context also influences attitudes to learner error correction, but this argument would seem rather tenuous in the context of this essay. Always remember the first R of the 3R Formula, i.e., whichever sources you select the absolute top criterion is that they must be *relevant*.

As an extension of this point, do not ever be tempted to 'pad out' your reference list by adding sources that *look* vaguely relevant but which you have *not* in fact consulted or actively used. Your course tutors will almost certainly pick up on such practices and you will lose marks.

Task 3.3

These students have committed academic misconduct due to *COLLUSION*. As a classmate, if you had been giving them some friendly advice, you could have reminded them to do their own work at all times and never to share their assignment answers.

Task 3.4a

Paraphrase b is the *only* one which is acceptable. The others can be rejected on the following grounds:

Paraphrase a: beyond the use of a reporting phrase and citation, this is the same as the original. This could be construed as PLAGIARISM which might lead to very negative consequences for the writer.

Paraphrases c, d and e: these cases have distorted the original meaning and are therefore misrepresenting what Chomsky said. While they would probably not be identified as cases of academic misconduct, a lecturer marking this work would almost certainly pick up on the inaccuracies and misrepresentations. This could potentially cost the student writer some marks.

Paraphrase f: this stands out as a very clear case of patchwriting. The same structure as the original has been kept with only a few lexical changes here and there. Again, this might not be considered as heinous a crime as outright plagiarism, but the student writer might still get a warning and also lose some marks.

Task 3.4b

As Pecorari and Petrić (2014) have pointed out, plagiarism is sometimes used as a catch-all term to cover a wide range of unacceptable practices. The problems found in poor academic writing in general, for example, such as weak referencing skills, poor citation and faulty paraphrasing are sometimes lumped in with more obvious cases of academic misconduct, such as procuring assignments from an essay mill, or directly passing off another student writer's work as if it were your own.

Task 3.4c

According to ... **(N)**
As ... has/have pointed out, **(A)**
... argues that **(N)**
Research by ... suggests that **(E)**
As ... see/sees it **(N)**
... claims that/has claimed that **(D)**
.. has/have demonstrated that **(E)**
... proposes that **(D)**
... defines x as **(N)**
... advocates **(N)**
... found that **(E)**
The results of X's study show/showed that **(E)**
... suggests/has suggested that **(D)**

Task 3.4d

Ding (2016) *claims that* engaging in continuing professional development can serve as a means of enhancing EAP practitioners' personal agency.

[the new connotation here is that the matter of whether CPD can boost EAP practitioners' personal agency is possibly open to debate. In the next clause, the writer may well go on to present a counter-argument]

As Lowton (2020) *has pointed out*, the number of private provider partnerships with UK has continued to increase.

[the new connotation here is that the writer agrees with Lowton and is now using those findings to support his/her own line of argument]

As Wenger (1998) *sees it*, learning is socially constructed.

[the new connotation here is that although this is being reported as Wenger's view, we cannot be sure of the writer's own stance]

As Swales (2019) *has pointed out*, a common failing of some of the published work on genre is that the writers often fail to make clear connections with classroom pedagogy.

[the new connotation here is that the writer agrees with Swales' view and is now using this point as supporting evidence for his/her own line of argument]

Task 3.5

There is no one answer to this task as what you discover will depend on which journals you choose to access, but you may well find that there are some citation differences between Arts and Humanities subjects, subjects belonging to the Social Sciences and subjects belonging to the Sciences.

Compare these illustrative examples:

Sample 1: Medicine [American Medical Association referencing style]
Source:
Casey SD, Joseph DiVito Jr., Lupow JB, Gulani, R. An Uncommon Cause of Acute Abdominal Pain: Primary Epiploic Appendagitis in the Emergency Setting. *Einstein Journal of Biology & Medicine.* 2016;31(1/2):17-19.
Text excerpt:
As this misdiagnosis indicated medical, rather than surgical, management, the correct diagnosis of PEA was obscured and its true incidence

falsely diminished (Ghahremani, 1992; Carmichael, 1985; Molla, 1998; Almeida, 1999; Rao, 1998).
   [example of non-integral/parenthetical citation]

Sample 2: Engineering [Vancouver referencing style]
Source:
Zhang Y, Zhao Q, Tan B, Yang J. A power system transient stability assessment method based on active learning. J Eng (Stevenage) [Internet]. 2021;2021(11):715–23. Available from: http://dx.doi.org/10.1049/tje2.12068.
Text excerpt:
Transient stability refers to the ability of the power system to transit to a stable state after suffering large disturbances [1].
   [example of in-text numeric style of citation – this style of citation is very common in science disciplines]

Sample 3: Arts & Humanities [APA referencing style]
Source:
O'Byrne, A. (2018). London and urban culture in eighteenth-century literature. *Literature Compass, 15*(2), e12437.
Text excerpt:
At the start of the century, as Cynthia Wall (1998) notes, the devastation wrought by the Great Fire of 1666 was still being worked through as "the demands of rebuilding the city generated an intense and widespread interest in urban redefinition that shaped a new set of technologies and a new set of literatures" (p. 9).
   [example of integral citation]

Task 3.6a

Many UK MA TESOL programmes require applicants to have at least two years practical teaching experience before commencing their studies. Though this stipulation might be perceived by some as an unnecessary administrative barrier, in pragmatic terms, it makes a lot of sense. As Bell (2021a) has pointed out, in-service teachers joining an MA TESOL programme with previous teaching experience will "already be familiar with things like lesson planning, ELT materials and classroom management" (p. 9). This clearly then places them in a more advantageous starting position than pre-service teachers, who by contrast will be learning such concepts from scratch.

Task 3.6b

When students with no previous teaching experience are accepted onto MA TESOL programmes which also lack a practical teaching component, one common problem is that they may then lack sufficient background knowledge to make much sense of all the new knowledge and skills that they will need to process. As Bell (2021a) points out, in some cases, this can even result in students graduating from their courses but then failing to make the necessary connections when they later start to work as teachers:

> .... a very common complaint from participants is that even after having successfully passed their Masters, they sometimes fail to see the *practical* relevance of what they covered on the course or apply this learning to their daily lived-in realities. In its extreme form, this is analogous to the English language learners who perform well in discrete-point grammar tests and can achieve high examination results, but then struggle to communicate when they find themselves in an English-speaking environment.
>
> (p. 10)

This issue not surprisingly invites some questions around the wider purpose of MA TESOL programmes, particularly in those cases when they are seen as fulfilling a gate-keeping function for entry to TESOL as a profession.

Task 3.7

Although EAP may have started life as a relatively minor sub-set of ESP, in more recent years, one might argue that it has now come into its own and can be viewed as a fully-fledged academic discipline in its own right. As Bell (2018) points out, EAP as a field of study:

> has considerably widened its scope and more explicitly marked out its boundaries. In so doing, EAP has evidently gained a much stronger sense of its professional identity. For example, while scholarly outputs dealing with EAP would once have appeared in the *ESP Journal*, they are now much more likely to be found in the pages of EAP's own dedicated journal, the *Journal of English for Academic Purposes* (*JEAP*).
>
> (p. 162)

All of the above can be seen as evidence to support the claim that EAP deserves to be treated as a bona fide academic subject.

Task 3.8

References

Cheddar, C. (1998). *The Wonderful World of Cheese*. The Dairy Press.

Emmental, A. (2021). Now we've got the cheese, what about the crackers? Retrieved from: http://www.gourmetadventurer.com/blogs/andy-emmental/crackers-matter.

Scamorza, L. (2009). The many many uses of mozzarella. In C. Halloumi & G. Feta (Eds.) *Cheese, Cheese, and More Cheese: A Definitive Guide* (pp. 221–240). The Gourmet Press.

Stilton, V. & Gouda, M. (2015). Is port always the best match? *Modern Cheese Lover*, 65(3), 22–36.

Additional Resources for Further Reading

Fox, T., Johns, J. & Keller, S. (2007). *Cite It Right: The SourceAid Guide to Citation, Research and Avoiding Plagiarism* (3rd ed.). Sourceaid LLC.

Neville, C. (2007). *The Complete Guide to Referencing and Avoiding Plagiarism*. McGraw-Hill Education.

Pecorari, D. (2008). *Academic Writing and Plagiarism: A Linguistic Analysis*. Continuum.

Pecorari, D. (2013). *Teaching to Avoid Plagiarism: How to Promote Good Source Use*. Open University Press.

Chapter References

Abasi, A.R. & Graves, B. (2008). Academic literacy and plagiarism: Conversations with international graduate students and disciplinary professors. *Journal of English for Academic Purposes, 7*(4), 221–233.

Alexander, O. (2009). *Understanding EAP Context-Teaching English Blog*. Retrieved from: http://www.teachingenglish.org.uk/blogs/olwyn-alexander/understanding-eap-context.

BALEAP. (2008). *Competency Framework for Teachers of English for Academic Purposes*. Retrieved from: https://www.baleap.org/wp-content/uploads/2016/04/teap-competency-framework.pdf.

Bell, D.E. (2018). The practice of EAP in Australia: A Rose by any other name? In L.T. Wong & W.L.H. Wong (Eds.) *Teaching and Learning English for Academic Purposes. Current Research and Practices* (pp. 161–177). Nova Science Publishers Inc.

Bell, D.E. (2021a). Linking theory with practice. *Modern English Teacher, 30*(3), 9–14.
Bell, D.E. (2021b). Accounting for the troubled status of English language teachers in Higher Education. *Teaching in Higher Education*. https://doi.org/10.1080/13562517.2021.1935848.
Bell, D.E. (2021c). *Using poetry as a means of promoting creativity and criticality in ELT*. Paper delivered at the 24-hour MATSDA International Language Learning Conference. Kuala Lumpur: Universiti Sains Malaysia.
Canagarajah, A.S. (1996). Appropriate methodology and social context. *ELT Journal, 50*(1), 80–82.
Casey, S.D., DiVito Jr., J., Lupow, J.B. & Gulani, R. (2016). An uncommon cause of acute abdominal pain: Primary epiploic appendagitis in the emergency setting. *Einstein Journal of Biology & Medicine, 31*(1/2), 17–19.
Chomsky, N. (1959). A review of B.F. Skinner's verbal behaviour. *Language, 35*(1), 26–58.
Crystal, D. (1997). *English as a Global Language*. Cambridge University Press.
Ding, A. (2016). Challenging scholarship: A thought piece. *The Language Scholar, 0*, 6–18.
Graddol, D. (1997). *The Future of English*. The British Council.
Hamp-Lyons, L. (2011). English for academic purposes. In E. Hinkel (Ed.), *Handbook of Research in Second Language Teaching and Learning* (Vol. 2, pp. 89–105). Routledge.
Hutchinson, T. & Waters, A. (1987). *English for Specific Purposes. A Learning-centred Approach*. Cambridge University Press.
Jackson, D.O. & Burch, A.R. (2017). Complementary theoretical perspectives on task-based classroom realities. *TESOL Quarterly, 51*(3), 493–506.
Kumaravadivelu, B. (2001). Toward a postmethod pedagogy. *TESOL Quarterly, 35*, 537–560.
Li, S. (2014). Oral corrective feedback. *ELT Journal, 68*(2), 196–198.
Lowton, R. (2020). The (T)EAP of the iceberg: The role of qualifications in teaching English for academic purposes. MA TESOL diss., University of Nottingham Ningbo, China.
Mackey, A., Park, H.I., & Tagarelli, K.M. (2016). Errors, corrective feedback and repair. In G. Hall (Ed.) *The Routledge Handbook of English Language Teaching* (pp. 499–512). Routledge.
O'Byrne, A. (2018). London and urban culture in eighteenth-century literature. *Literature Compass, 15*(2), e12437.
Pecorari, D. (2003). Good and original: Plagiarism and patchwriting in academic second-language writing. *Journal of Second Language Writing, 12*(4), 317–345.
Pecorari, D. & Petrić, B. (2014). Plagiarism in second-language writing. *Language Teaching, 47*(3), 269–302.
Pollock, E. (2012). Feedback and correction. *English Teaching Professional, 83*, 51.
Russell, J. & Spada, N. (2006). The effectiveness of corrective feedback for the acquisition of L2 grammar. A meta-analysis of the research. In J.M. Norris & L. Ortega (Eds.) *Synthesizing Research on Language Learning and Teaching* (pp. 133–164). John Benjamins.
Swales, J.M. (1990). *Genre Analysis: English in Academic and Research Settings*. Cambridge University Press.
Swales, J.M. (2014). Variation in citational practice in a corpus of student biology papers: From parenthetical plonking to intertextual storytelling. *Written Communication, 31*(1), 118–141.

Swales, J.M. (2019). The futures of EAP genre studies: A personal viewpoint. *Journal of English for Academic Purposes, 38*, 75–82.
Wenger, E. (1998). *Communities of Practice: Learning, Meaning and Identity.* Cambridge University Press.
Zhang, Y., Zhao, Q., Tan, B., & Yang, J. (2021). A power system transient stability assessment method based on active learning. *Journal of Engineering,* (11), 715–723. http://doi.org/10.1049/tje2.12068.

4 Becoming a More Confident and Proficient Academic Writer

Introduction

This short chapter focuses on some of the different knowledge and skills you will need to master in order to become a more confident and proficient academic writer.

It opens by presenting an overview of some fundamental features of effective academic writing, such as clear structuring, use of appropriate lexis, awareness of hedging devices and supporting all of your claims with relevant evidence.

This chapter then provides some detailed guidance and practice on the mechanics of how to build a coherent academic argument and how to develop a credible personal stance.

Additional resources for your further reading are listed on page 92.

4.1 Fundamental Features of Effective Academic Writing

In order for it to be considered effective, all academic writing is likely to have several fundamental features in common. These will be discussed under the sub-headings below.

4.1.1 *The Importance of Clear Structuring*

Whenever and whatever you write academically, there needs to be a clear overall structure, so that your ideas flow and the different points are all properly linked together. In a good piece of academic writing, the reader should be able to follow the writer's thoughts easily and there will always be a sense of order and underlying logic.

You can achieve this in your own writing by learning to use **signposting language** effectively. As the name suggests, signposting language refers to words and phrases which serve as a signpost or direction marker for the reader in signalling the specific points that are going to be made and the order in which they will appear. Look at an example of some signposting language in the excerpt from an essay opening in the box below. The relevant parts of the text have been highlighted for you:

> The question of which ELT methods and approaches are likely to provide teachers and learners with the best results has been a highly controversial topic. Some writers (e.g., Holliday, 1994; Canagarajah, 1999) have taken the stance that methodologies are an extension of the cultural and political implications of teaching English in general and, as such, carry sinister imperialistic overtones; others (e.g., Adamson, 2004) have viewed methodological developments more benignly, likening the broad range of different methods and approaches to changes in fashion. Others still (e.g., Kumaravadivelu, 2001) have criticised methodologies for not sufficiently catering to the realities of non-Western teaching contexts.
>
> In this essay, I will carry out a critical comparison of two conceptually very different ELT methodologies: Grammar Translation and Communicative Language Teaching. As a framework for my analysis, I will contrast the differences and similarities of the approaches advocated by each methodology using five pedagogical dichotomies commonly found in ELT. These are outlined below:
>
> i. Teacher-centred vs. learner-centred
> ii. Low tolerance of learner errors vs. high tolerance of learner errors
> iii. Permitted use of the L1 vs. prohibited use of the L1
> iv. Deductive vs. inductive approaches to pedagogy
> v. Language as a system vs. language as a practical tool for communication
>
> **i. Teacher-centred vs. Learner-centred**
>
> As several of the post-millennium writers on methodologies (e.g., Adamson, 2004; Waters, 2012; Richards & Rodgers, 2014) seem to agree, Grammar Translation Methodology (GTM) fundamentally takes a teacher-centred approach to pedagogy.

In this example, the writer makes it very clear for the reader what the essay is going to focus on. After a few opening comments to set the general context, there is a direct statement of purpose – "In this essay, I will...." – followed by more specific detail on the different points that will be covered – "As a framework for my analysis, I will...". The writer also then uses a numbered list and a bolded sub-heading to make the intended structure of the essay even more explicit.

I will discuss use of the First Person in more detail below, but for now, simply note the way in which it is being used here to signpost the writer's intentions. Use of numbered lists and sub-headings can also be a helpful means of highlighting exactly how a piece of academic writing will be structured. In the case of the latter though, you must be careful not to *overuse* them, as too many sub-headings can make a piece of academic writing look fragmented and 'bitty', especially if there is very little text under each point. As a general rule of thumb, each time you use a sub-heading, make sure that you provide sufficient written detail before you use one again. In the essay excerpt above, for example, I would expect there to be around 300–500 words of discussion under the teacher-centred vs. learner-centred sub-heading, before the writer switches to the next sub-heading about tolerance of learner errors.

4.1.2 Use of the First Person

In the example essay opening in the box above, the writer explicitly uses the First Person to show what will be covered – "In this essay, I will...". In the past, this style of writing used to be frowned upon and students were generally advised to avoid all use of the First Person in their academic prose and instead adopt a more impersonal style, e.g., "This essay will..."; "In this essay, the writer will...".

Modern thinking on this issue has changed significantly and use of the First Person is now considered to be much more acceptable. This does *not* mean that you should begin every single sentence with 'I', however, nor does it mean that all lecturers are necessarily 100% supportive of First Person usage; some may still prefer their students to write more impersonally. As always, the best approach is to check what is required with your course tutors and adjust your writing style accordingly. Creating a more impersonal and indirect style remains a feature of academic writing in general, as I will discuss below in the section under 'Hedging', but a much greater tolerance for First Person usage now means that rather clumsy phrases such as "As far as the author of this paper is concerned" or what has sometimes been termed 'the Royal We' – "We are of the opinion that" – are generally no longer needed.

4.1.3 Hedging and the Avoidance of Sweeping Generalisations

When I am marking and correcting my own MA students' written work, one of the most common problems I find is that their writing can come across as being too dogmatic. Contentious issues are often presented as if they were accepted facts and there is an over-use of sweeping generalisations, when the writing should actually be much more tentative in its tone. As I have mentioned above, using an impersonal and indirect style is still a core feature of academic writing and one of the ways in which good academic writers achieve this is by their effective use of hedging strategies. Look at the short academic writing excerpts (a), (b), and (c) in the box below. In each case, the relevant hedging language has been shown in italics:

> a. Communicative Language Teaching (CLT) *tends to place more emphasis* on learner-centred pedagogy. This does not mean there will never be any instances of teachers taking a more central role – the PPP model is a good example of when they do – but compared to more traditional methodologies such as Grammar Translation, *it is generally acknowledged* (e.g., Hall, 2011; Richards & Rodgers, 2014) that CLT *usually* puts greater priority on learner-centredness.
> b. *Few could deny that* use of the L1 has been a contested issue in English Language Teaching. Early methodologies such as Grammar Translation were explicit in their insistence that all instruction should be carried out in the learners' mother tongue, but the thinking on this *arguably* changed quite dramatically with the introduction of alternative methodologies such as the Oral Approach (Richards & Rodgers, 2014). Under these new orthodoxies, *it was suggested that* learners *might* develop their language skills more effectively if all classroom instruction were carried out in the target language (L2). *For the most part*, this style of pedagogy has been enthusiastically embraced by subsequent methodologies, particularly CLT (Adamson, 2004; Hall, 2011).
> c. Most modern writers *appear to be* in broad agreement (e.g., Adamson, 2004; Richards & Rodgers, 2014; Waters, 2012) that Grammar Translation Methodology (GTM) chooses to take a highly deductive approach to pedagogy. This contrasts quite sharply with the approaches of other methodologies, which *may be* more inductive in nature.

Hedging language is used in academic writing to make the writer's opinions sound less dogmatic and to allow for the possibility of other interpretations. Modal verbs such as 'may' and 'might' can be very useful when expressing these different shades of meaning, as can the use of modifying adverbs such as 'generally', 'usually' and 'quite'. Note also that in the examples above, the writer hedges with the use of verbal structures such as 'tends to', 'it was suggested that' and 'appears to be'. All of these phrases help to keep the tone of the text tentative, impersonal and indirect.

In example (a), if the student had written "Communicative Language Teaching (CLT) places more emphasis on learner-centred pedagogy", this would not in itself be wrong, but as no direct supporting evidence has been provided for the claim (see Section 4.1.5), it might elicit a feedback comment or two in the margin from the marker such as 'Who says?' or 'How do you know?'. Careful use of hedging language helps to avoid this kind of reader reaction. Similarly, in example (b), when discussing the use of L2 in classroom instruction, the student writes "For the most part, this style of pedagogy has been enthusiastically embraced by subsequent methodologies...." Use of 'For the most part' in this sentence is important because it allows for the possibility that there may be some exceptions. If the student had left this hedging phrase out and simply stated that *all* subsequent pedagogies have exclusively used the L2, a tutor marking the work might justifiably comment that this is not entirely true and then go on to point out that not *every* pedagogical approach has chosen to follow this rule. The judicious use of a little bit of hedging language here makes all the difference.

Check Your Understanding: Independent Task 4.1a

Re-write statements (a)–(e) using appropriate hedging devices so that the writing sounds less dogmatic.

a. In Communicative Language Teaching methodology, there is no need for the teacher to correct learners' mistakes.
b. Task-based learning is more effective than the audio-lingual approach because the learners are using language for a purpose rather than blindly repeating drills.
c. Communicative Language Teaching is not suitable for use in China because of large class sizes.
d. Asian students are reluctant to give their opinions in class.
e. If teachers fail to correct their students' linguistic errors, they will fossilise.

Some suggested answers to this task have been provided on page 90.

4.1.4 Use of Appropriate Academic Lexis

Part of becoming a good academic writer means learning to recognise and use appropriate academic lexis. A common problem with many students' writing, particularly those for whom English is not their first language, is that the words they choose are too informal or belong more to an oral rather than a written register. Some contrastive examples showing how the verbs used in academic language differ from those found in more General English writing or speaking are listed in the box below:

General English	Academic English
Make/do	**Carry out/conduct** Research *carried out by/conducted by* Jones (2022) suggests that … NOT Research made by…. Research done by …
Reckon/figure	**Believe** Most contemporary writers *believe that* … NOT Most contemporary writers reckon… Most contemporary writers figure…
Figure out	**Conclude** Based on his findings, Smith (2021) *has concluded that*… NOT Smith (2021) has figured out that…
Say	**State/point out** Jones (2021) *has stated that/has pointed out*…. NOT Jones (2021) has said that…
Guess	**Surmise/content/hypothesise** Based on these findings, Parker (2018) *surmises that/contends that/hypothesises that*… NOT Parker (2018) guesses that…

Check Your Understanding: Independent Task 4.1b

Re-write statements (a)–(e) using more appropriate academic lexis (Note that the actual citations here are fictional)

a. Hopkins (1999) reckons that not correcting learners' errors will lead to fossilisation.
b. Thomas and Hamilton (2015) have said that learner-centred pedagogies may be less popular in Asia.
c. Johns (1989) figured out that needs analysis should be about more than identifying only target situation needs.
d. There was some research done by Leyland (1979) which showed that pre-teaching vocabulary items can help with learners' comprehension.
e. Green and Black (2012) made some research on process-based approaches to writing.
f. Researchers guess that pre-reading activities can help to activate learners' schemata.

Some suggested answers to this task have been provided on page 90.

4.1.5 Supporting All Claims with Evidence

Although I have saved it to the end of my list of fundamental features, one crucial aspect of Western-style academic writing is that except for those statements which are universally acknowledged as being true, e.g., 'Rain makes uncovered outdoor surfaces wet', all claims need to be supported with evidence. In most academic writing, such evidence is typically drawn from the relevant academic literature, e.g., 'As Cheddar (2021) has pointed out, port is frequently a welcome accompaniment to cheese'; 'According to Scamorza (2020), mozzarella goes well with basil and balsamic vinegar'; 'Mediterranean cuisine often pairs white cheese with black olives (Feta & Halloumi, 2021)'. If you are still unsure of how to use integral and non-integral citations as supporting evidence like this, go back and review the relevant sections of Chapter 3.

Do bear in mind though that evidence for your claims is not always going to come from the academic literature alone; in some cases, you will also need to evidence what you say by drawing directly on your own data. As I will discuss in the following chapter, when writing a linguistic analysis report for example, you will need to evidence any claims that you make not only by drawing on examples from the wider literature but also by linking them to specific quotations from the data which you yourself have gathered during your analysis (see pages 104–110). Depending on the type of essay you are writing, drawing on your personal experience, either as a teacher or a learner, can also sometimes constitute a form of supporting evidence. In such cases, you might first support a claim by referencing the academic literature then add further strength to this by providing some personal examples from your own experience.

In each case though, the same general principle remains true: unless you are stating a universally acknowledged truth, whenever you make a claim in academic writing, you *must* always check to make sure that you are providing relevant supporting evidence.

4.2 Building a Coherent Academic Argument

When you decide to build an academic argument, some of the first things you need to be clear about are your thesis statement(s), the specific points you want to make, the order in which you will present them and the evidence you will use in support.

> **Check Your Understanding: Independent Task 4.1c**
>
> The short excerpt below shows some student writing about Grammar Translation Methodology (GTM). Identify any parts which you think could be improved based on the guidance that has been provided for you in Sections 4.1.1 to 4.1.5, and also what was covered in Chapter 3.

GTM dominated European and foreign language teaching for nearly a century. But the rigorous format of instruction was questioned and rejected by learners later in that era. First in GTM, learners are likely to burn out by learning over-rigid grammar rules. As time goes by, learners' motivation and innovation are likely to fade away in memorising an enormous number of useless grammar rules and attempting to produce translations of tedious literary prose, which severely deprives learners' creative nature and also overlooks the communicative nature of language. In addition to learners' burnout, teachers may also experience burnout. In the absence of context, teachers have to follow one-dimensional teaching practices and have limited opportunity to have meaningful interaction with students. What's more, GTM is believed to serve read-and-write learners and those with good memories, but cannot benefit every type of learner (Peters, 1934).

A suggested answer to this task has been provided on page 91.

Look at the academic writing excerpt in the box below. This comes from a passage in which the writer is trying to argue that some of the methodologies and pedagogies found in General ELT may not be directly transferable to the types of teaching required in English for Academic Purposes (EAP) contexts:

When considering what might be the most appropriate methodologies and pedagogies for EAP, it can be instructive to examine some of the methodological swings, which have occurred in the history of ELT in general.

As most of the post-millennium writers on ELT appear to agree (e.g., Adamson, 2004; Kumaravadivelu, 2006; Bell, 2007; Hall, 2011; Waters, 2012; Richards & Rodgers, 2014; Thornbury, 2017) the history of ELT has been marked by several methodological pendulum swings. These have typically led to methodological issues in language teaching being presented as a series of binaries or dichotomies. An illustrative (though by no means exhaustive) selection of these is presented below:

- To use the L1 in the classroom or not to use the L1
- To be teacher-centred or to be learner-centred
- To teach deductively or to teach inductively

- To correct student errors or not to correct student errors
- To focus primarily on form or to focus primarily on function
- To prioritise accuracy or to prioritise fluency

The first methodological dichotomy on this list, whether teaching should or should not permit use of the L1, has been a long-standing debate in ELT and continues to attract attention from modern writers (e.g., Zulfikar, 2018). Early methodological thinking such as that espoused by proponents of the Grammar Translation Method, insisted that the students' L1 should play a central role in their instruction. Indeed, such learners were encouraged to learn their L2 through the active medium of their L1, translating from one language to the other and drawing direct linguistic comparisons. With the advent of methodologies such as the Oral Approach (Spiro, 2013; Richards & Rodgers, 2014), the thinking on this was then completely reversed and use of the L2 now came to the fore. Under this new orthodoxy, use of the L1 was effectively banned and henceforth, both teachers and learners were expected to carry out all of their classroom communication only in the target language. The dominance of this L2-only approach largely continued with the development of later methodologies, most notably with the appearance of Communicative Language Teaching in the late 1970s and early 1980s, and its hegemony has continued unabated (and it must be said largely unchallenged) until the present day.

While I am certainly not about to suggest that there should be a unilateral return to the days of Grammar Translation, in the case of EAP teaching, I think it is nonetheless worth considering a little more critically whether the prevailing L2-only methodological rule is necessarily the best fit in every context. I am personally aware of situations in my current geographical location of China, where students in Chinese-medium universities are required to engage with EAP texts, but where both the students' and the teachers' communicative level is simply not sufficiently high enough to do absolutely everything in the classroom via the medium of English. In such cases, rather than taking what might be termed a fundamentalist approach to language teaching pedagogy and insisting on the constant use of the L2 alone, surely it would make much better sense to take a more pragmatic stance and look at what might be achieved by judicious use of the L1 *in conjunction with* the L2. Such approaches have in fact already been suggested in some of the more recent research around the role of translanguaging pedagogy (e.g., Mazak, 2017; Rabbage, 2019). In the expanding number of international contexts in which L2 teachers of English significantly outnumber those for whom English is their L1, I would personally contend that translanguaging pedagogy may well have some interesting implications not only for ELT in general, but also for EAP.

> Adapted from Bell, D.E. (2023). *English for Academic Purposes: Perspectives on the past, present and future.* Channel View Publications/Multilingual Matters.

It can be helpful to deconstruct this piece of writing and look at the different ways in which the writer goes about building his argument. As a means of doing this, we can start by identifying his opening thesis statement and then list the different points he has decided to make:

Opening Thesis Statement:
If we are going to consider methodology and pedagogy in EAP, then we should begin by looking at how methodology and pedagogy have been treated in General ELT.

Point 2:
Historically speaking, methodological approaches in General ELT have often been presented as binaries or dichotomies.

Point 3:
One particular dichotomy, use or non-use of the L1, has received lots of attention and continues to be debated.

Point 4:
Non-use of the L1 has tended to dominate.

Point 5:
We should question whether non-use of the L1 is appropriate in all contexts.

Point 6:
In some situations, rather than insisting on L2 only, judicious use of the L1 in conjunction with the L2 may in fact be preferable.

Point 7:
Recent research on translanguaging pedagogy seems to support this view.

Point 8:
As the number of teachers using English as an L2 outnumbers those who use English as their L1, translanguaging pedagogy may have some important implications for both General ELT and EAP.

As I have advised under Section 4.1.5, look at how the writer brings in supporting citations for his claims in the examples below:

> As most of the main post-millennium writers on methodology appear to agree (e.g., Adamson, 2004; Bell, 2007; Hall, 2011; Kumaravadivelu, 2006; Richards & Rodgers, 2014; Thornbury, 2017; Waters, 2012) the history of ELT has been marked by several methodological pendulum swings.
>
> …whether teaching should or should not permit use of the L1 has been a long-standing debate in ELT and continues to attract attention from modern writers (e.g., Zulfikar, 2018).
>
> With the advent of methodologies such as the Oral Approach (Richards & Rodgers, 2014; Spiro, 2013), the thinking on this was then completely reversed and use of the L2 now came to the fore.
>
> Such approaches have in fact already been suggested in some of the more recent research around the role of translanguaging pedagogy (e.g., Mazak, 2017; Rabbidge, 2019).

Note also how the writer makes his own personal stance explicit:

> When considering what might be the most appropriate methodologies and pedagogies for EAP, it can be instructive to examine some of the methodological swings which have occurred in the history of ELT in general. While I am certainly not about to suggest that there should be a unilateral return to the days of Grammar Translation, in the case of EAP teaching, I think it is nonetheless worth considering a little more critically whether the prevailing L2-only methodological rule is necessarily the best fit in every context.
>
> I am personally aware… of situations in my current geographical location of China, where students in Chinese-medium universities are required to engage with EAP texts, but where both the students' and the teachers' communicative level of English is simply not sufficiently high enough to do absolutely everything in the classroom via the medium of English.
>
> … rather than taking what might be termed a fundamentalist approach to language teaching pedagogy and insisting on the constant use of the L2 alone, surely it would make much better sense to take a more pragmatic stance and look at what might be achieved by judicious use of the L1 in conjunction with the L2.
>
> … I would personally contend that translanguaging pedagogy may well have some interesting implications not only for ELT in general, but also for EAP.

As I discussed earlier in this chapter, some lecturers may still frown on the direct use of the First Person when showing your personal stance, so this is something worth checking with the academics in your own context. Even if all direct mentions of 'I' are removed from the above example though, it should still be clear what the writer is arguing. Whenever you build a written academic argument, your own stance must always be evident.

This chapter has examined some of the different mechanics which underpin effective academic writing. In providing the guidance that I have, however, I am mindful that for some readers, there may perhaps be a danger of my advice being perceived as too prescriptive.

There are, of course, many different ways in which to tackle academic writing, and in providing the examples and models above, I am certainly not suggesting that there is only one approach. Further ideas and suggestions for how to improve your academic writing can be gleaned from the additional resources listed on page 92.

I do very strongly believe, however, that as a general guiding principle, learning to *notice* features of writing, deconstruct how they operate and then re-apply them to your own particular contexts can help to make the journey from novice to accomplished academic writer a significantly shorter one.

Suggested Answers to Independent Tasks

Task 4.1a

a. In Communicative Language Teaching methodology, there **may be somewhat less of a need** for the teacher to correct learners' mistakes.
b. Task-based learning is **often considered to be** more effective than the audio-lingual approach because the learners are using language for a purpose rather than blindly repeating drills.
c. Communicative Language Teaching **may perhaps be less** suitable for use in China because of large class sizes.
d. Asian students **may sometimes be** reluctant to give their opinions in class.
e. If teachers fail to correct their students' linguistic errors, **there can be a danger that** they will fossilise.

Task 4.1b

a. Hopkins (1999) **contends** that not correcting learners' errors will lead to fossilisation.
b. Thomas and Hamilton (2015) have **suggested** that learner-centred pedagogies may be less popular in Asia.

Becoming a More Confident and Proficient Academic Writer

c. Johns (1989) **concluded** that needs analysis should be about more than identifying only target situation needs.
d. There was some research **carried out** by Leyland (1979) which showed that pre-teaching vocabulary items can help with learners' comprehension.
e. Green and Black (2012) **conducted** some research on process-based approaches to writing.
f. Researchers **hypothesise** that pre-reading activities can help to activate learners' schemata.

Task 4.1c

From an academic writing perspective, there are several problems with what this writer has produced. One of the first things which should jump out at the reader is the very evident lack of supporting evidence for almost every claim. The writer opens by saying that GTM dominated language teaching for almost 100 years until it was later questioned and rejected, but no evidence is offered to support this. Similarly, the writer claims that GTM learners are likely to burn out by over-learning 'rigid' grammar rules. However, as it stands, this can only be considered to be the writer's personal opinion, as there is no corroborating evidence offered in support.

Closely allied to the issue of the writer not providing any supporting evidence for claims, there is an over-use of sweeping generalisations, too much dogmatic writing and far too many unsubstantiated personal judgments. In the case of the latter, note the value-laden judgments inherent in statements such as '**useless** grammar rules' and '**tedious** literary prose'. How do we *know* that the grammar rules are 'useless' or that the literary prose is 'tedious'? These are highly subjective statements by the writer, which may or may not be valid. As discussed under Section 4.1.3, this excerpt could have been vastly improved had the writer adopted a more tentative tone with better use of hedging language.

A final issue with this writing concerns the closing reference to Peters (1934). It should be obvious that much has changed in English Language Teaching since 1934, but the writer is presenting this source as if it were a conclusive view. As I discussed in Chapter 3, as an operational rule of thumb, unless older sources are universally recognised as being seminal texts, or are being presented to provide a specific historical contrast, academic writers should always be drawing on citations which are as recent and as pedagogically up to date as possible.

Additional Resources for Further Reading

Cottrell, S. (2005). *Critical Thinking Skills: Developing Effective Analysis and Argument*. Palgrave Macmillan.

Lea, M. & Steiner, B. (2000). *Student Writing in Higher Education*. Open University Press.

Levin, P. (2004). *Write Great Essays! A Guide to Reading and Essay Writing for Undergraduates and Taught Postgraduates*. Open University Press.

Silver, M. (2003). The stance of stance: A critical look at ways stance is expressed and modelled in academic discourse. *Journal of English for Academic Purposes*, 2, 359–374.

Wallace, M. & Wray, A. (2011). *Critical Reading and Writing for Postgraduates*. Sage Publications.

Chapter References

Adamson, B. (2004). Fashions in language teaching methodology. In A. Davies & C. Elder (Eds.) *The Handbook of Applied Linguistics* (pp. 605–622). Blackwell.

Bell, D.E. (2023). *English for Academic Purposes: Perspectives on the Past, Present & Future*. Channel View Publications.

Bell, D.M. (2007). Do teachers think that methods are dead? *ELT Journal, 61*(2), 135–143.

Canagarajah, A.S. (1999). *Resisting Linguistic Imperialism in English Teaching*. Oxford University Press.

Hall, G. (2011). *Exploring English Language Teaching. Language in Action*. Routledge.

Holliday, A. (1994). *Appropriate Methodology and Social Context*. Cambridge.

Kumaravadivelu, B. (2001). Toward a postmethod pedagogy. *TESOL Quarterly*, 35, 537–560.

Kumaravadivelu, B. (2006). *Understanding Language Teaching: From Method to Postmethod*. Lawrence Erlbaum.

Mazak, C.M. (2017). *Translanguaging in Higher Education: Beyond Monolingual Ideologies*. Channel View Publications.

Peters, M.O. (1934). An experimental comparison of grammar-translation method and direct method in the teaching of French. *Modern Language Journal, 18*, 528–542.

Rabbage, M. (2019). *Translanguaging in EFL Contexts: A Call for Change*. Routledge.

Richards, J.C. & Rodgers, T.S. (2014). *Approaches and Methods in Language Teaching* (3rd ed.). Cambridge University Press.

Spiro, J. (2013). *Changing Methodologies in TESOL*. Edinburgh University Press.

Thornbury, S. (2017). *Scott Thornbury's 30 Language Teaching Methods*. Cambridge.

Waters, A. (2012). Trends and issues in English language teaching methods and methodology. *ELT Journal, 66*(4), 440–449.

Zulfikar, Z. (2018). Rethinking the use of L1 in the L2 classroom. *Englisia, 6*(1), 43–51.

5 Dealing with Different Types of Written Coursework Assignments

Introduction

This chapter sets out to examine three different types of written coursework assignments you will be likely to encounter on your MA TESOL/MA Applied Linguistics programme: discursive essays, tasks requiring linguistic analysis and assignments which ask for reflective writing such as learner diaries. In each case, this chapter suggests ways in which the different assignments should be approached and then offers detailed guidance and practice on specific aspects of the actual writing. At the end of this chapter, an example of some typical MA TESOL/Applied Linguistics marking criteria is provided to illustrate how your written work may ultimately be judged and graded.

Additional resources for your further reading are listed on page 118.

5.1 Dealing with Academic Essays

Discursive essays are probably the most frequent type of written coursework assignment which you will encounter on an MA TESOL/MA Applied Linguistics programme. While all essays are likely to have certain things in common, depending on the nature of the essay type, there may also be some important differences. It is worth examining these in more detail.

5.1.1 'Compare and Contrast' Type Essays

As the name suggests, this type of essay is asking you to compare and contrast something. The something in question might be two different approaches, e.g., a typical assessment found on Research Methods modules asks students to compare the relative strengths and weaknesses of qualitative methods and quantitative methods, or it might represent different theories and beliefs, e.g., an assessment from Applied Linguistics might ask you to compare two different writers' views on the validity of the Critical Period Hypothesis.

DOI: 10.4324/9781003269854-5

> **An example of a typical 'compare and contrast' type essay**
>
> Write an essay of circa 4,000 words in which you critically compare and contrast two specific ELT methodologies which have been covered in this module. Your essay should discuss what you see as being the possible merits and defects of each methodology and provide a critical overview of what the main issues have been in their application. Your discussion here should aim to cover both theoretical and practical perspectives.
>
> You should provide evidence to support all your claims by making appropriate references to the relevant academic literature. You may also refer to your own experiences as a language learner and/or teacher. Your writing must follow accepted APA academic style conventions throughout and must include a full references list at the end in which you list all the sources that you have consulted.

As with all academic assignments, it can help to break the writing process down into a series of discrete stages or steps. Some suggestions for how you might go about doing this have been outlined below:

Step 1

First make sure you fully understand what the assignment requires

What exactly is being asked of you? A useful way of checking your understanding here is to go through the assignment rubric very carefully, highlighting each of the key phrases, so that you don't miss anything important.

Look at the example above of a typical 'compare and contrast' MA TESOL essay task. As suggested in the advice just given, the most important parts of the rubric have been highlighted for you.

In sum, this essay is asking the writer to do nine things:

1. Write around 4,000 words of original text.
2. Critically compare and contrast two specific ELT methodologies covered in the module.
3. Discuss the respective merits and defects of each methodology.
4. Identify what the main issues have been in their application.
5. Draw on both theoretical and practical perspectives.
6. Support all claims with evidence from the academic literature.
7. Bring in any insights from their own experiences either as a teacher or learner.

8. Follow APA academic style conventions throughout.
9. Include a full references list at the end.

Step 2

Decide what you are going to focus on

In the case of the essay above, this would first mean deciding which methodologies you are going to compare and contrast. Although you have a completely free choice here, basic common sense should tell you that it would probably be better to choose two methodologies which are quite different from one another, rather than choosing two methodologies which are very similar. That way, you will potentially have more things to write about in your essay.

Step 3

Read up as much as you can on your chosen topic areas

In the case of the essay above, once you know which methodologies you are going to compare, then you would need to read up as much as you can about them. You would need to understand what their strong points have been, what their weak points have been, the issues that they have faced and the theories that they have been based on – essentially anything and everything relevant to the assignment task from the academic literature that you can find.

Step 4

Based on your reading, create tables, mind maps or bullet-point lists which will allow you to capture the main points or features 'at a glance'

In the case of the essay above, if you had decided to compare Grammar Translation Method (GTM) with Communicative Language Teaching (CLT), a preliminary bullet-point summary of the key features for GTM might look something like this:

Grammar Translation Method

- Based on a detailed analysis of grammatical rules
- Primarily concerned with teaching learners to read and write
- Heavy reliance on bilingual word lists
- Focus on understanding at the sentence level
- Emphasis on accuracy
- Deductive approaches to pedagogy
- Learners' native language used as the language for instruction

---

Step 5

Put your mind maps, tables or bullet-point lists side by side and look for the differences and similarities. Decide which of these points you are going to comment on in your essay and in which order you will present them

In the case of an essay comparing GTM and CLT, completing this step might lead you to produce something like this:

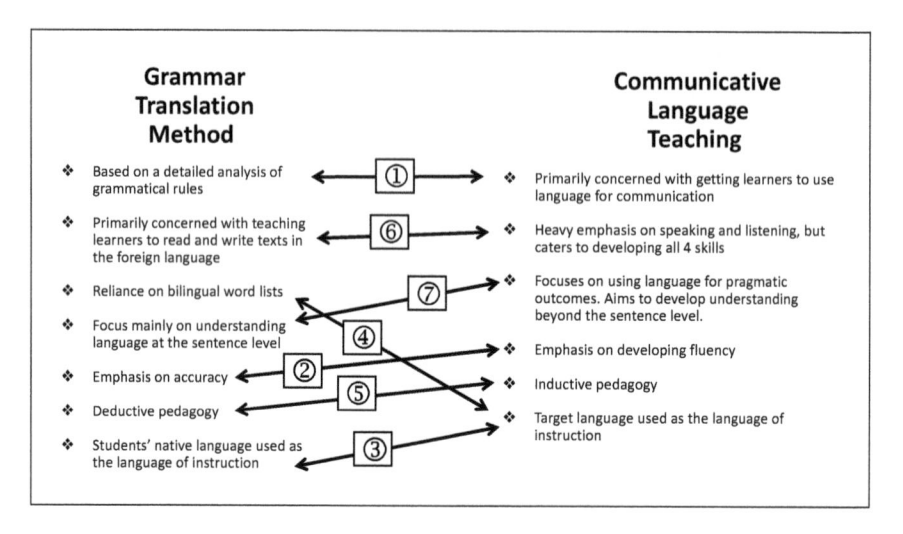

Grammar Translation Method		Communicative Language Teaching
❖ Based on a detailed analysis of grammatical rules	←— ① —→	❖ Primarily concerned with getting learners to use language for communication
❖ Primarily concerned with teaching learners to read and write texts in the foreign language	←— ⑥ —→	❖ Heavy emphasis on speaking and listening, but caters to developing all 4 skills
❖ Reliance on bilingual word lists	⑦	❖ Focuses on using language for pragmatic outcomes. Aims to develop understanding beyond the sentence level.
❖ Focus mainly on understanding language at the sentence level	④	❖ Emphasis on developing fluency
❖ Emphasis on accuracy	←— ② / ⑤ —→	❖ Inductive pedagogy
❖ Deductive pedagogy		❖ Target language used as the language of instruction
❖ Students' native language used as the language of instruction	←— ③	

Step 6

Make sure that you have matching evidence to support your points

As we have already discussed, one of the key features of academic writing is that you must always be able to support your points with appropriate evidence. This typically means that you will need to find other writers who have said the same, or similar things, as you yourself are saying.

As covered earlier, a good academic essay will contain a balanced mix of *citations*, i.e., when you only list another writer's name and the publication date, and *quotations*, i.e., when you list another writer's exact words and the publication date plus page number.

While doing your background reading for an essay, it can be a good habit to create a logbook of any useful citations or quotations, which you can then later draw on when you are looking for examples as supporting evidence. If you do this, however, you will need to make absolutely sure that you keep an exact note of where your citations and quotations came from, e.g., (Jones, 2022, p. 250), so that you can properly reference the source later. One of the most frustrating things when preparing for an academic assignment can be coming across a really good quotation which you

Dealing with Different Types of Written Coursework Assignments 97

intend to use in your own writing, but then not being able to locate the full academic reference when you actually decide to cite it later. It pays, therefore, to be as focused and systematic as you can in all your background reading and essay planning and keep detailed records of all the texts that you access.

In the case of the example about GTM and CLT from Step 5 above, the addition of supporting evidence from the wider academic literature might result in you writing a paragraph which looks something like this:

> Perhaps the first point to be made when comparing GTM and CLT is that in pedagogic terms, they fundamentally follow a very different ethos. As Richards and Rodgers (2014) have pointed out, GTM is based on a detailed analysis of grammatical rules. CLT, on the other hand, is primarily concerned with getting learners to use language for communication (Widdowson, 1978; Hall, 2011).

Step 7

Start mapping out the general structure of your essay

By this stage, you should have gathered together quite a lot of information. If you had been diligently following the previous steps, you would now have a list of all the different points you wanted to include in your essay and you would also have a range of sources (both citations and direct quotations) which you could use in conjunction with those points as supporting evidence.

The next thing you would need to decide is how exactly your essay should be structured. In most basic terms, as you probably know already, the rhetorical structure and flow of most academic essays traditionally tends to follow three distinct stages:

The Introduction:
>General statements to set the scene and provide a context and some signposting for what is coming.

The Body:
>A detailed discussion of the main essay content, point by point, with lots of supporting evidence from the wider literature.

The Conclusion:
>An analysis of what you believe the different points you have covered in the body might suggest, leading to a closing statement (or series of statements) in which you draw everything together and make your own position clear.

Step 8

Start drafting your essay

Different people approach this stage in different ways: some simply start from the beginning of the essay and keep on writing until they reach the end; others choose to focus on particular sections and start by drafting those first, then go back and forth, later weaving everything together. There is no right or wrong answer for this – you will need to find which writing approach is the most effective for you.

Whichever technique you use, you need to recognise from the outset that the process of academic writing is highly *cyclical*, i.e., you will need to keep going back over what you have written and continue making refinements. You will almost certainly never just write something once.

Becoming a good academic writer means taking the time to refine and polish your writing until you get it into the best possible shape. At all times though, while you are doing this, you must always keep asking yourself:

Am I doing **what the task requires of me?** Am I **fully answering the essay question?** Is all of my writing **relevant?**
Am I writing **critically** and **evaluatively**, or too descriptively?
Am I always **supporting what I say with relevant and adequate evidence?**
Am I **following academic conventions correctly?**
Am I **making myself clear?** Do my different **points and arguments hang together logically?** Does everything **flow in a coherent direction?**

Step 9

Refine your essay

As I explained under Step 8, producing good academic writing is *always* a highly cyclical process, which will require you to go back over what you have written several times. Once you have a full draft of the essay, you should read through everything again (and again... and again!) checking very carefully each time for the following:

That the different points you are making **flow** and that there is a **discernible structure and underlying logic in their order**
That **your arguments make sense and that you have provided sufficient support for them**
That **the tone of your language is sufficiently tentative and that you have used hedging devices well**; that **you have avoided any sweeping generalisations**
That your **use of language is accurate** and there are **no typos, grammatical mistakes or other stylistic errors**

Dealing with Different Types of Written Coursework Assignments 99

That you have used your own words at all times, have paraphrased effectively and not committed any acts of plagiarism or other forms of academic misconduct

That you have followed academic conventions appropriately and correctly cited and referenced all of your sources

Step 10

Prepare the References List/Bibliography

As discussed in Chapter 3, when you produce an academic essay, you will usually be required to create a references list or bibliography at the end, in which you list all the different sources that you have consulted.

This list should present the sources in *ascending* alphabetical order (a–z) and must conform to the same academic style conventions which you used for any in-text citations in the essay body, i.e., if you decided to follow APA conventions when citing sources, then you must stick with APA conventions when compiling the final references list.

If you are in any doubt, your course handbook will most probably specify which academic conventions are preferred, or you could always ask your course tutor. You can also download specific academic style guides by searching online.

Check Your Understanding: Independent Task 5.1a

The academic writing excerpt below shows the introduction to an essay in which the writer was asked to critically compare and contrast the relationship between ELT theory and ELT classroom practice.

From a structural point of view, there are arguably five different rhetorical stages in this introduction – can you identify them? How do you think the next paragraph will begin?

A suggested answer to this task has been provided on page 114.

The relationship between theory and practice and the extent to which one should inform the other is an issue which has resonated across a great many human endeavours, not just English Language Teaching. Thanks to the work of pioneering psychologists such as Kurt Lewin (1890–1947), it might even be argued that the idea of there being nothing more practical than a good theory has now entered our collective consciousness. In the specific case of English Language Teaching, however, the question of whether theories and methodologies can help teachers to improve what they do in their classrooms continues to be hotly debated. In discussing this issue, rather than treating theory as an abstract concept, I believe that it is first necessary to specify which particular theories we are talking about, as clearly some theories will have more relevance to teachers than others. A closely related point is the matter of when and how teachers should be exposed to such theories in the first place. A final consideration, and one which I believe is highly pertinent to each of these cases, is the matter of teachers' underlying values and beliefs and how these are formed and take shape. In this essay, I will be discussing each of these core areas in turn.

5.1.2 'Discussing a Quotation' Type Essays

As we have already learned, when dealing with an academic assignment, the first thing you need to make sure of is that you fully understand what the task is asking you to do. In the case of a quotation-type essay, this means that you must first check that you have understood the meaning of the quotation.

Look at the example below of a typical quotation-type essay task from an MA TESOL:

> Theory may inform teachers' decisions, but with regard to methods and classroom methodology, teachers will still be guided by their sense of what is and what is not plausible.
>
> (Hall, 2011, p. 120)
>
> Do you agree with Hall's statement? Why/why not? What role(s) do you believe theories and methodologies have in informing teachers' classroom practice?
>
> Write an essay of circa 4,000 words in which you discuss the above. Provide examples by drawing on specific historical developments in language teaching methodology and support your arguments with reference to the relevant academic literature. Your writing must follow APA academic conventions throughout and must include a full reference list as the end in which you list all the sources you have consulted.

Before you could start preparing for this essay, you would first need to check that you have understood what Hall is saying. A useful way of concept-checking this would be to have a go at reformulating the quotation using your own words. If you were to do this for the example above, then you might end up with something like the text listed in the table below:

Table 1 An Original Quotation and an 'Unpacked' Quotation

Quotation	What I Think It Means in My Own Words
'Theory may inform teachers' decisions, but with regard to methods and classroom methodology, teachers will still be guided by their sense of what is and what is not plausible.'	Theory may play a role in what teachers do, but teachers will always decide for themselves what does and doesn't work based on their firsthand experience.

Having unpacked what is meant by the quotation, you would next need to go through a similar concept-checking process to make sure that you are clear on what the task itself requires:

Table 2 An Original Assignment Rubric and an 'Unpacked' Assignment Rubric

Assignment Rubric	What I Think It Means in My Own Words
Do you agree with Hall's statement? Why/why not? What role(s) do you believe theories and methodologies have in informing teachers' classroom practice?	Are teachers guided by theory? Why do I/don't I think so? Which theory/theories are important? How? When? Where? How do theories and methodologies link with what happens in the classroom?

Unlike the compare and contrast essay in Section 5.1, Step 5, this quotation-type essay requires you to take a personal stance and to decide whether you agree or disagree with what Hall has claimed. For essays which require this kind of writing, after deciding where you stand on a given matter, you will then need to think of the different points which you can bring in as your supporting evidence. As we discussed under Section 5.1, Step 6, a good academic writer will be able to draw on both citations and quotations when doing this.

Look at an example of this principle in action below, where the writer first uses a quotation from Brown, then draws on relevant supporting citations from Ellis, Prabhu and Borg:

> Teachers' underlying beliefs and personal values will always play an important role in determining what they do in their classrooms. Brown (2007) discusses this at some length:
>
> > If... you believe that non-verbal communication is key to successful second language learning, you will devote some attention

> to non-verbal systems and cues. If you perceive language as a phenomenon that can be dismantled into thousands of discrete pieces and those pieces programmatically taught one by one, you will attend carefully to an understanding of the discrete forms of language. If you think language is essentially cultural and interactive, your classroom methodology will be imbued with sociolinguistic strategies and communicative tasks.
>
> (p. 7)
>
> Other writers (e.g., Prabhu, 1990; Ellis, 1997) have also agreed that teachers' values and beliefs hugely influence their classroom practice. To assist in the development of more effective teacher training programmes, we might wish to ask ourselves how these values and beliefs are formed in the first place. Research on teacher cognition by Borg (2003) suggests that...

Check Your Understanding: Independent Task 5.1b

Look at the example 'quotation-type' essay below. Go through the steps which were suggested above and identify:

i. What you think the quotation means
ii. What you think this essay is asking you to do

> ... no idealized teaching method can visualize all the variables in advance to provide situation-specific suggestions that practicing teachers need to tackle the challenges that confront the practice of their everyday teaching.
>
> (Kumaravadivelu, 2012, p. 18)

Some might argue that this criticism by Kumaravadivelu immediately negates the value of pursuing language teaching methodology. Do you agree with such a view, or are there in fact some benefits which have been gained in exploring different approaches and methods?

Write an essay of circa 4,000 words in which you discuss the above. Provide examples by drawing on specific historical developments in language teaching methodology and support your arguments with reference to the relevant academic literature. Your writing must follow APA academic conventions throughout and must also include a full references list at the end in which you list all the sources that you have consulted.

A suggested answer to the task has been provided on page 115.

5.1.3 'Critically Evaluate' Type Essays

An essay which requires you to make a critical evaluation is asking you to weigh up the pros and cons of something and to examine it from a range of perspectives. Depending on the exact wording of the task, as part of your evaluation, you may also be asked to take a particular stance or reach a certain conclusion. Look at this example essay title below from an MA Applied Linguistics programme:

> Critically evaluate the extent to which becoming proficient in a second language is reliant on learners copying and internalising examples of sounds and structures. Can this feature alone account for successful Second Language Acquisition, or as applied linguists, do we need to consider other dimensions?

Most of the features of effective academic writing that we have already discussed in this chapter would continue to be relevant for this essay. However, a key thing in this case would be first to identify the relative strengths and weaknesses of learning by imitation ('copying and internalising'), as discussing this is likely to form the main thrust of the essay content. As per the second half of the essay question, the writer would then need to consider whether learning a second language also draws on other processes.

Check Your Understanding: Independent Task 5.1c

Look at the 'critically evaluate' essay title in the box above. What are some of the main theories about Second Language Acquisition that writing this essay will most likely require you to discuss?

A suggested answer to this task has been provided on page 115.

5.2 Dealing with Linguistic Analysis Tasks

Although discursive essays are likely to represent the most common form of academic writing that you will encounter on an MA TESOL or MA Applied Linguistics programme, you may also sometimes be required to carry out tasks which are more report-like in nature. The most typical of such tasks are those which require you to carry out some form of linguistic analysis. These are often encountered in Applied Linguistics modules looking at discourse, or on MA TESOL modules dealing with linguistic aspects of English for Specific Purposes (ESP).

5.2.1 Which Dimensions of a Text Should I Analyse?

There are many different tools and models which can be applied when analysing the linguistic features of a given text. The discussion which follows does not intend to be exhaustive in this regard, but some of the main things that a linguistic analysis should be paying attention to include:

a. *Lexico-grammatical features (Field)*

When looking at a given text, one thing that a linguistic analysis will almost certainly focus on is the specific features of lexis and grammar which the text exemplifies. Based on the work of Michael Halliday (1978) and what has come to be known as Systemic Functional Linguistics (SFL), these features are often grouped together under the broader heading of 'Field'.

One such lexico-grammatical feature immediately worth looking at is verb forms. A linguistic analysis of a given text might thus seek to examine how verbs are being used in terms of their tense and their voice. As an early textual analysis by Barber (1962) revealed, for example, verbs used in scientific writing tend to favour the Present Simple tense. In the scientific texts which Barber analysed, use of the Present Simple tense represented a whopping 64% of his sample, whereas other verb tenses appeared significantly less frequently, e.g., Present Progressive 0.6%; Present Perfect 1.7%; Future Simple 3.7%. Barber's analysis of scientific prose also concluded that when it comes to voice, scientific texts are much more likely to employ verb forms using the passive than they are using the active.

Another area of interest with verb forms revolves around relative levels of certainty and use of hedging. As Myers (1990) has argued, scientific writing typically uses hedging strategies to reduce the likelihood of face-threatening activities and to avoid creating a tone of writing which could run the risk of offending fellow researchers. A linguistic analysis of a given text might thus wish to investigate specific aspects of verb use such as hedging and modality.

Beyond verbs, a linguistic analysis might also consider lexico-grammatical features such as nominalisation. As Liardét (2016) has pointed out, nominalisation (the use of verbal nouns ending in suffixes such as *-ation*, *-ity*, *-ment* or *-ness*) is a particularly common feature of academic prose. One of the reasons for this is because nominalisation allows complex information to be packaged into a phrase which is, grammatically speaking, quite simple. For example, as Bloor and Bloor (2004) have argued, by using nominalisation, a process can then become the head of a nominal group as in phrases such as 'muscular *contraction*' or 'technical *information*'. Nominalisation may also be used to allow the nominal to become the classifier, as in phrases such

Dealing with Different Types of Written Coursework Assignments

as *'contraction* rate' or *'information* technology'. In the case of scientific writing, nominalisation further allows all reference to people to be omitted. This can help to give descriptions of scientific knowledge a more objective reality and, in so doing, facilitates the expression of general scientific truths.

b. *The assumed relationship between the writer of a text and the reader (Tenor)*

No texts ever exist in isolation; all are written with particular audiences in mind. Depending on who the audience of a given text is presumed to be, writers adjust their choice of lexis and content to meet the knowledge level of their readers. A text written for those who are already experts in a specific subject area will naturally look very different to a text written for novices, or for those who only have a layperson's understanding. In Hallidayan terms, when a linguistic analysis discusses the *tenor* of a text, these are the dimensions it is investigating.

c. *The format that a given text takes (Mode)*

From a linguistic point of view, texts can be classified as oral or written. A politician's speech might belong to the former, while an academic article would clearly represent the latter. In some text types though, this oral-written distinction is much less clear-cut. Emails and text messages, for example, though evidently forms of writing, in fact share many features more commonly found in oral communication. A linguistic analysis drawing on Halliday's SFL principles would seek to comment on issues like this under the heading of *mode*.

d. *Specific structural and rhetorical features of text types (Genre)*

Although there are now several different ways in which researchers approach genre and this has resulted in competing terminologies, at its root, genre refers to the identification and analysis of the structural and rhetorical features which allow texts to be classified as certain types, e.g., nobody would confuse a restaurant menu with a technical manual, but what exactly is it that makes each of these text types instantly recognisable as such? Genre analysis can provide linguists with a practical toolkit to help them investigate and answer such questions. Thanks to the pioneering work of John Swales (1990), genre analysis has been particularly useful in the domain of academic writing and as such plays an important role in English for Academic Purposes. Building on Swales' work, Vijay Bhatia (1993) has also applied principles of genre analysis to the study of professional texts such as unsolicited sales letters.

e. *Miscellaneous linguistic devices*

Depending on the nature of the text being analysed, writers may need to identify different linguistic devices. In certain contexts, some of these will be more relevant than others. A linguistic analysis of a piece of academic writing such as a journal abstract, for example, is almost certainly going to be looking at different things than an analysis of, say, a print advertisement or a technical instruction manual. For each text type, the analyst will need to be aware of the specific linguistic devices most commonly used by that medium. A selection of the devices typically found in print advertisements, for example, is detailed below:

Deviant Spelling in Brand Naming, e.g., *Irn Bru; KiteKat; Sunkist*
Puns, e.g., *Wool. It's worth more. Naturally* (American Wool Council)
Ellipsis, e.g., *Does she, or doesn't she? Only her hairdresser knows for sure* (Clairol)
Lexical Boost, e.g., *Deeply Replenished, Beautiful Fluidity* (Nexxus)
Phonetic Word Play, e.g., *Cerealously chocolatey* (Quaker Oats)
Rhyme, e.g., *A Mars a Day Helps You Work Rest and Play* (Mars Chocolate)
Pseudo-Science, e.g., *Uses Hyaluronic Acid. Powerful hydrator that keeps your skin cells hydrated and plumped* (Boutique)
Rhetorical Questions, e.g., *If your pay packet was £1 short each week, who would really notice?* (Christian Aid)
Alliteration, e.g., *skin perfecting power* (Dior)
Professional Endorsement, e.g., *The #1 Dermatologist Recommended Skincare* (Boutique)
Use of Commands, e.g., *Buy one, get one free!* (Tower Records)
Mention of Statistics, e.g., *90% of women experienced a visible skin transformation* (Dior)
Appeals to Nature, e.g., *Naturally luminous minerals* (Clinique)
References to Time, e.g., *Beauty enhancement day after day* (Dior)
Promises to Solve a Particular Problem, e.g., *reduces the appearance of spots and redness* (Dior)

Check Your Understanding: Independent Task 5.2a

Find a print advertisement which focuses on a female cosmetic or other beauty product. Carry out a linguistic analysis of any text the advertisement contains by drawing on the principles which have been discussed under a–e above. What are some of the specific things that you might wish to comment on?

A suggested answer to this task has been provided on pages 115-116.

5.2.2 What Form Should a Textual Analysis Take?

As a linguistic analysis tends to be more like a report than a discursive essay, it will follow a slightly different structural format. For example, it is likely to draw more extensively on the use of headings, sub-headings and tables. As with all academic writing though, there will still need to be effective use of signposting language to help guide the reader and claims will still need to be supported with references to the relevance academic literature. Unlike a discursive essay however, as a linguistic analysis is usually based on a specific sample of text, claims will also need to be supported by a detailed cross-referencing of the actual language in the sample.

Look at this example of a typical linguistic analysis assignment from an MA TESOL programme:

> Write an analysis of up to 3,000 words in which you identify and discuss the main linguistic features of a particular sample of text. This sample may be representative of EAP texts, e.g., a series of academic journal abstracts, or ESP texts, e.g., a collection of business letters, technical manuals or print advertisements. You should include scans of your chosen sample texts as an appendix.
>
> Your analysis is expected to cover issues such as structure, core lexis and any other linguistic features that you feel to be worth mentioning. Where possible, it should also refer to the wider academic literature and draw on any relevant previous research findings. You must follow APA conventions throughout, and include a full references list at the end, detailing any academic sources which you have consulted.

If you tackled this assignment and decided to examine a series of academic journal abstracts, your analysis might follow a rhetorical structure like this:

The Introduction:
>Some general statements about academic journal abstracts being representative of a particular genre, followed by a brief synopsis of what other writers have said about this. Specific signposting language to indicate which abstracts your own sample includes and an outline of the framework you will use for analysing these.

The Body:
A detailed analysis of the different linguistic features of your sample abstracts, each discussed under a series of headings and sub-headings.

The Conclusion:
Some commentary on the extent to which the language in your sample either conforms to or departs from what others have identified as representative features of this text type. If you have identified any differences, then perhaps also some critical analysis of why you think these divergences might have occurred.

After carrying out a linguistic analysis of the move structures in a selection of abstracts from two different journals (Applied Linguistics and TESOL Quarterly) look at how a student presented and supported her claims in this short excerpt from the analysis body section:

The Simple Present tense (frequency = 86) and Simple Past tense (frequency = 77) are the most commonly used tenses in my sampled abstracts from the two journals, each massively outnumbering the use of the Present Perfect tense (frequency = 11). In the TESOL Quarterly abstracts, the Simple Present tense appears with a significantly higher frequency in the Topic, Background, Conclusion and Implications moves. However, in the Niche and Purpose moves, the Applied Linguistics abstracts draw on either the Present Passive or the Present Simple, while TESOL Quarterly seems to favour either the Present Perfect or the Simple Past:

Applied Linguistics Abstract 1: Niche
   ... little **is known** about how teaching professionals engage with existing research or carry out their own research.

TESOL Quarterly Abstract 7: Niche
   However, few studies **have examined** how the processing of formulaic sequences interacts with...

Applied Linguistics Abstract 3: Purpose
   The present study **aims to** examine the issue from a diachronic perspective.

TESOL Quarterly Abstract 6: Purpose
   This study **investigated** the potential of discipline-related television programmes as sources for...

Check Your Understanding: Independent Task 5.2b

Based on the principles of genre analysis, how many separate move structures can you identify in the academic conference abstract below and what different functions do they serve?

Needs Analysis for Continuing Professional Development of Chinese Teachers of English
16th Asia TEFL International Conference, Macau, June 2018

There is widespread recognition of the desirability of continuing professional development for Chinese teachers of English (Yan, 2005; Xu & Connelly, 2009; Edwards & Li, 2011). However, obstacles to the implementation of communicative language teaching in China (Li & Baldauf, 2011; Xiaoshan, 2011; Rao, 2013) tend to limit the design and content of teacher development courses.

The presentation reports on the methods and findings of needs analyses conducted with groups of teachers prior to their attendance on teaching methodology courses at the University of Nottingham Ningbo China. These findings are compared with the results of surveys completed by teachers at the end of their courses in order to determine what type of professional development activities are most useful and beneficial for Chinese teachers of English. One of the most significant findings is that teachers highly valued the opportunity to participate in demonstration lessons taught by the trainers, and micro-teaching carried out in groups, both of which were based on the textbooks that the teachers normally use in their own schools.

A suggested answer to this task has been provided on page 116.

5.3 Dealing with Reflective Writing Tasks

Compared to the other types of academic writing already discussed in this chapter, reflective writing tasks are, relatively speaking, probably the least common of all. However, you may still sometimes encounter them on an MA TESOL or MA Applied Linguistics programme, so it is worth considering what they involve and how they should best be approached.

One very typical reflective writing task is when an assignment asks you to keep a learner diary. This often happens on MA TESOL courses, especially those with a teaching practicum component, when your tutors may want to see some evidence of you critically reflecting on personal experiences, such as a series of different lessons you have taught or observed. In the MA TESOL programme, which I currently direct at the University of Nottingham Ningbo China for example, one of our elective modules requires students to keep a learner diary for the entire duration of the second semester. In this case, students are asked to reflect critically on four different things: their understanding of the different weekly academic input sessions they are exposed to; their experience of peer microteaching; different lessons they observe; and finally, their experience of teaching practice at a local school. The learner diary is then submitted for formal evaluation and carries a weighting of 30% of the students' overall module grade.

Unlike the essay formats which this chapter has already discussed, most reflective writing is probably *not* going to follow a traditional 'Introduction-Body-Conclusion' rhetorical structure. However, this is not to say that none of the advice already offered on these elements will not be relevant. You will still need to structure your points in a coherent and logical manner; you will still need to draw on the wider academic literature as support for your claims; and you will still need to make good use of signposting language and devices such as headings and sub-headings. Perhaps the biggest difference though between the style of writing in an academic essay and that found in a learner diary is that the latter will involve much more explicit sharing of your personal thoughts and writing in the First Person, i.e., in this style of writing, you can more directly give your opinions and there will be somewhat less of a need for hedging and tentative language. When reading a learner diary, your marking tutor will principally be looking for evidence of how clearly and convincingly you can express your own thoughts and critically evaluate your personal experiences, while making relevant connections between theory and practice. These skills lie at the very heart of critical reflection.

5.3.1 The Difference between Description and Critical Reflection

One problem which I frequently encounter when assessing my students' learner diaries is that their writing often ends up becoming pure description, rather than proper critical reflection.

Look at the two learner diary writing excerpts below. Which one do you think is best? Why?

Dealing with Different Types of Written Coursework Assignments 111

TEXT A

Peer Micro-Teaching 1

I taught my first peer micro-teaching session on March 14, 2022. This lasted for 15 minutes, and my topic was how to teach students skimming and scanning. I gave my classmates a text about famous tourist sites in London. I first asked them to skim the text to get the main ideas, then I asked them to scan for specific points. I was pleased that my classmates could answer all my questions. However, I noticed that in his feedback afterwards, the observing tutor told me to think more carefully about my timing.

TEXT B

Peer Micro-Teaching 1: March 14, 2022

In my first peer micro-teaching session, I decided that I would teach my classmates some reading strategies such as skimming and scanning. To do this, I decided to use a text about famous tourist sites in London. I chose this text because I felt that it would lend itself well to both of those strategies and thus be a realistic reflection of how readers might approach such a reading passage in real life. If someone was encountering a brochure like this for the first time, for example, they might skim it first, just to see whether it is worth reading, then scan for more specific detail in any of the sections which they thought looked more interesting. As we learned in the input session on how to teach reading, I agree that if we want to teach learners specific reading strategies, it makes sense to choose texts which learners would naturally approach in those ways, as this can then help to make their learning more practical and meaningful.

At the start of the session, I began by quickly showing my classmates the front page of the brochure and I asked them what they thought the text would be about. From the front cover photographs of Big Ben and Buckingham Palace, my classmates could easily identify that the text would probably be about tourist sites in London. I think this pre-reading activity immediately engaged their interest and made them want to read the text. As various scholars have argued (e.g., An, 2013; Anderson, 2004) doing something like this can also help to activate learners' schemata and get them making some predictions and thinking about relevant vocabulary. As we learned in an earlier input session, preparing students for reading in these ways can also be much more motivational than simply giving them a reading text 'cold'.

It should be self-evident from the above that Text B is more critically reflective, and is therefore a much more successful piece of writing than Text A. Instead of just describing facts, e.g., 'my topic was how to teach students skimming and scanning', Text B shows that the writer has put some critical thought into things and can provide a rationale to support his/her choices, e.g.,

> I decided to use a text about famous tourist sites in London. I chose this text because I felt that it would lend itself well to both of those

strategies and be a realistic reflection of how readers might approach such a reading passage in real life.

The writer of Text B is also able to make explicit connections between what the theories about reading instruction say and how these have then been applied in the class, e.g.,

> I think this pre-reading activity immediately engaged their interest and made them want to read the text. As various scholars have argued (e.g., Anderson, 2004; An, 2013) doing something like this can also help to activate learners' schemata and get them making some predictions and thinking about relevant vocabulary.

As Text B shows, to be awarded high marks in a coursework assignment which asks you to produce critically reflective writing, your discussion of the content will need to include sufficient detail and depth. Tutors will want to see demonstrable evidence of you thinking about how theories relate to practice and showing that you have some critical awareness of how to make such connections between these and your own experiences.

> **Check Your Understanding: Independent Task 5.3**
>
> Write one or two paragraphs (400–500 words) in which you critically reflect on whether classroom teaching should be delivered entirely in the target language (L2) or if use of the learners' mother tongue (L1) may also be permitted.
> As in the example above, you should write predominantly using the First Person and draw on examples taken from your own experiences, either as a teacher or a learner. Where relevant, also try to link what you say with supporting citations from the wider academic literature. Close this piece of writing by reaching a personal conclusion one way or the other.
> A sample answer for this task has been provided on page 117.

5.4 Marking Criteria

When your MA lecturers mark and grade your work, they will almost certainly be doing so by following an established set of marking criteria. These are essentially a set of institutionally agreed descriptors and grade bands, which can be used to help markers accurately determine and categorise the relative value of a piece of writing. As the sample marking guide below shows, student academic writing is usually judged on how well it meets the definitions for criteria spanning a range of different areas:

Dealing with Different Types of Written Coursework Assignments   113

Table 3 Example of Grade Descriptors and Marking Bands

Grade Band	Structure and Organisation	Knowledge and Understanding	Practical Application	Use of Language
80+ High distinction	Demonstrates an exceptionally high ability to organise material during which different perspectives are balanced.	Demonstrates an exceptionally high knowledge of the topic and how it fits with the wider field with sophisticated critical analysis.	Demonstrates an exceptionally high ability to draw implications from theory/research for professional practice and explore these critically.	Demonstrates fluent application of academic language and conventions. Handles language with an exceptional level of linguistic sophistication.
70–79 Distinction	Demonstrates a high level of skill in selecting, synthesising and organising material.	Demonstrates a very broad and detailed knowledge of the topic with significant evidence of criticality.	Demonstrates the ability to draw implications from theory/research for professional practice and explore these in depth.	Demonstrates a very high awareness of academic language and conventions. Handles complex language skilfully.
60–69 Merit	Demonstrates the ability to select and organise material very effectively.	Demonstrates a broad knowledge of the topic with good evidence of criticality.	Demonstrates a high ability in applying theory to practice.	Demonstrates a good awareness of academic language and conventions.
50–59 Pass	Demonstrates a satisfactory level of structure and organisation. Meets the task requirements.	Demonstrates an adequate knowledge of the topic. Shows some capacity for criticality.	Demonstrates the ability to apply theory to practice. Shows evidence of adapting theory to specific contexts.	Demonstrates a satisfactory command of academic language and conventions.
40–49 Soft fail	Demonstrates poor organisational ability with frequent irregularities.	Demonstrates limited knowledge of the topic.	Demonstrates little capacity to apply theory to practice.	Demonstrates limited awareness of academic language and conventions.
30–39 Hard fail	Fails to organise the material coherently and/or address the needs of the task.	Fails to demonstrate knowledge or understanding of the topic and/or task.	Fails to relate theory to practice.	Fails to demonstrate a grasp of academic language and conventions.

Make sure that you familiarise yourself with the institutional marking descriptors which will be used to judge your academic coursework. If you can get into the habit of using these as a self-checking mechanism before submitting your assignments, it will help you to tighten up your academic writing and in so doing get better grades.

Suggested Answers to Independent Tasks

Task 5.1a

Table 4 Different Moves in an Assignment Response

The relationship between theory and practice and the extent to which one should inform the other is an issue which has resonated across a great many human endeavours, not just English Language Teaching.	1. A general statement: something that most people would agree to be true.
Thanks to the work of pioneering psychologists such as Kurt Lewin (1890–1947) it might even be argued that the idea of there being nothing more practical than a good theory has now entered our collective consciousness.	2. Some evidence for the opening general statement.
In the specific case of English language teaching, however, the question of whether theories and methodologies can help teachers to improve what they do in their classrooms continues to be hotly debated.	3. A quick synopsis of the key issue.
In discussing this issue, rather than treating theory as an abstract concept, I believe that it is first necessary to specify which particular theories we are talking about, as clearly some theories will have more relevance to teachers than others. A closely related point is the matter of when and how teachers should be exposed to such theories in the first place. A final consideration, and one which I believe is highly pertinent to each of these cases, is the matter of teachers' underlying values and beliefs and how these are formed and take shape.	4. Detailed topic statements to indicate the direction in which the essay will be going.
In this essay, I will be examining each of these core areas in turn.	5. A signposting phrase to confirm how the essay will be structured.

Based on the structural overview which has been outlined above, the next paragraph of this essay is most likely to be dealing with those theories which the writer considers to be important.

Dealing with Different Types of Written Coursework Assignments 115

Task 5.1b

Table 5 An Original Quotation and an 'Unpacked' Quotation

Quotation	What I Think It Means in My Own Words
'... no idealized teaching method can visualize all the variables in advance to provide situation-specific suggestions that practicing teachers need to tackle the challenges that confront the practice of their everyday teaching.'	No one method can ever deal with everything – there are simply too many variables involved in teaching and these are often context-specific.

Table 6 An Original Rubric and an 'Unpacked' Rubric

Assignment Rubric	What It Means
Some might argue that this criticism by Kumaravadivelu immediately negates the value of pursuing language teaching methodology. Do you agree with this stance, or are there in fact some benefits which have been gained in exploring different approaches and methods?	Has the search for an effective methodology just been a waste of time? Has the field of ELT benefitted from exploring different approaches and methods? If so, how? What are my own opinions on these issues?

Task 5.1c

Your critical evaluation for this task is likely to draw on the following theories:

Behaviourism and behaviourist theories of language learning, e.g., the work of B.F. Skinner and its application to methodologies such as audio-lingualism (ALM)

Cognitivism and the role of universal grammar, e.g., the work of Noam Chomsky

The acquisition-learning hypothesis and the natural order hypothesis, e.g., the work of Stephen Krashen

You will most probably also be making some mention of interaction hypothesis, constructivism and social constructivism, and the notion of communicative competence.

Task 5.2a

Print advertisements, especially those targeting cosmetics and other beauty products, often make use of several linguistic techniques. A detailed analysis might well draw attention to:

Deviant spelling, e.g., *Pro X Clear*

Use of lexical boost, e.g., a *total* skin care solution; *leading* dermatologists; *consistently* clear skin

Use of professional endorsements, e.g., leading *dermatologists;* skin *scientists; clinically proven* technology; *professional* expertise

References to time, e.g., see amazing results *in as little as four weeks*

Alliteration, e.g., *b*lemishes and *b*reakouts; *c*onsistently *c*lear skin; *Potent. Proven. Professional*

Promises to solve a particular problem, e.g., *reduce* and *help prevent* frustrating blemishes and breakouts; *even* texture and *minimise* the look of pores; professional expertise together with a skin-transforming experience *provides an answer*

Use of command forms, e.g., *see* the proof

Task 5.2b

There are four main moves in this text. They can be identified as follows:

Example Move Structures in a Conference Abstract

Needs Analysis for Continuing Professional Development of Chinese Teachers of English
16th Asia TEFL International Conference, Macau, June 2018 *[used with permission from P. Beech]*

There is widespread recognition of the desirability of continuing professional development for Chinese teachers of English (Yan, 2005; Xu & Connelly, 2009; Edwards & Li, 2011).	Establishing the Topic
However, obstacles to the implementation of communicative language teaching in China (Li & Bauldauf, 2011; Xiaoshan, 2011; Rao, 2013) tend to limit the design and content of teacher development courses.	Identifying a Problem
This presentation reports on the methods and findings of needs analyses conducted with groups of teachers prior to their attendance at teaching methodology courses at the University of Nottingham Ningbo China. These findings are compared with the results of surveys completed by teachers at the end of their courses in order to determine what type of professional development activities are most useful and beneficial for Chinese teachers of English.	Describing the Research
One of the most significant findings is that teachers highly valued the opportunity to participate in demonstration lessons taught by the trainers, and micro-teaching carried out in groups, both of which were based on the textbooks that the teachers normally use in their own schools.	Detailing the Findings

Task 5.3

As most modern writers on language teaching methodology agree (e.g., Hall, 2011; Spiro, 2013; Richards & Rodgers, 2014) the question of whether classroom teaching should be conducted in the target language (L2) or in the learners' mother tongue (L1) has been a dichotomous issue throughout the history of language teaching. While early methodologies such as Grammar Translation (GTM) advocated that everything should be done using the L1 alone, more modern approaches such as Communicative Language Teaching (CLT) have taken the completely opposite stance, arguing that all teaching should be carried out in the L2. My own take on this issue has also reflected this pendulum swing, but somewhat surprisingly, perhaps in the opposite direction. When I first started teaching in the 1980s, CLT had taken language teaching by storm and my teacher trainers at that time were adamant that only the L2 should be used. At first, I embraced this pedagogic principle enthusiastically and did all my teaching only in English, never ever resorting to using my learners' native language or allowing them to do so. However, there were times when I found myself thinking that on certain occasions perhaps some *principled* use of their L1 might not be such a bad thing. When trying to explain some of the finer points of grammar, for example, or show the different nuances between closely related lexical items, I could see that some of my adult learners were getting frustrated and it was clear that despite my best efforts, either a few people were still not fully understanding or, as I discovered later, had in fact completely *misunderstood* what I was trying to teach them. At times like these, I began to wonder if it might not be more effective for me sometimes to draw explicitly on my learners' L1 knowledge. Learning means drawing on different types of knowledge, after all, so why should we put artificial restrictions on that process? Adult learners are already proficient users of their L1 and they can be encouraged to draw on these skills to help them learn an L2. Rather than just blindly following a blanket methodological ruling which insists on one thing or another, my current way of thinking, therefore, is to adjust my teaching style to meet the specific demands of a given context. If I am trying to build oral fluency with my learners, then obviously it makes sense for them to have as much exposure to the L2 as possible and on such occasions, I try to keep away from anything which might disrupt their flow. If I am teaching a particular grammatical point, however, then nowadays I may sometimes ask my learners to make explicit comparisons invoking both their L1 and L2. For

> me, the key issue here is that my approach will always depend on what exactly I am trying to achieve. As far as I am concerned, it is impossible to fix a ruling which amounts to one size fits all; pedagogic principles *always* need to be adapted to meet the particular demands of specific learners and specific contexts.

Additional Resources for Further Reading

Fairclough, N. (2010). *Critical Discourse Analysis: The Critical Study of Language*. Routledge.

Godfrey, J. (2018). *How to Use Reading in Your Essays*. Bloomsbury.

Judge, B., Jones, P. & McCreery, E. (2009) *Critical Thinking Skills for Education Students*. Learning Matters.

Chapter References

An, S. (2013). Schema theory in reading. *Theory and Practice in Language Studies*, 3(1), 130–134.

Anderson, N.J. (2004). *Exploring Second Language Reading: Issues and Strategies*. Beijing Foreign Language Press.

Barber, C. L. (1962). Some measurable characteristics of modern scientific prose. In J.M. Swales (Ed.) *Contributions to English Syntax and Philology*, 1988. *Episodes in ESP* (pp. 1–16). Pergamon.

Bhatia, V.K. (1993). *Analysing Genre: Language Use in Professional Settings*. Longman.

Bloor, T. & Bloor, M. (2004). *The Functional Analysis of English*. Hodder Arnold. https://doi.org/10.4324/9780203774854.

Borg, S. (2003) Teacher cognition in language teaching: A review of research on what language teachers think, know, believe, and do. *Language Teaching*, 36(2), 81–109.

Brown, H.D. (2007). *Teaching by Principles: An Interactive Approach to Language Pedagogy* (2nd ed). Pearson Education.

Edwards, V. & Li, D. (2011). *Confucius, constructivism and the impact of continuing professional development of teachers of English in China*. British Council Research Papers.

Ellis, R. (1997). *The Study of Second Language Acquisition*. Oxford University Press.

Hall, G. (2011). *Exploring English Language Teaching. Language in Action*. Routledge.

Halliday, M.A.K. (1978). *Language as a Social Semiotic: The Social Interpretation of Language and Meaning*. Arnold.

Kumaravadivelu, B. (Ed). (2012). *Language Teacher Education for a Global Society*. Routledge.

Li, M. & Baldauf, R. (2011). Beyond the curriculum: A Chinese Example of issues constraining effective English language teaching. *TESOL Quarterly*, 45(4), 793–803.

Liardét, C.L. (2016) Nominalization and grammatical metaphor: Elaborating the theory. *English for Specific Purposes, 44*, 16–29.

Myers, G. (1990). *Writing Biology: Texts in the Social Construction of Scientific Knowledge.* University of Wisconsin Press.

Prabhu, N.S. (1990). There is no best method - Why? *TESOL Quarterly, 24*(2), 161–176.

Rao, Z. (2013). Teaching English as a foreign language in China: Looking back and forward: Reconciling modern methodologies with traditional ways of language teaching. *English Today, 29*(3), 34–39.

Richards, J.C. & Rodgers, T.S. (2014). *Approaches and Methods in Language Teaching* (3rd ed.). Cambridge University Press.

Spiro, J. (2013). *Changing Methodologies in TESOL.* Edinburgh University Press.

Swales, J.M. (1990). *Genre Analysis: English in Academic and Research Settings.* Cambridge University Press.

Widdowson, H.G. (1978). *Teaching Language as Communication.* Oxford University Press.

Xiaoshan, Z. (2011). Communicative language teaching obstacles and strategies. *IEEE*, 641–643.

Xu, S. & Connelly, F.M. (2009) Narrative inquiry for teacher education and development: Focus on English as a foreign language in China. *Teaching and Teacher Education, 25*, 219–227.

Yan, C. (2005). INSET Participation and Certification: a case-study from China. *Journal of In-Service Education, 3*, 471–484.

6 Teaching Observation and Practice

Introduction

This chapter focuses on some of the more practical elements you may need to engage with during your Masters' studies. Teaching observation and practice probably represent the most common manifestations of these, although a small number of MA programmes worldwide may also sometimes include internships and work placements.

This chapter opens by considering the relationship between theory and practice and suggests that you will get more out of your studies if you can try to make the connections between these two areas explicit. It then looks at teaching observation and discusses some of the tools and mechanisms which are typically used for this. Next, it examines the traditional stages of a classroom observation cycle before turning its attention to some different dimensions of lesson planning.

The closing sections of this chapter discuss common approaches to teaching practice on Masters' programmes and also consider the importance of critical reflection.

Additional resources for your further reading are listed on page 138.

6.1 The Relationship between Theory and Practice

A commonly voiced criticism of many Masters' programmes worldwide, not only those involving TESOL/Applied Linguistics, is that their focus may sometimes be perceived as being overly theoretical. When working on different MA programmes over the years, I have often heard students say that although they enjoyed doing their Masters, after they had graduated from the course, they found that they somehow 'couldn't really use' what they had been taught because the content had never been made sufficiently relevant to their individual contexts. The latter part of this comment may well be true. When I was a student at different stages in my own career, I have often sat through lectures in which the material being presented was highly abstract and there were no explicit links being forged between the research theories and what their ramifications might be for teachers and

DOI: 10.4324/9781003269854-6

learners. However, I think it would be grossly unfair of me if I were to place *all* the blame for this at the lecturers' door. I would also have to acknowledge that as an MA student, I should have been prepared to take more individual agency myself and to have learned how to reflect more deliberately on the ways in which educational theories might be usefully linked with my own day-to-day practices.

As the famous psychologist Kurt Lewin (1890–1947) has often been quoted as saying, 'There is nothing quite so practical as a good theory.' Certainly from my current perspective as an MA programme director, I do now very firmly believe that in order for students to get the most out of their TESOL/Applied Linguistics studies, they should be encouraged to make as many connections as they can between what the theories say and how these might then be effectively applied in real life.

In what has since gone on to become a highly influential and oft-cited publication from 1987, N.S. Prabhu suggested that although educational theories undoubtedly have their place, teachers will still always be guided by their own sense of plausibility. In other words, teachers will gradually build their own theoretical sense of what works and does not work based on their accumulated experiences and the impact that these then have on their professional values and beliefs. I wholeheartedly agree with Prabhu on this, but would add that from my own experience as a teacher educator, I also believe that most novice teachers' developmental trajectories can be greatly enhanced if they are *actively and explicitly encouraged* to engage with and reflect on the relationship between theory and practice right from the outset.

To get you thinking along these lines, the Independent Task 6.1a below asks you to do this with regard to some very common educational theories you are likely to encounter in MA TESOL/Applied Linguistics programmes.

Check Your Understanding: Independent Task 6.1a

The theories and hypotheses below are all commonly discussed in TESOL and Applied Linguistics. What *practical* implications does each of these have for language learning and teaching?

a. Behaviourist Theory
b. Social Constructivist Theory
c. Monitor Hypothesis
d. Affective Filter Hypothesis
e. Schema Theory

A suggested answer to this task has been provided on page 135.

122 *Teaching Observation and Practice*

As part of your MA TESOL/Applied Linguistics, you will undoubtedly be exposed to many different theories, some of which may well include the examples I have provided in the independent task above. If your lecturers fail to make the practical applications of such theories relevant, do not be shy about asking them to do so. Also, always be prepared to think critically about such matters yourself. This means that when you encounter different educational theories, do not just learn and then regurgitate them as established facts. Instead, subject them to your own critical scrutiny and try to evaluate their validity in more practical and personally contextualised terms. If you are able to show some evidence of doing this in your academic writing, you will almost certainly be awarded higher marks. As discussed in Chapters 3 and 5, engaging with material appropriately at the Masters' level should always involve a strong element of criticality and you will be expected to go beyond mere description.

Check Your Understanding: Independent Task 6.1b

As I have suggested above, you should always be trying to engage with educational theories *critically*, not just learning them as if they were established facts.

A critical evaluation of theories means evaluating whether or not they consistently make sense, identifying any weaknesses or contradictions and then considering if there are any counterviews.

What objections or counterviews might you therefore legitimately raise in critically evaluating the following theory-based proposals?

a. 'Teachers must immediately correct their language learners' mistakes and model the correct answer. If they fail to do this, then those linguistic mistakes will become ingrained as bad habits and the fossilization of errors will take place' [**Behaviourist Theory**]
b. 'Acquiring linguistic items based on appropriately-tuned comprehensible input will give far better results than deliberately setting out to learn language forms' [**Monitor Hypothesis**]
c. 'Using language to complete group work tasks will result in your learners' greater linguistic fluency than having them individually translate sentences from one language to another' [**Social Constructivist Theory (linked with some basic tenets of Task-Based Learning) being contrasted with Grammar Translation Methodology**]

As far as possible, try to support your points with practical examples from your own experience, either as a teacher or as a learner.

A suggested answer to this task has been provided on page 136.

6.2 Teaching Observation

Teaching observation on MA TESOL/Applied Linguistics programmes can take a variety of forms. Some taught modules may formally require you to complete a full cycle of classroom observation with designated teachers and classes of students; others may be much less structured and simply suggest that you informally engage in a few teaching observations as part of your own continuing professional development.

Whatever the stance that your course takes on teaching observation, you will probably get more out of the experience if you approach it systematically and consider how you might most effectively use different observation tools and mechanisms. When looking at classroom observation more holistically, it can also be helpful to conceptualise observation itself as a cycle, i.e., as a process with different stages.

6.2.1 Observation Tools and Mechanisms

Although the work is now becoming a little dated, Michael Wallace (1991) includes some very useful sections on different approaches to classroom observation in his book *Training Foreign Language Teachers*. As Wallace documents, historically speaking, over the years there have been several different ways in which classroom observations have been handled. The original system-based approaches such as those from the 1960s and 1970s (e.g., Bellack et al., 1966; Sinclair & Coulthard, 1975, Fanselow, 1977) have gradually given way to more ethnographic (e.g., Hammersley & Atkinson, 1983) and what Wallace termed ad hoc methods (e.g., Wallace, 1981; Ramani, 1987; Brown, 1988). For a more contemporary overview of these, I can highly recommend Matt O'Leary's excellent book, *Classroom Observation. A Guide to the Effective Observation of Teaching and Learning* (Routledge, 2014).

For the purposes of this current discussion, however, my intention is simply to raise your awareness that if you are asked to carry out classroom observations, then the process can be made more enriching and significantly less 'messy' if you prepare some tools and mechanisms in advance. One such tool that I try to pass on to my own MA students is the concept of a running commentary.

As the name suggests, a running commentary requires the observer to create a blow-by-blow written record of everything which is observed happening in a given lesson. Although there are various proformas which can be created for doing this, I usually provide my students with a document which looks something like the material shown in the box below:

124 *Teaching Observation and Practice*

⏱	*Record of observed activity*	*Interaction*	*Observer questions and comments*

NAME OF TEACHER OBSERVED: .... CLASS: .... NUMBER OF STUDENTS: ....
NAME OF OBSERVER: .... DATE OF OBSERVATION: .... DURATION: ....

A form like this (which in total might run to five or six pages in length: bear in mind that I am only showing the front cover page here) allows the observer to keep a detailed written record of everything he/she observes as an ongoing stream of consciousness. In the first column, for example, the observer makes a note of the time when different activities start and finish. In the second column, a record can be kept of each different activity. In the centre column, the observer makes a note of the observed interaction patterns and finally, the column on the right allows the observer to jot down any questions or comments.

I first learned about this approach to doing a running commentary almost 25 years ago when I was working as an EAP tutor at Bilkent University in Turkey. One of the undoubted highlights of my employment at that time was the fact that Bilkent offered its staff a surprisingly rich selection of professional development opportunities. These often took the form of accredited training courses, which meant that one was not only professionally developing but also accruing useful academic qualifications. I learned, for example, how to carry out classroom observations using running commentaries as part of an extremely valuable year-long postgraduate Diploma on Teacher Training. To this day, I remain indebted to the trainers, Deniz Kurtoglu-Eken and Marion Heron, for their many useful insights.

One such insight was that we were advised to do our observation running commentaries in pencil rather than ink. Apart from the fact that writing in pencil generally seems to allow one's handwriting to go a lot faster, the added advantage is that any mistakes which inevitably creep in can then later very easily be erased before a clean copy of the commentary is shared with the observee.

When they are done well, running commentaries like this can serve as a snapshot of everything which an observer sees happening in a class. An example of what the first part of one might look like after completion is shown in the box below:

| NAME OF TEACHER OBSERVED: Karen | CLASS: 7b | NUMBER OF STUDENTS: 32 |
| NAME OF OBSERVER: Doug | DATE OF OBSERVATION: 24/10/22 | DURATION: 90 mins |

🕐	Record of observed activity	Interaction	Observer questions & comments
09:00	T greets the class. Asks Ss to take out hmwk from the prev. lsn.	T-SS	
	T says, 'Can anyone answer question 1?' SILENCE FROM SS.	T-SS	Ss seem v. subdued. Why do you think that is?
09:06	'OK. Tina- what did you write?'	T-S	
	Tina: 'errr, I'm not sure but I think it's a kind of flower'	S-T	?? What could you do here to avoid putting individuals on the spot?

There are a few things worth commenting on here. Perhaps the first point to be made is that observers need to be able to react quickly when writing down a record of what they see. This process can be significantly speeded up if observers develop their own form of note-taking or shorthand. As in the example above, in order to save time, instead of writing the word out in full, 'teacher' can be reduced to just 'T' and 'Student' or 'Students' can be more simply captured as 'S' or 'Ss'. Observers may also wish to devise their own symbols or abbreviations to capture particular moods or emotions. An exclamation mark next to a comment might signify surprise, for example, or it could be used to highlight something that seems problematic. A smiley-face on the other hand might indicate something very positive, while a string of question marks might signify an issue which the observer would later like to explore with the observee in more detail.

A further point worth stressing here is that in the column for recording the observed activities, the observer should strive to be as non-judgmental as possible and simply write down what he/she sees happening. When this is done effectively, it leads to a neutral and objective blow-by-blow account of everything which occurred. This element of neutrality can become very important later on when discussing the details of the observed lesson with the observee. In this regard, it is not unknown for people to deny quite vehemently that they did whatever the observer says they did, but having an objective written record of the events can help to counteract this.

Of course, the types of classroom observation you may be asked to engage in as part of an MA TESOL/Applied Linguistics are not meant to be evaluative, nor will they have any longer-term consequences in terms of annual performance appraisals. The likelihood of the observer and the observee ending up at loggerheads over differences of opinion should therefore be greatly minimised. Nonetheless, the process of being observed and then discussing one's teaching performance with someone else still has the potential to become emotionally fraught. From my own experience, even when observations are being carried out entirely from a collegial and developmental perspective, the more that observers can do to avoid sounding judgmental and to allay their observees' concerns in this regard, the better.

Having stated above that running commentaries should be completed by hand using pencil, I am mindful that in this day and age, many people might prefer to go through the process by typing their commentary on a laptop or tablet. My advice on this would be to find whichever system works best for you. Either way, if you can master the skills of taking an effective running commentary, I am confident that you will find the process of classroom observation a much more rewarding experience than if you simply sit in lessons and take occasional notes, or if you try to keep everything that you see happening around you in your head.

> **Check Your Understanding: Independent Task 6.2a**
>
> Create a running commentary document based on the guidance above and try it out while observing one of your friends or peers teaching a class.
>
> Which aspects of doing the running commentary did you find easy? Which ones were more difficult?

6.2.2 The Observation Cycle

Your classroom observations should be carefully planned events, not just random happenings. To get the most out of the experience, it can also be helpful to approach classroom observation as a cycle which has distinct phases. One typical way of doing this is to break down the process itself into three clear stages: a pre-observation, an observation and then a post-observation.

In the pre-observation stage, the observer typically sits down for a face-to-face meeting with the observee and asks him/her to talk through the lesson to come. The pre-observation stage is also the time when the overall purpose of the observation will be confirmed, such as whether or not the observer will be looking out for anything in particular, e.g., use of the board; amount of teacher talking time; balance of interaction patterns etc., or if the observation will be more holistic in nature. On some MA TESOL modules, you may be asked to pair up with a buddy and then take turns observing each other's classes, focusing on particular elements each time. This diet of elements will often be designed to reflect some of the discrete topics which may have been covered in the module's taught input sessions, e.g., effective use of instructions; techniques for classroom management; approaches to scaffolding activities etc. and might then also tie in with further discussion of these same topics in a reflective diary (see my discussion of this in Chapter 5). By the end of the pre-observation meeting, both the observer and the person being observed should have a shared understanding of what is expected to happen. They will have agreed on how long the observer should remain in the class and whether or not the purpose of the observation will be made clear to the students. The observer will also have been provided with a lesson plan and copies of the teaching materials that will be used.

During the observation itself, the observer will usually aim to sit to one side of the class and keep his/her presence as unobtrusive as possible. As I have touched on above, the purpose of the observation is often explained to the students in advance, so that they are not wondering why there is suddenly a stranger in their classroom, but beyond this, there should be no need for the observer to get involved in any of the activities. To all intents and purposes, he/she will simply be there as a fly on the wall, quietly taking a running commentary and observing what is going on. From a practical perspective, if an observation is intended to cover just a portion of a full lesson, it can be helpful to have the observer seated near the door, so that at the designated time, he/she can slip out with minimum disruption.

The post-observation stage, as the name would suggest, represents a face-to-face meeting between the observer and the observee, scheduled for some point after the lesson has taken place. There is no fixed rule on the timing for this, but obviously it makes sense to have the post-observation meeting as soon as possible after the observed lesson, so that everyone's impressions can remain fresh. When I go through observation cycles myself, schedules mutually permitting, I usually try to have my post-observation meetings no later than close of business on the next day.

The main purpose of the post-observation stage is to discuss the lesson and critically deconstruct the different things which the observer may have seen happening. To help guide and get the most out of this exchange, the observer should begin by sharing a clean copy of the running commentary with the observee; this can then be gone through step by step and used as a springboard for discussions. As I have commented above, the observations you may be asked to carry out on an MA TESOL/Applied Linguistics programme are never going to be evaluative or managerial in nature, so there should not be any element of the observer criticising or 'talking down' to the observee. All the comments and questions which the observer has written down on the running commentary should have been motivated by aiming for all parties concerned to reach a better understanding of teaching and learning. The post-observation meeting offers some extremely rich possibilities in this regard and can serve as a catalyst for the further professional development of both the person who was observed and the person who did the observing.

As I started this section of the chapter by saying, developmental classroom observations should always be carefully planned events. This means that there needs to be due consideration of the time which should be devoted to them. In the tri-partite cycle I have been describing, at least 20–30 minutes would be devoted to the pre-observation stage, the observation itself should last for either the full lesson, or in the case of classes which go beyond an hour at least 40–45 minutes, then a further 30–40 minutes would be assigned to the post-observation stage. In total, all of this clearly adds up to a significant time investment. However, as I have stressed, if you are going to get the most out of them, classroom observations do need to be taken seriously.

> **Check Your Understanding: Independent Task 6.2b**
>
> Arrange a classroom observation with one of your peers in which you go through the cycle I have described above then later arrange for that person to do the same thing with you.
>
> When both observation cycles are complete, discuss what you each learned from the experience.

6.3 Lesson Planning

I think it is fair to say that most students enrolled on MA TESOL/Applied Linguistics these days are likely to have had some prior experience of teaching, particularly in the case of TESOL. However, in some parts of the world, as I have already explained, such Masters' programmes may still be willing to accept students without any relevant work experience. In these cases, no prior knowledge of lesson planning can be assumed, so it is worth examining some of the fundamental considerations which go into planning an effective lesson.

6.3.1 Different Conceptualisations of Lessons

Before you begin to plan a lesson, it can be helpful to take a few steps back and think about the notion of lessons in more abstract conceptual terms. When you start to do this, you will soon come to realise that there are in fact many different ways in which the idea of a lesson can be conceptualised. Your personal understanding of what a lesson might look like is then likely to have some important ramifications for how a given lesson and the respective roles of the teacher and the students will be organised during your planning.

Several different ways of conceptualising a lesson are listed in the box below. If you were asked to choose one, which of these metaphors represents the closest match with how you yourself might conceptualise a lesson?

If we now 'unpack' the above, it should be clear that each metaphor carries a slightly different set of tacit assumptions. In some cases, such as a shopping trip or a consultation with a doctor, the emphasis is

> Different metaphors for a lesson:
>
> - A symphony
> - A carefully choreographed dance
> - A football match
> - A consultation with a doctor
> - A conversation between friends
> - A dinner menu
> - A freestyle jazz session
> - A shopping trip
>
> Adapted from Ur (1991).

transactional, reflecting a process of give and take which is expected to result in some kind of tangible outcome. In others, such as a conversation between friends, the emphasis is falling more on interaction and on the sense of a social relationship between the protagonists. Here, there is also the underlying assumption that the process of interaction itself will lead to particular outcomes. In other cases, the key message embedded in the metaphor is that of a very carefully staged and planned event. This becomes evident in those conceptualisations which see lessons as being like a choreographed dance, a football match or a symphony. In each of these cases, the protagonists will always have very clearly defined roles and are expected to work closely together to achieve specific results. In marked contrast to such carefully structured events, the freestyle jazz session is conceptually much looser and there is a recognition that lessons may need to be flexible and might therefore develop in any number of different ways and directions.

As this exercise shows, the ways in which we conceive of a lesson can be expected to have an impact on how the lessons we plan are structured and the roles that we expect the different protagonists will play.

Check Your Understanding: Independent Task 6.3a

After reading through the explanations above and perhaps now thinking more deeply about the different ways in which a lesson might be conceptualised, has your personal choice of metaphor changed or remained the same?

Are certain metaphors likely to be more popular in your country/culture than others? Why do you think this might be?

6.3.2 Different 'Ingredients' in Lessons

Although individual teachers will approach their lesson planning in their own idiosyncratic ways, there are nonetheless likely to be several key 'ingredients' which all lessons will have in common. If you are a novice teacher, it can be useful to think about what these might be.

The starting point for any lesson should be a consideration of its aims and objectives; the different purpose(s) the lesson is intended to achieve. Like a piece of music, lesson aims can be conceptualised as being either major or minor. Most lessons will have one or two major aims, which will be seen as their main objective, then a series of minor aims, which will be seen as subsidiary outcomes. In a class on reading, for example, the main aims of the lesson might be to give students practice in developing the skills of skimming, scanning and inferring author's meaning, while the subsidiary aims might be for them to notice and then practice a particular language point.

Once the aims have been set, most lessons will then consist of a series of activities through which the teacher anticipates that the aims will successfully be achieved. Deciding on which activities should be included, in turn, then opens up a series of other considerations around the timing of activities, the order in which individual activities should be presented and the desired interaction patterns for each. Wrapped around all of this, there will also then be questions around the contextualisation of learning and how the given content and activities should be presented as part of a coherent whole. As a sub-component of this, the transition from one activity to another will become another important consideration, as will the extent to which individual learning points are consolidated and recycled. Just as when cooking, the overall quality of a dish will depend firstly on the selection of the ingredients and secondly on how successfully the chef is able to combine them, the quality of a lesson will also largely depend on how skilfully the teacher understands and is able to handle each of these different dimensions.

> ### Check Your Understanding: Independent Task 6.3b
>
> One of the key ingredients mentioned above was the notion of contextualisation and ensuring that topics and activities are placed within a coherent whole.
>
> Imagine that you are going to teach a group of English learners a reading lesson, the main theme of which will be Stanley Milgram's famous social science experiment on obedience to authority from 1963 and the dangers of blindly following orders.
>
> How might you contextualise the opening of such a lesson? What wider purpose(s) would such contextualisation serve?
>
> A suggested answer to this task has been provided on page 137.

6.3.3 Approaches to Writing Lesson Plans

Different institutions approach lesson plans in different ways. Some may require their teachers to follow a particular format or style; others may be more flexible and leave everything up to the individual. However, the main purpose of *any* lesson plan is to act as a guide and blueprint for what will be taught. As such, it is worth remembering that lesson plans are first and foremost *practical* documents and this will be reflected in the different types of information they include. For instance, there will always be some detail provided on the nature of the class that is going to be taught, i.e., the number of students, the lesson topic and the class duration. There will also always be some mention of the desired aims and objectives. As I discussed in the previous section, lesson aims are often divided into main aims and subsidiary aims and these will usually be clearly stated at the top of the lesson plan. In the main body of the lesson plan, there will then be some detail on the individual activities, along with an indication of the different timings and intended interaction patterns. As I suggested in the previous sub-section, when planning a lesson, some thought always needs to be put into how one activity should transition to another and how the learners' development will be adequately supported and scaffolded. A common weakness with many novice teachers is that such scaffolding can be markedly absent and their activities appear to jump from one to the other without any clear sense of progression or purpose. In a well-developed lesson plan, there should be a clear relationship between each of the constituent parts with no sudden surprises or deviations. I am mindful that on the face of it, this advice may seem to be in opposition to the idea of the freestyle jazz session which I mentioned earlier, but if the direction and flow of a lesson suddenly *does* end up changing, then at the very least, the teacher should be able to provide a pedagogical justification and explain how this fits in with the whole. In short, things usually happen for a reason and teachers should always be able to defend their pedagogic choices and decisions.

6.4 Teaching Practice

As I started this chapter by saying, not all MA TESOL/Applied Linguistics around the world include a focus on teaching practice. Some MAs are predicated on the assumption that their students' practical classroom teaching knowledge and skills should be developed elsewhere, possibly by having them take one of the certificate or diploma courses, as I will discuss in Chapter 10. If one of the course entry requirements is that applicants must have a minimum number of years of previous teaching experience, then there may also be the tacit assumption that the participants are already competent in the classroom and need no further instruction.

Check Your Understanding: Independent Task 6.3c

Look at the short excerpt from a lesson plan below. The teacher was intending to have a class of 20 Junior High School students take part in a class debate on the merits and defects of zoos.

What feedback might you give to this teacher regarding the importance of including adequate staging and scaffolding?

Part of an Example Lesson Plan

Mins.	Planned Activities	Int.	Materials Needed/Comments
15	SS work in groups to brainstorm for the language of opinions, i.e. how to ask others what they think; how to give their own opinion; how to agree/ disagree; how to suggest alternative courses of action etc.	SS	I will give the groups sheets of A3 paper and marker pens for them to write down their ideas.
10	T asks each group to present their findings. Other groups listen and make a note of any key phrases they didn't have on their list.	SS-SS	
20	T writes on the W/B: 'Zoos show a shocking disregard for animals' rights and should be closed down'. T divides the class into two halves. One side will argue that zoos should be abolished; the other side will argue that zoos serve an important societal function and should be maintained.	SS-SS	I will show SS some pictures of depressed looking animals.

A suggested answer to this task has been provided on page 138.

For other Masters' programmes though, formal teaching practice may represent either a core or elective modular component. Before you enrol on an MA TESOL/Applied Linguistics, you may wish to consider whether or not you want/need a programme which includes this dimension, what form any such teaching practice might take and what the process is likely to require of you.

Some typical approaches to the different kinds of teaching practice found on Masters' programmes are outlined below.

6.4.1 Peer Micro-Teaching

On the MA TESOL programme at my own institution, peer micro-teaching currently represents a core component of our TESOL Observation and Practicum module in the second semester. As the name suggests, peer micro-teaching involves students in the delivery of small-scale (micro) instruction (teaching) to their classmates (peers).

You may be surprised to learn that the topics chosen for peer micro-teaching, especially when it is carried out for the first time, often may not have anything to do with language teaching at all. This is because the main purpose of that first exposure to peer micro-teaching is usually just to give novice teachers a taste of the different elements that teaching involves. When considered from this perspective, there is actually no need for the topic to be restricted to TESOL and students can be given the choice of teaching their classmates pretty much anything they want. In the case of my own institution, however, this always comes with the caveat that whichever topic they decide to choose, students must try to *teach* their peers rather than lecture.

This distinction does need to be made explicit because more often than not, when they are first asked to teach a given topic, students typically end up preparing an oral presentation using PowerPoint slides which they then talk through point by point, as if they were delivering a lecture. Rather than following such a didactic lecture format, we ask that a successfully executed micro-teaching session should instead try to show some evidence of more student-centred activities. In an attempt to make this even more explicit, in more recent years we have banned the use of PowerPoint slides completely, as we find that this then forces our students to think more creatively about what they want to teach and how they are going to teach it. As indeed Luke Meddings and Scott Thornbury originally proposed in the principles of their Dogme approach to ELT from 2009, it might be argued that the modern reliance on technology has, in some ways, had an unnecessarily restrictive effect on teaching. By returning the classroom to its original state of grace when 'all there was, was a room, a few chairs, a blackboard and a teacher', we find that our trainee teachers are more likely to develop a better understanding of core pedagogic principles than if we allow the use of PowerPoint slides to dominate.

After the first taster session, most subsequent peer micro-teaching sessions will begin to focus more explicitly on ELT and these typically follow a three-part sequence:

The Briefing Stage:
    when the students are told what to teach and receive some guidance on how this might be carried out.
The Teaching Stage:
    when the micro-lesson itself is taught. This is usually video-recorded.

The Analysis Stage:
> when the recording of the micro-lesson is played back, discussed and critically analysed by the tutor/class as a whole.

It is worth noting here that some institutions may also include a fourth stage to micro-teaching typically known as 'The Reteach' when students are asked to teach the same lesson again, albeit this time taking on board the feedback from stage 3.

Whether there are three or four stages, the underlying purpose of peer micro-teaching should always be to allow novice teachers the opportunity to develop their teaching knowledge and skills in a safe, non-threatening and supportive environment.

6.4.2 Team Teaching/Teaching Your Own Class

In contrast to peer micro-teaching, both team teaching and teaching your own class will involve real-life students and the focus now will be explicitly on the teaching of language. Different institutions are likely to have different ways of arranging this. Some may draft in language learners to be used as guinea-pigs for their Masters' students by offering members of the public a free course. In other cases, the institution may have made arrangements with local schools and colleges for their MA students to go there as trainee teachers. One advantage of the latter is that it can allow for some useful exposure to different student types. In the case of my own institution, over the years we have established good working relations with a range of Primary, Junior High and Senior High Schools across our city, which means that we are usually able to offer our students teaching practice across a range of educational contexts and ability levels.

Whichever way your own institution chooses to organise teaching practice, it is likely that you will be required to teach a given number of lessons, either alone or as part of a small team. Some of those lessons will then be observed and perhaps also formally assessed by your MA programme academic staff.

6.5 The Importance of Critical Reflection

Since the pioneering work of educationalists such as David Kolb and Donald Schön in the 1970s and 1980s, the notion of critical reflection has now permeated almost every discipline in Higher Education, not just TESOL/Applied Linguistics.

As I suggested at the beginning of this chapter during my discussion of the relationship between theory and practice, if you are to get the most out of your postgraduate studies, learning how to critically reflect will become a very important skill for you to develop.

Within the context of an MA TESOL/Applied Linguistics, the process and application of critical reflection may take several forms. First of all, you will need to reflect on the input you are being exposed to in the taught input sessions and try to reconcile this with what you already know, from your perspective as either a language teacher or a language learner. In these cases, critical reflection will involve you evaluating the validity and reliability of various theories and concepts and matching them with your existing knowledge base and what you have learned from your previous experiences.

Another form of critical reflection is likely to come into play a little later in the semester when you get back your first sets of grades and corrected coursework from your lecturers. In this case, you will be reflecting on the feedback you have been given, looking critically at your work and identifying the areas in which you need to improve. The critical reflection you will be engaging in this time arguably has a more practical and immediate application because you will be using the outcomes of your reflection to inform and guide your future performance.

Finally, as I have discussed throughout this chapter, if your MA programme includes a teaching observation and practice component, then there will be ample opportunities for your ongoing critical reflection, either on the teaching of others, or on how you engage with teaching yourself.

Check Your Understanding: Independent Task 6.5

Take some time to critically reflect on the different ideas that have been presented in this chapter. Write down your thoughts and any immediate reactions. If the chapter has raised any questions for you, how will you now go about finding the answers?

Suggested Answers to Independent Tasks

Task 6.1a

a. **Behaviourist Theory** has practical implications for the use of language drills. It underpinned the approach taken by the Audio-lingual Method. It also has some practical implications for how teachers might approach error correction.
b. **Social Constructivist Theory** has practical implications for the use of pairwork and groupwork in teaching. Ideas around peer learning also draw on this theory.

c. **Monitor Hypothesis** has practical implications for how much exposure to raw language teachers should provide their students.
d. **Affective Filter Hypothesis** has practical implications for how teachers deal with their students as people and the extent to which learning is impacted by motivation and feelings.
e. **Schema Theory** has practical implications for the teaching of reading. Pre-reading activities such as predicting the content of a text draw on the principles of Schema Theory.

Task 6.1b

a. Immediately correcting learners' errors *may* (or may not) improve their accuracy, but either way, it is certainly likely to have a negative effect on the learners' fluency. If the teacher jumps in and corrects them every single time they make a grammatical mistake, learners are likely to lose their confidence about speaking and become unwilling to speak aloud in class. The desire to correct mistakes therefore needs to be balanced with a wider awareness of what other perhaps unintended effects this might have.
b. There are several different ways of looking at this. For one thing, it can be very difficult for teachers to gauge what constitutes appropriately tuned input, especially in a mixed-ability class of learners. Some students may follow what is going on whereas others may become hopelessly lost and slip further behind. Conversely, if the level is too easy, students are likely to become bored and may simply not engage. Another point worth considering is that adult learners in particular tend to be more aware of their preferred learning styles. Some learners may prefer to be taught something directly rather than being left to figure everything out for themselves. Those in favour of comprehensible input may not be giving this factor sufficient attention. A final issue concerns the practicalities of time and the environment in which most foreign languages are taught. Children acquire their first language after literally tens of thousands of hours of input over a number of years. Second-language learners do not have such a luxury. They typically need to master certain elements of a given language within a given timeframe and for a specific purpose, e.g., to pass an examination. Under these constraints, formal teaching and the process of *explicit* learning (as opposed to *implicit* acquisition) may in fact be more fit for purpose.

c. The suggestion that learners will learn language more effectively if they are using it to 'do things' in cooperation with others continues to be a popular notion in ELT methodology. However, there are also some counterviews. One of the common drawbacks with task-based learning is that students may successfully complete the task but not use much language in doing so, or at least only use the language drawn from their existing store. Similarly, traditionally speaking, we might say that translating from one language to another has fallen out of methodological favour, but the recently emerged interest in translanguaging (e.g., see Mazak, 2017) is forcing teachers and researchers to reconsider the relationship between the learners' L1 and their target L2. Rather than avoiding all use of the L1 and telling learners never to translate between languages, it may well be that more judicious use of these dimension can be helpful for learners in acquiring an L2. This is especially the case with adult learners, who will be able to bring more advanced cognitive skills and their prior experience to the language learning context.

Task 6.3b

If you were going to teach a reading lesson using a text about Stanley Milgram's famous experiment on obedience, there are various ways in which you could contextualise things. Given that the Milgram experiment was originally inspired by the trial of the war criminal Adolf Eichmann, you could perhaps start such a lesson by showing some photos from the Second World War era, e.g., pictures of soldiers rounding up prisoners in a concentration camp, and then ask the students what the pictures show. You could then build on their answers by asking them if they would always be prepared to obey orders from someone they perceived to be a superior. This could then be extended to a discussion on whether or not obeying orders can ever justifiably be used in someone's defence, if it then results in them carrying out acts which they themselves should know to be morally and ethically wrong.

The purpose of such contextualisation is to activate the students' schemata and get them thinking about the topic before they read. As part of this, depending on how exactly the pre-reading stage is handled, teachers might also use it to introduce students to any difficult vocabulary.

Task 6.3c

If this lesson is considered from a PPP methodological perspective, the teacher has essentially missed out the second P, i.e. the need for some controlled practice *before* the students are launched into the free production stage. In the first activity, the teacher had the students brainstorm for some target language which might be used in debates, but then there was no detailed focus on this language in terms of its appropriateness, levels of formality or how one set of phrases might differ from another. Without at least *some* kind of scaffolding of this nature, it is debatable how well prepared the students would be for the ensuing discussion.

Additional Resources for Further Reading

Mann, S. & Walsh, S. (2017). *Reflective Practice in English Language Teaching: Research-based Principles & Practices*. Taylor & Francis.

O'Leary, M. (2014) *Classroom Observation. A Guide to the Effective Observation of Teaching and Learning.* Routledge.

Pang, M. (2016). Pedagogical reasoning in EFL/ESL teaching: Revisiting the importance of teaching lesson planning in second language teacher education. *TESOL Quarterly, 50*(1), 246–263.

Wallace, M.J. (1991). *Training Foreign Language Teachers. A Reflective Approach.* Cambridge University Press.

Chapter References

Bellack, A.A., Kliebard, H.M., Hyman, R.T. & Smith, F.L. (1966). *The Language of the Classroom.* Teachers College Press.

Brown, R. (1988). Classroom pedagogics: A syllabus for the interactive stage? *The Teacher Trainer, 2*(3), 13–17.

Fanselow, J.F. (1977). Beyond RASHOMON - Conceptualising and describing the teaching act. *TESOL Quarterly, 11*(1), 17–32.

Hammersley, M. & Atkinson, P. (1983). *Ethnography: Principles in Practice.* Tavistock Publications.

Kolb, D.A. (1984). *Experiential Learning: Experience as the Source of Learning and Development.* Prentice Hall.

Mazak, C.M. (2017). *Translanguaging in Higher Education: Beyond Monolingual Ideologies.* Channel View Publications.

Meddings, L. & Thornbury, S. (2009). *Teaching Unplugged.* DELTA Publishing.

Milgram, S. (1963). Behavioral study of obedience. *Journal of Abnormal and Social Psychology, 67*, 371–378.

Prabhu, N.S. (1987). *Second Language Pedagogy.* Oxford University Press.

Ramani, E. (1987). Theorizing from the classroom. *ELT Journal, 41*(1), 3–11.

Schön, D.A. (1983). *The Reflective Practitioner: How Professionals Think in Action.* Temple Smith.

Sinclair, J.M. & Coulthard, R.M. (1975). *Towards an Analysis of Discourse.* Oxford University Press.

Ur, P. (1991). *A Course in Language Teaching.* Cambridge University Press.

Wallace, M.J. (1981). Toward a skill-based analysis of EFL teaching skills. *TESOL Quarterly, 15*(2), 151–157.

7 Planning Your Dissertation

Introduction

This chapter focuses on the very early stages of planning your MA TESOL/Applied Linguistics dissertation. It provides advice on how you should go about choosing a relevant topic and suggests a series of steps which can help you to narrow down your focus and create suitable research questions. It then explores some different ontological research paradigms and critically evaluates the relative suitability of these when they are applied to different areas of research inquiry. The penultimate section of this chapter provides an example of a real-life MA TESOL/Applied Linguistics dissertation proposal and gives you practice in drafting a proposal of your own. It then closes with a discussion of what you should realistically expect from your supervisor and provides some tips on how to get the most out of the MA supervisor-supervisee relationship.

Additional resources for your further reading are listed on page 170.

7.1 Choosing a Suitable Topic

Worth 60 credits of the final degree and representing some 15,000 words of text, the MA TESOL/Applied Linguistics dissertation usually represents the biggest piece of independent written work you are likely to encounter as a Master's student. Although some people may have had to do a scaled-down dissertation as part of their undergraduate studies, for most students, completing a Master's dissertation will be their first experience of the specific academic demands this kind of work requires. It is especially important, therefore, to make sure that you are starting your dissertation journey by heading in the right direction. The vital first stage in this process involves you choosing a suitable topic.

7.1.1 Where Do I Begin?

Most students feel quite daunted by the prospect of writing a dissertation, especially if English is not their first language, so try not to worry if this also applies to you – such initial feelings of fear and apprehension are perfectly normal. Producing 15,000 words of original writing is no easy feat

DOI: 10.4324/9781003269854-7

and undoubtedly represents a significant piece of work, especially if you are only used to writing essays in the 3,000- to 4,000-word range. However, once you break the dissertation writing process down into smaller chunks, you will find that the task soon becomes significantly more manageable.

From the outset, you need to be clear about what a dissertation is, how it differs from other types of academic work and what it will require of you. At the Masters' level, a dissertation represents an extended piece of discursive academic writing, during which you carry out independent research on a topic of professional interest to practitioners in your field. In the case of MA TESOL/Applied Linguistics dissertations, this research is usually *primary* in nature, i.e., it will require you to gather and then critically evaluate original data of your own. By going through this process, you are basically serving a researcher apprenticeship. In writing your Masters' dissertation, you will be demonstrating to the university that you are able to formulate credible research questions and make principled choices about the different ontological/epistemological paradigms and research methodologies which could be used in answering them; position your topic and research questions appropriately within the existing academic literature; interpret, analyse and critically evaluate your results; make logical inferences about what those results might mean; and then finally, draw some wider conclusions around the significance of your entire research project for the field as a whole.

It should be clear from the above that a dissertation represents much more than just a big essay. Aside from the fact that it requires you to gather original data, a dissertation also differs from other Masters' coursework in that the topic and title for your writing will not be given to you; you are expected to come up with this content by yourself.

A step-by-step approach to assist you in doing this is outlined below:

Step 1

Decide which *broad* area of TESOL/Applied Linguistics you might be interested in exploring.

Dissertation writing usually takes place towards the end of your period of study, so by the time you are asked to start thinking about a topic, you are likely to have been a Master's student for quite a few months. This means that you will already have been engaging with various forms of TESOL/Applied Linguistics subject matter. Indeed, chances are that you will have written different coursework essays on these subject areas as part of your other taught modules. By this stage in a Master's, most people have a general idea of the topics they like and those they are not so keen on. You might, for example, know that you particularly enjoy learning about Second Language Acquisition, aspects of teaching reading and writing, or approaches to analysing grammar. Conversely, you might have decided that you are not so interested in psycholinguistics, testing and evaluation, or teaching young learners. At the end of the day though, TESOL and Applied Linguistics are diverse fields with lots of different subject areas, so it is

142 *Planning Your Dissertation*

important to choose a topic that you are genuinely interested in and want to find out more about. You are going to be doing a lot of reading and writing about this subject after all, so it most definitely helps if your opening feelings about it are positive.

As a first step, make a descending rank-ordered list of the top three subject areas that you know you like and are interested in. These may also be things that you already have some professional knowledge or firsthand experience of.

After completing this exercise, your notes might look something like this:

Possible Areas for a Dissertation Focus

MA TESOL	*MA Applied Linguistics*
English for academic purposes	Second Language Acquisition
Teacher training	Pragmatics
Classroom management	Sociolinguistics

Step 2
Brainstorm around your topic areas to think of more specific sub-topics. It can be useful to go through this process by making a mind map.

Once you have identified some broad areas of interest, the next step is to break each subject down into a series of potential sub-topics. Going through this process will get you thinking about the different dimensions of a given topic and how it might be approached from a variety of angles. One advantage of doing this as a mind map is that it allows you to capture a lot of different information at a single glance.

In the case of my example of English for Academic Purposes, if you were to complete a mind map in the way that I am suggesting, your results might look something like this:

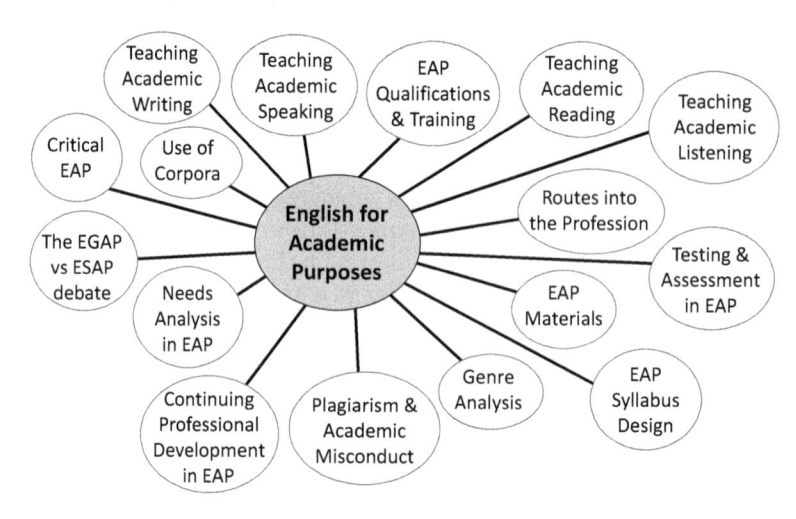

Mind map centred on "English for Academic Purposes" with branches to: Teaching Academic Writing, Teaching Academic Speaking, EAP Qualifications & Training, Teaching Academic Reading, Teaching Academic Listening, Critical EAP, Use of Corpora, Routes into the Profession, The EGAP vs ESAP debate, Testing & Assessment in EAP, Needs Analysis in EAP, EAP Materials, Continuing Professional Development in EAP, Plagiarism & Academic Misconduct, Genre Analysis, EAP Syllabus Design.

Needless to say, this mind map is not meant to represent a *definitive* guide to every possible sub-topic of EAP, but it should at least give you some idea of how a broad topic area can be broken down into many different parts.

Step 3

Choose a couple of your sub-topic areas and try to break them down into even more specific topics. It can be helpful to frame these as a series of different questions.

Under your chosen sub-topics, it should be possible for you to create a list of even more specific further sub-topics. When you do this, try to frame the new topics as questions you are curious about.

If you were to do this for the EAP example above, the results might look like this:

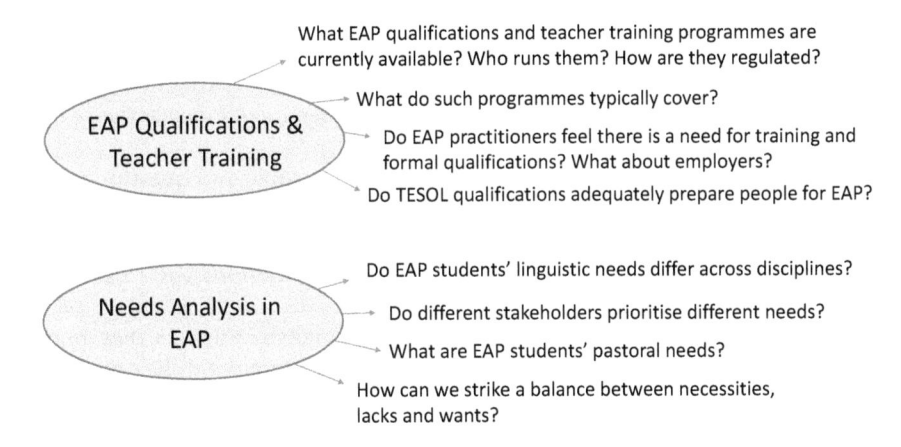

EAP Qualifications & Teacher Training
- What EAP qualifications and teacher training programmes are currently available? Who runs them? How are they regulated?
- What do such programmes typically cover?
- Do EAP practitioners feel there is a need for training and formal qualifications? What about employers?
- Do TESOL qualifications adequately prepare people for EAP?

Needs Analysis in EAP
- Do EAP students' linguistic needs differ across disciplines?
- Do different stakeholders prioritise different needs?
- What are EAP students' pastoral needs?
- How can we strike a balance between necessities, lacks and wants?

Step 4

Now try to turn some of the information you generated from Step 3 into an interesting title and one or more *specific* research questions that you would like your dissertation to answer. Don't worry if you are not entirely happy with what you first produce for this: everything is still just provisional at this stage.

Once you have generated some specific questions related to a sub-topic, these can then be tweaked and further refined so that they become a possible focus for your dissertation. Based on the example above, an MA TESOL student might thus tentatively decide on the following title and research questions:

144 *Planning Your Dissertation*

An Example Dissertation Topic with Research Questions

TITLE	'All of our staff are fully qualified....' The Role of Qualifications in EAP
RESEARCH QUESTION 1	*Which qualifications do EAP recruiters typically recognise?*
RESEARCH QUESTION 2	*How well do the existing TESOL qualifications prepare teachers for the realities of working in EAP?*
RESEARCH QUESTION 3	*Is there a need for more bespoke professional qualifications in EAP?*

Step 5

Look at your chosen topic and proposed research question(s) from Step 4 and then ask yourself the following:

1. Is my topic *relevant* for an MA TESOL/Applied Linguistics? Is it *academically credible*?
2. Is there *literature* available on my topic? Has anybody else already looked at it? Will my research *add anything* to the existing field?
3. Is the research itself 'do-able'? Can my proposed question(s) actually *be answered*?
4. Are there any *logistical constraints* around my topic and question(s)?
5. Are there any *ethical constraints* around my topic and question(s)?
6. *How* will I go about investigating my topic and answering my question(s)? Which specific *paradigms* and *research methods* will I use?

Not all of these questions are necessarily as straightforward as they may first seem, so it is worth unpacking them in a little more detail below:

1. *Is my topic relevant for an MA TESOL/Applied Linguistics? Is it academically credible?*

It should be obvious that if you are enrolled on an MA TESOL/Applied Linguistics, then your dissertation will need to focus on a topic relevant to one of those fields. It wouldn't really be appropriate, for example, for an MA TESOL dissertation to be investigating strategies for learning Spanish, Mandarin Chinese or some other modern language. Such topics might be a slightly better fit with an MA Applied Linguistics, although even then, it would still depend on how exactly the research questions were being framed. Similarly, if an MA Applied Linguistics student decided to write their dissertation on pedagogic approaches to materials design in ELT, this would probably be more appropriate for an MA TESOL. In my current role as an MA TESOL course director and dissertation module convener, when I screen initial dissertation proposals, a small number each year are instantly rejected on the grounds that they are a poor fit with the target subject area. At all times, your dissertation topic MUST match well with your named degree. If you are thinking carefully about potential topics and using your common sense though, this goal should not be too difficult to achieve.

The second part of question 1 is arguably somewhat trickier – is your chosen topic academically credible? Every year, I see dissertation proposals which are broadly *relevant* in terms of their topic choice, but which then badly fall down in terms of their academic credibility. To make sure that your work adequately meets this criterion, the focus of your investigation must be worthwhile; you need to be researching a topic which has genuine academic rigour and depth. In this regard, you must be very careful not to choose research questions to which the answers are already known, or which common sense tells you will be blindingly obvious. I personally like to call this the 'rain makes you wet' problem and it is surprising how easy it can be for novice researchers to fall into this trap. If the topic of your research questions is in danger of evoking a 'So what?' response, then it most probably means that you have not chosen a subject with enough academic depth, or that the answers you are likely to find will not be sufficiently meaningful.

Look at this example:

An Example of a Proposed Student Dissertation Topic

Proposed topic	An investigation of communicative language teaching
Proposed research question	Do students enjoy using CLT activities in class?
Proposed methodology	Questionnaires administered to 50 High School students

In this case, the research question is too shallow. The student merely proposes to ask 50 High School students if they find CLT activities enjoyable. This is a good example of what I was saying above about research questions evoking a 'So what?' response. Even if all 50 students say yes, they enjoy using CLT activities as part of their English learning, or no they hate it, do either of these responses really matter? Is such a result likely to be of professional interest, or to have any real significance for other practitioners in the field? I suspect not. Although an investigation of CLT is appropriate for an MA TESOL, as it stands, this particular research question would almost certainly be rejected on the grounds of it having weak academic credibility.

Check Your Understanding: Independent Task 7.1a

Look again at the proposed research question about Communicative Language Teaching above. How might you work with this student and help them to refine their topic/research question so that it has more depth and academic credibility?

A suggested answer to this task has been provided on page 164.

2. *Is there literature available on this topic? Has anybody else already looked at it? Will my research add anything to the existing field?*

One of the early acid tests you should apply when testing the validity of an MA dissertation proposal is to check whether your chosen topic has attracted any interest from the wider academic literature. On this point, I usually advise my own Masters' students that if they are unable to find much literature on their topic, then they should go back to the drawing board and try to think of something else.

It is worth remembering here that for a Master's dissertation, you are generally only expected to add something credible to the existing knowledge base; you are NOT usually expected to come up with an earth-shattering piece of novel research which nobody else on the planet has ever thought of. The requirement to break new ground like this becomes much more important at the doctoral level, but even then, very few theses truly manage to do so. The harsh reality is that most academic research tends to involve the re-framing and re-positioning of existing knowledge. At the risk of sounding unduly cynical, in most social sciences research, there is usually very little that is absolutely revolutionary or *truly* new.

In the case of your Masters' dissertation, confirming from the outset that there is literature available on your topic becomes especially important because as an integral part of the dissertation writing process, you will be expected to carry out a literature review and situate your own research questions within that wider academic framework. As I have already mentioned above, writing a Master's dissertation is essentially an academic rite of passage and can be considered as a researcher apprenticeship. As one part of this process, you will be judged on how well you can identify, locate, and critically engage with the relevant academic literature. For each of these reasons, when you are first deciding on your dissertation topic and research questions, it is very important indeed to check how well your ideas fit in with the existing literature. I will be looking at the finer details of how to structure and carry out an MA TESOL/Applied Linguistics literature review in the next chapter.

Check Your Understanding: Independent Task 7.1b

How would you check to see if there is literature available on your topic? What different steps might you go through?
A suggested answer to this task has been provided on page 165.

3. *Is the research itself 'do-able'? Can my proposed question(s) actually be answered?*

Similar to the issue I have described above on academic credibility, a further difficulty which students often encounter when first drafting a dissertation proposal is that the research they say they are interested in doing is simply not 'do-able'. This may be because the sheer scale of the project is too ambitious and would take more time for them to investigate than the time they have available, or (more commonly in my experience) because the actual questions they are asking are, in research methodology terms, simply unanswerable. In practice, this latter point can often be much trickier than it sounds, so it is worth us looking at it in more detail.

When considering whether your research questions are 'do-able', you always need to be mindful of concepts such as methodological validity and reliability. In this regard, I often find that my Masters' students initially come up with research proposals which might first *seem* to meet all the relevant criteria on the surface, but which then fall down in terms of their research validity when they are subjected to closer scrutiny.

Consider this example:

Another Example of a Proposed Student Dissertation Topic

Proposed topic	A critical comparison of ELT methodologies
Proposed research question	Which is the most effective: GTM or CLT?
Proposed methodology	Observation of a series of taught lessons
	Interviews with students
	Interviews with teachers

The proposal above appears broadly relevant in terms of the topic choice – a critical analysis of different ELT methodologies certainly fits well within the scope of an MA TESOL. However, the research question itself is essentially unanswerable: if you think about it, how is it possible to say that one methodology is more effective than another? When the student who submitted this topic later discussed it with me, she confessed that her original thinking was that by setting up and observing two different types of lessons – one being taught using Grammar Translation techniques and the other being taught using communicative approaches – and then interviewing the students and teachers, she hoped she would be able to 'prove' that one is more effective than the other. At one level, such thinking is seductively plausible, but the student had neglected to consider what other unseen variables might lead to English language learning success or failure. She had also failed to specify what exactly she meant by 'effective', as this is clearly a highly subjective term: what constitutes 'effective' in the case of one group of learners might well be something entirely different to what would be considered 'effective' for another. There were also some academic credibility issues with the proposed methodology – the student said that she would observe classes and then interview students and teachers, but as she later conceded when I asked her to think about this in more detail, none of those approaches would allow her to measure what constitutes effectiveness with any sense of objective reliability. Watching

148 *Planning Your Dissertation*

two different activities, an observer might well conclude that one is more effective than the other, but this would unavoidably be a highly subjective impression. A different observer might reach an entirely different set of conclusions. In sum, for each of the above reasons, as the somewhat crestfallen student finally accepted, this topic could not be accepted as an MA TESOL dissertation research proposal in its original form. Thankfully, this story ultimately had a happy ending in that we were able to make some adjustments to the proposal so that the research questions were worded a little differently and therefore became more 'do-able', but this serves as a good example of why it is very important to apply acid test number three: whichever dissertation research questions you formulate, they must always be answerable.

I will be returning to examine some of the wider issues around methodological validity and reliability in more detail under Section 10.2.

Check Your Understanding: Independent Task 7.1c

Look again at the example dissertation topic above which proposes to compare GTM and CLT. How might *you* help the student tweak this topic to make it more 'do-able' and have stronger research validity?

A suggested answer to this task has been provided on page 165.

4. *Are there any logistical constraints around my topic and question(s)?*

As I have commented above, some dissertation proposals ultimately turn out to be not very 'do-able' simply because they are too ambitious in their scope. As well as thinking about research validity and academic credibility, it is therefore also very important to consider the logistical practicalities. An MA TESOL student once gave me a dissertation proposal in which she claimed she wanted to investigate approaches to English learning in rural high schools in the far West of China. The topic itself looked worthwhile, and the research questions were very interesting and academically valid, but when I asked her if she knew anybody in the West of China, or had any contacts in the rural high schools there, I was rather surprised when her answer was no. When I then asked how she intended to carry out the ethnographic fieldwork for her research, and also how she would cover the significant expenses she would undoubtedly incur with flights, accommodation and living costs, it was clear that she had not given any thought to these practical dimensions. In this case, although it passed muster in academic terms, the topic the student had chosen was too impractical and ultimately just not feasible for her logistically. In the end, we agreed that it would make far better sense for her to investigate ELT practices in her home city;

at least that way, she would be able to get easier access to relevant teachers and schools through her local networks.

The example above is admittedly quite extreme and it was rather surprising for me that the student in question had not been able to identify for herself what seemed to me to be quite obvious logistical barriers. Sometimes though, the underlying logistical challenges to a given research proposal may not be so immediately apparent. In their enthusiasm to identify an interesting topic, students can often overlook the practicalities. For example, a different student once submitted an MA TESOL dissertation proposal in which she claimed she wanted to investigate subject lecturers' attitudes to academic literacy development at our home institution. The topic and research questions for this were broadly fine, but when I asked her how she intended to gain access to these academic subject lecturers, or which specific subject areas she would focus on, it was clear that she had not considered any of those details. Upon closer questioning, it turned out that she did not know any of the academics she was hoping would become involved in her research and she had not even considered how she might get in touch with them, or who the relevant gatekeepers would be. In this case, there was an even bigger logistical problem in that the timeframe she had tentatively identified for her interviews to take place had been set during a period when most university academic staff would already be on their annual leave and unavailable for consultation. Had she been left entirely to her own devices and gone ahead with the dissertation as originally defined, this dimension alone would have made the student's data gathering almost impossible.

The key learning point to be taken from each of these examples is that when you are putting together your dissertation research proposal, right from the outset, you need to be thinking very carefully indeed about all the practical angles and making sure that you have identified any logistical barriers.

5. Are there any ethical constraints around my topic and question(s)?

Closely related to logistical concerns, when you start to draft a dissertation proposal, you also need to consider potential ethical constraints. Most of the research that is carried out on MA TESOL/Applied Linguistics programmes is usually not so contentious in this regard, but there are still some things for you to be aware of. If you are intending to have any contact with minors, for example, then there will be ethical procedures around getting informed consent which you will definitely need to take into account in your planning. I once had an MA TESOL student who intended to carry out classroom observations of teaching and learning at a local primary school, but in the end, getting the appropriate consent from the school and (some of) the children's parents proved to be an unexpectedly lengthy and complicated process. In the final analysis, these difficulties almost derailed the entire dissertation. As with logistics, ethical considerations are therefore something which needs to be carefully considered from the outset.

6. *How will I go about investigating my topic and answering my question(s)? Which paradigms and research methods will I use?*

As I touched on above in my discussion of academic credibility, once you have identified a likely topic area and potential set of research questions, you need to give careful thought to your research methodology. One of the most common problems I encounter with my Masters' students (and unfortunately also some of my doctoral candidates) is that they fail to make a good match between what they *say* they want to investigate, and *how* they then intend to go about doing so. The most typical manifestation of this problem results in a methodological overkill in which students try to apply too many different paradigms and approaches all at the same time. I often read proposals, for example, in which my students say that they will use questionnaires, then interviews, then focus groups, then classroom observations and sometimes even field ethnography on top. While there *may* sometimes be valid reasons for combining such a variety of methods, and I am not suggesting here that the practice will always be categorically wrong, more often than not, when they are challenged to defend such methodological choices, I find that my students are unable to do so. It most typically transpires that their choice of methodology has simply been a knee-jerk reaction, in which they try to apply everything and anything that they have ever read about or received instruction on during their research methods module. Instead of doing this, I encourage my students to be much more *selective* about their methodological choices and to make sure that there is always a credible and justifiable match between the topic(s) they are investigating and the ways in which they intend to go about doing so. In this regard, as I will discuss in more detail under Section 10.2, most MA TESOL/Applied Linguistics research broadly falls into one of three possible paradigms: qualitative research, quantitative research or mixed-methods research, the latter of which may represent *either* a mix of different approaches selected from the first two paradigms, or a mix of complementary approaches which usually belong to one paradigm or the other.

At the risk of me over-generalising, I think it is safe to say that most of the student research I encounter on MA TESOL/Applied Linguistics dissertations these days tends to belong to the qualitative paradigm. Some of this is undoubtedly due to fashions and trends in the current social sciences research Zeitgeist, but given the nature of TESOL in particular, where understanding feelings and opinions now tends to play a greater role than measuring large-scale statistics and establishing the objective validity of scientific facts, it is probably no great surprise that qualitative research methodology has started to dominate. This is not to suggest, however, that quantitative approaches have no place. Over the years, I have also supervised several successful TESOL/Applied Linguistics dissertations in which students have taken a quantitative approach to their data gathering and analysis. As a researcher, the key question you must always be asking yourself is *which research paradigm and methodology represents the best fit with what I am investigating*. As part of this, and as I have already commented, you also need to be thinking about how well everything then fits with the logistics and more practical issues. A given Master's student, for example, might first decide that he wants to take a quantitative approach to his dissertation research by sending out questionnaires to hundreds of different recipients, but in the end, the sheer logistics of such an undertaking might prove impractical in the limited time available. In such a case, settling on a smaller scale qualitative approach might be more feasible and appropriate.

Check Your Understanding: Independent Task 7.1d

Look back at the example dissertation topic described under Step 4 which proposed to investigate the role of qualifications in EAP. Does this meet all the requirements listed under Step 5 on page 144? Which methodological approaches could be used to answer the three research questions?

A suggested answer to this task has been provided on page 166.

7.1.2 How Should I Manage My Time?

As with any large-scale project, producing a successful Master's dissertation has a lot to do with effective time management. From the very start of the planning process, I therefore always encourage my students to map out a formal project timeline to help them structure and manage the different stages in their research and writing up.

When setting yourself a project management timeframe, it can be helpful to start from the end date and steadily work backwards. In the case of our own Masters' programmes, the final submission deadline for dissertations each year is usually August 31, so I ask my students to begin by looking at that date and then work backwards to set themselves a series of staged completion milestones. I usually recommend that the full dissertation should be in a complete first draft form by the end of the first week of August, as this then gives students at least three more weeks to check through everything, act on any feedback they receive from their supervisor and make any final revisions before the work is handed in. Another point worth stressing while we are discussing this time management dimension of writing up a dissertation is that the writing-up process itself is almost never entirely linear or chronological; in other words, you shouldn't necessarily expect to be producing your chapters in the order that they will finally appear. Indeed, you may well find that Chapter 1 and the Introduction section to your dissertation is one of the last parts that you will write. I will discuss the order and general organisational structure of dissertations in more detail in the following two chapters, but for now, it is simply worth noting that many students begin their writing up with Chapter 2, the Literature Review. They then might progress to writing up Chapter 3, the Methodology chapter, before moving on to Chapters 4 and 5, leaving Chapters 6 and 1 to the very end.

There is no one-size-fits-all approach to producing a successful dissertation, but whichever systems are followed, you should aim to break the process down into achievable goals. You might, for example, give yourself a timeframe of six to eight weeks in which to research and complete your writing up of the Literature Review. Working on this would then become your main daily focus for that period. As with all large-scale writing projects, when it comes to doing the actual writing up, as with the traditional advice which is often dispensed on loading a paintbrush, your approach should be little and often. As far as possible, you should definitely try to write something every day. A modest daily production target of 300–500 words very soon adds up to a substantial amount and is a much more effective approach than leaving everything to the very last minute and then struggling to produce thousands of words under pressure. As I have commented elsewhere in this book, producing good quality academic writing is invariably a highly cyclical process, which involves going back over the same text several times. When you are first planning your dissertation writing timeframe, it is therefore very important to allow yourself enough time and to factor this cyclical revision process in.

A sample dissertation completion timeline is detailed below:

A Proposed Dissertation Timeline

By end of January	Formal submission of dissertation topic and research questions
By mid-February	Decide on methodology, get necessary ethics approvals and start gathering data; identify and start compiling relevant literature
By end of March	Complete write-up of Literature Review chapter
By mid-April	Complete all gathering of data; start coding and analysing data
By mid-May	Complete write-up of Methodology and Results chapters
By end of June	Complete write-up of Discussion and Conclusion chapters
By end of July	Complete Introduction chapter and abstract and have first full draft ready
End of August	Give everything a final polish and submit final dissertation by August 31

Check Your Understanding: Independent Task 7.1e

Despite having submitted his formal proposal in January (this was duly approved by the course director, albeit with a recommendation for minor revisions to the wording of his research questions) an MA TESOL student decides not to do any further work on his dissertation until after he has completed all of the required coursework for the second semester. The final submission deadline for this is May 15. After handing in his final piece of coursework, the student decides to give himself a two-week holiday to recharge his batteries; he therefore only starts to look at his dissertation from the first week of June.

The student then decides that he wants to make some changes to the way he was originally intending to gather his data. This necessitates the completion of a new set of ethics forms, which his supervisor now decides need to be scrutinised and approved at the Faculty level. Unfortunately, the Faculty Ethics Committee has formally ceased to meet for the year, as the university taught semester has finished and the members are already taking their annual leave or are away doing research. In order to get the new ethics forms approved, Chair's Action is required and this takes another ten days, as the Chair of the committee is now out of the country and not regularly accessing his email. The new formal ethics approval is finally granted on June 20.

On June 22, the student contacts the academic staff he wants to interview, but over ten days later, he has still not received any replies. This suggests to him that nobody is available or wants to take part in his study. In a panic, the student now contacts his supervisor and asks if he can change his topic to something else. By July 5, the student is busy refining a new set of proposal forms but even if these are approved, there is now almost no chance for him to complete his research and write everything up in time for the August 31 dissertation submission deadline. In fact, it is looking increasingly likely that the student will either need to request an extension, be forced to submit incomplete work or now formally defer his MA studies until the start of the next academic year.

Where did this student go wrong? What should he have done differently in terms of his time management? If you had been one of his classmates, what friendly advice might you have given him?

A suggested answer to this task has been provided on page 167.

7.2 Deciding on an Appropriate Research Paradigm

As I have discussed above, matching an appropriate research paradigm and methodological approach with your research question(s) is a vital part of the dissertation writing process. If you have enrolled on a research methods module as part of your Masters, you will no doubt be provided with invaluable advice and guidance from your lecturers on how the different ontological research paradigms and approaches to research methodology operate. If you have not had the option of completing a research methods module, then you should definitely be reading extensively around the topic of research methodology and aiming to learn as much as you can by yourself. There are lots of very useful resources you can consult in this regard and your supervisor or MA course leader is sure to provide you with a recommended reading list, but a small selection of particularly helpful texts is provided below:

- Brown, J.D. & Rodgers, T.S. (2002). *Doing Second Language Research.* Oxford University Press.
- Creswell, J.W. (1998). *Qualitative Inquiry and Research Design. Choosing among Five Traditions.* Sage.
- Dörnyei, Z. (2007). *Research Methods in Applied Linguistics.* Oxford.
- Flick, U. (2009). *An Introduction to Qualitative Research* (4th ed.). Sage.
- Litosseliti, L. (Ed.) (2018). *Research Methods in Linguistics* (2nd ed.). Bloomsbury.
- McKay, S.L. (2006). *Researching Second Language Classrooms.* Lawrence Erlbaum.
- Miles, M.B. & Huberman, M.A. (1994). *Qualitative Data Analysis.* Sage.
- Paltridge, B. & Phakiti, A. (2015). *Research Methods in Applied Linguistics.* Bloomsbury.
- Rasinger, S.M. (2013). *Quantitative Research in Linguistics* (2nd ed.). Bloomsbury.
- Rose, H., McKinley, J. & Briggs Baffoe-Djan, J. (2020). *Data Collection Research Methods in Applied Linguistics.* Bloomsbury.
- Schwandt, T. A. (2001). *Dictionary of Qualitative Inquiry* (2nd ed.). Sage.
- Silvermann, D. (2010). *Doing Qualitative Research* (3rd ed.). Sage.

As I will discuss in more detail in the following chapter, when you come to write up the Methodology chapter for your dissertation, you will need to begin by providing a brief justification for the methods you have chosen. Once you start reading around research methodology, it can be very helpful to keep a bank of any useful quotations and citations that you come across. Just as you are required to support your arguments for academic writing in general either by paraphrasing or quoting directly from the relevant literature, when you write your Methodology chapter, you will need to provide supporting evidence for your claims by drawing on the different sources you have consulted about research methods.

7.2.1 Understanding Ontology and Epistemology

The term ontology basically refers to the different ways in which reality can be conceptualised and perceived, whereas epistemology refers to the different ways in which human knowledge can be approached and understood. These two constructs play an important role in academic research because they inform and underpin the different paradigms and methodological choices open to researchers. While it is not necessary for you to gain a *deep* understanding of ontology and epistemology, you do need to be aware of what the main issues are, and to appreciate how these can have an impact on the different methodological choices that are open to you when you carry out academic research.

Most writers on research generally agree that there are four main ontological philosophies or paradigms: *positivism, postpositivism, constructivism* and *pragmatism*. Positivists take the stance that reality can be understood objectively because it is governed by a series of immutable laws and principles. Under the positivist paradigm, reality is perceived to be quantifiable and measurable. Postpositivists, on the other hand, subscribe to a modified version of positivism which is somewhat less rigid in its outlook. One of the core tenets of postpositivism, for example, is that perceptions of reality can only ever be an approximation and will never be entirely accurate. Postpositive researchers thus recognise and value objectivity as an important guiding principle. In marked contrast to positivism and postpositivism, constructivist ontology sees reality as being open to *several* different interpretations, depending on who is involved and in which contexts the action is taking place. Rather than perceiving reality as something fixed and immutable, constructivists therefore see it as being co-constructed through a social lens. The final category of research ontology, pragmatism, emphasises the problem-solving dimension of research. In this regard, we might conclude that pragmatism is not really a paradigm in the same way as positivism or constructivism, in that it gives more freedom for researchers to pick and mix from whichever approaches are felt to be the best match in solving a particular issue. By its nature, pragmatism thus tends to sit well with mixed-methods research.

From an epistemological standpoint, the four different ontological paradigms can have various ramifications for the approaches taken in research methodology. Positivists and postpositivists, for example, will usually try to distance themselves from what they are investigating, so that they can achieve a more objective and accurate representation of the reality. In the case of a classroom observation, this might result in a highly positivist observer sitting quietly at the back of the room and unobtrusively carrying out the observation by using a highly structured instrument. A constructivist observer, on the other hand, might approach this process very differently and deliberately choose to become involved in the classroom activities as an active participant. From a constructivist perspective, it could be argued that this closer involvement of the researcher is likely to assist with the development of greater trust between the researcher and the research subjects. This would then presumably make the subjects more willing to open up more about their feelings and emotions, which would allow for the gathering of richer data. However, it is important to recognise that there is no 100% 'right' or 'wrong' answer here – both approaches are valid in their own way, but each may yield slightly different results. Being aware of how ontology and epistemology can have an impact on such matters lies at the very heart of research methodology design.

7.2.2 *Quantitative or Qualitative?*

The most common methodological dichotomy facing researchers is whether their approach should be quantitative or qualitative in nature. As the names suggest, quantitative research is concerned with *quantifying* aspects of the issue under investigation, while qualitative research puts more emphasis on the overall *quality* of the experience, in other words, on understanding the research participants' feelings and beliefs. It follows that quantitative research usually involves large sample sizes and requires the application of statistics for analysis. Qualitative research, on the other hand, tends to favour smaller sample sizes and there is much less of a concern with statistical validity.

I will be examining some of the specific approaches to quantitative and qualitative research in more detail in the next chapter, when I discuss how to write the Methodology chapter of your dissertation, but for now, it is simply worth noting these basic distinctions between the quantitative and qualitative paradigms and thinking about which aspects of TESOL/Applied Linguistics research are likely to represent the most appropriate match with each.

Check Your Understanding: Independent Task 7.2a

Which research paradigm do you think would fit best in each of the following situations, quantitative or qualitative? If you think that either of them might be possible, then explain how the specific approaches would be different.

i. A researcher wants to look at how a group of High School students have performed on one particular section of an ELT placement test.
ii. A researcher wants to better understand teachers' beliefs about how to teach reading.
iii. A researcher is interested in whether non-native English teachers face hiring discrimination compared to native English speakers.
iv. A researcher wants to investigate the frequency of specific grammatical forms in scientific reports.
v. A researcher wants to investigate whether English language teachers are more likely to favour MA TESOL or MA Applied Linguistics in their choice of qualifications.
vi. A researcher wants to investigate the academic and socio-cultural adjustment problems faced by Chinese first year students at an EMI institution.

A suggested answer to this task has been provided on page 167.

7.2.3 Mixed Methods

As I have already described above, some approaches to research methodology are highly pragmatic in nature and choose to mix different methods. One of the most commonly claimed advantages of taking a mixed-methods approach is that it can help with the triangulation of results data. This arguably leads to greater research validity and reliability. However, from my own experience, there can sometimes be a danger that MA TESOL/Applied Linguistics students become over-preoccupied with these issues and therefore end up choosing mixed-methods research as a default position. As I have argued throughout this chapter, it is better to be more discerning about your methodological choices in this regard and not fall into the trap of trying to cover too much ground. If there is a clear *advantage* in you taking a mixed-methods approach, and there are no competing factors, then naturally it is fine for you to do so, but you shouldn't automatically assume that you *have to*. Sometimes mixed methods simply add layers of unnecessary complexity and as, I have already argued, can result in a methodological overkill. As long as you can provide a principled justification for whatever research methodology you choose, you will not be marked down for not having brought in lots of alternative approaches. When you are writing your dissertation, remember that there will always need to be a sensible balance struck between the questions you are trying to answer and the research methods you choose to apply in doing so.

158   Planning Your Dissertation

Check Your Understanding: Independent Task 7.2b

Look again at items (ii), (iii), (v) and (vi) from Independent Task 7.2a. How might these be investigated using a mixed-methods approach?
A suggested answer to this task has been provided on page 168.

7.3 Completing a Formal Proposal

Most institutions will require their Masters' students to submit their dissertation proposals for formal approval. The exact details of this will differ from institution to institution, but in most cases, institutions will have a designated format in which proposals should be submitted. This paperwork typically requires students to complete information on the general topic and their chosen research question(s), as well as giving some indication that they have had a preliminary look at the available literature, have thought about their methodological approach and have considered any logistical and/or ethical issues.

A sample dissertation proposal form is provided for your reference below:

A Sample Dissertation Proposal Form

NAME:	XXXX	STUDENT ID:	XXXX

PROGRAMME: MA Applied Linguistics
PROPOSED TOPIC/TITLE:
RESEARCH QUESTIONS:

Brief outline of your research objectives and your proposed methodology (two to three paragraphs. 250–400 words in total)
Two to four keywords:
Are any significant resources required? (It is your own responsibility to investigate this and ensure that sufficient resources are available for you to complete the project)

Check Your Understanding: Independent Task 7.3a

Now look at the following example of a Master's student dissertation proposal. Consider whether this proposal is likely to be accepted as it is, or if further revisions or even a complete re-submission is required.

If you were evaluating this submission, what comments might you make?

A suggested answer to this task has been provided on page 169.

A Completed Dissertation Proposal

Name	XXXX	Student ID	XXXX
Programme		MA TESOL	
Proposed topic/title	Formulaic sequences and IELTS: an investigation of Academic Writing Task 2		
Research questions	RQ1: How many and what different kinds of formulaic sequences are used in IELTS Writing Task 2? RQ2: Do the number and types of formulaic sequences differ between Band 6.0 and Band 8.0? RQ3: Do the formulaic sequences used in samples match the IELTS official criteria? RQ4: Are IELTS test-takers aware of the role played by formulaic sequences when being awarded their final scores?		

The main objective of my research is to investigate whether importance should be attached to the teaching of formulaic sequences when preparing students for the IELTS Writing Task 2. Formulaic sequences often receive attention in discussions on oral testing but there are few studies which have examined their use in writing. Formulaic sequences are not classed as one of the formal assessment criteria for IELTS but they may feed into student performance under the categories of lexical resources and coherence/cohesion. I suspect that effective use of formulaic sequences will contribute to students being awarded higher test scores but that most test-takers are probably not aware of this correlation.

My research proposes to answer the four questions I have posed using a mix of quantitative and qualitative methods. In the case of the former, 20 Task 2 model answers (ten from Band 6 and ten from Band 8) will be selected from IELTS preparatory coursebooks. The relative frequency of formulaic sequence use will be calculated and the sequences themselves will be categorised whether they are representative of lexical resources or coherence/cohesion. For the qualitative part of the study, 20 test-takers will be interviewed (ten who achieved IELTS 6.0 and ten who achieved IELTS 8.0) to investigate their awareness of formulaic sequences in IELTS writing.

Check Your Understanding: Independent Task 7.3b

Based on everything you have learned in this chapter, now try to draft a formal dissertation proposal of your own.

There is no suggested answer to this task but you can self-check your work by comparing it with the examples which have already been provided.

7.4 What to Expect from Your Supervisor

As soon as your dissertation proposal has been formally accepted, you will ordinarily then be assigned a supervisor. This person is usually a member of the MA academic staff, so you are likely to know them already, although in some cases, you might be assigned a supervisor from outside the school or department. As ever, different institutions tend to handle their internal processes differently and as with most of academia, there is no one-size-fits-all approach. Most commonly, however, MA course directors try to match up the topics that their students are researching with the academic expertise of the available staff. This can be especially helpful when you come to do your Literature Review, as an academic who already knows something about your particular area will obviously be in a good position to recommend core readings and can help you to frame your research questions accordingly. If an academic already has research expertise in your area, they will also be able to give you sterling advice on which research paradigms and methodological approaches are likely to be the best fit with your topic. If it turns out that your supervisor doesn't have specific expertise in the area you are investigating though, this is not necessarily a cause for alarm. There is also a school of thought here, which contends that supervisors with a more general background can play a valuable role because their advice will be more dispassionate and objective. One of the slight drawbacks of having a supervisor with expertise in your chosen subject area is that they can sometimes become over-domineering and start moulding you into a version of themselves. Experienced supervisors are well aware of this problem and usually manage to avoid the temptation, but those who are new to the supervisor role may find it difficult to keep things in balance. As with all human interactions, the supervisor-supervisee relationship needs to be managed with mutual respect and on principles of give and take. It is worth us considering some of the key features of the relationship here, so that you have a clear idea of what to expect.

As I started by saying above, supervisors are usually assigned after proposals have been formally approved. In some cases, your proposal may have been approved on the understanding that you will need to make further tweaks with the help of your supervisor; in other cases, your proposal may have been approved outright, in which case you can get on with your work and will only need to approach your supervisor when you feel it is necessary.

Every supervisor tends to handle the supervision process slightly differently. Some are extremely hands-on and will expect to have formal progress meetings with you every month; others may be much more relaxed and will generally allow you to take the lead. These are the sorts of details that it is worth sorting out with your supervisor quite early on, usually in the first meeting, so that both parties have clear expectations of one another and do not later find themselves at loggerheads. In the case of my own institution, we usually aim to get our MA TESOL students started on their dissertation

Planning Your Dissertation 161

writing process quite early, usually around the end of January. This means that they will be working with their supervisors for a period of some six to seven months. Other institutions may deal with this differently. Even within the same institution, there may be some variance from programme to programme. While our full-time MA TESOL cohort tends to start their dissertation journey in January-February, our MA Applied Linguistics students don't usually formally begin until March-April. In our own institutional case, this is largely due to the respective size of the student cohorts and the logistics involved around supervision. Our MA TESOL programme currently has over 70 enrolments, for example, and the teams of supervisors routinely have around 15 or more supervisees each. Our MA Applied Linguistics programme is much smaller in scale, so there is a little less time pressure. As I have argued throughout this book, you can and should be prepared to expect such individual variations from institution to institution.

Once your supervisor has been formally appointed, it is very likely that he or she will call an initial face-to-face meeting with you. As I have intimated above, this is when you can both set some ground rules on how the supervision process is most likely to operate. One thing you do need to be aware of here is that most institutions will set a maximum time allowance for each dissertation supervisee. In the case of my own MA TESOL students, for example, we usually allow a maximum of six hours supervision time for each individual student. This time covers the period between February and August and is also meant to cover time spent on answering emails and giving feedback on any drafts. Six hours is not a huge amount of time, so the allowance does need to be used wisely. I might thus see every one of my supervisees for a 20-minute meeting at the beginning, but then each subsequent meeting will be more spread out and handled on a case-by-case basis. Most supervisors are happy to treat the time allowance with some flexibility – unless you have been abusing the system, nobody is going to be setting a stopwatch on your meeting times – but you still need to treat the time seriously and not waste it. I will be returning to this point again in the section below.

7.4.1 *Some Tips for Getting the Most Out of the Supervisor-Supervisee Relationship*

a. *Be clear on the ground rules from your very first meeting and try to stick to them*

As I have indicated above, the supervisor-supervisee relationship will ideally be a case of give and take, with both parties adjusting to the needs and communication styles of the other. If you feel that you need more (or less) academic guidance from your supervisor though, you should politely raise this with them as soon as possible. Some students do not bother to contact their supervisors for months on end, but then complain bitterly about not having received sufficient guidance if they later fail their dissertation. Remember that as an adult, you are expected to take full responsibility for your own learning and development. If your supervisor is not contacting you, then you should be contacting them.

b. *Own your research topic and take personal agency*

At the end of the day, your dissertation is YOUR work. Your supervisor is there to help guide you and provide professional advice, but they will not be writing the dissertation for you, nor will it be their fault if the final quality of the dissertation is poor. You yourself must take personal agency throughout the dissertation writing process and do all that you can to achieve a good result. Your supervisor is only there as an experienced guider to help you meet this goal.

c. *Do not expect a proofreading service*

This is especially important if English is not your first language. Most of the students I currently supervise fall into the NNES category and as a result, there are usually grammatical and/or stylistic weaknesses in their academic writing. When I provide feedback on drafts, I usually *do* end up making some linguistic corrections, but I do not go through every sentence line by line checking for accuracy. There are various software packages which are designed to help you to check your work in this regard, or alternatively, you can pay for the services of a professional proofreader. Ensuring that your work is presented to the highest possible academic standards once again falls under your own personal agency banner.

d. *Manage the supervision time allowance wisely and do not waste it*

As I have already explained above, most institutions will set a maximum individual time allowance for supervisory consultations. With this in mind, you should prepare well for all the meetings with your supervisor and make sure that you know exactly what questions you want to ask. Do not squander your allowance on trivia. Going to meetings with only a very vague idea of what you want to achieve is a waste of both your own and your supervisor's time. The better prepared you are, the more successful the supervision outcome is likely to be.

A further issue with time concerns your management of the overall project timeframe, and whether or not a supervisor will be able to give you feedback on a full draft. This process differs from institution to institution, and from supervisor to supervisor, but as long as you have allowed them sufficient time to do so, most supervisors will be happy to cast their eyes over a final full draft of your dissertation and point out any remaining weaknesses. The key thing here is to allow them sufficient time for this to happen. As I have already explained, in my own institution, I routinely supervise upwards of 15 MA TESOL dissertations each year and this comes on top of my doctoral supervisions. Given the August 31 submission deadline, it is clearly not going to work if all 15 MA TESOL supervisees send me their full dissertation drafts on August 25 and then expect to receive my detailed feedback. Even if I were magically able to read and provide comments on everything in such a short timeframe, the students themselves would probably not have sufficient time to make any necessary revisions. It is absolutely vital, therefore, that you manage your project timelines carefully.

e. *Try not to be unduly defensive or to argue with your supervisor*

In my own experience of Masters' supervision, this is thankfully a rare occurrence, but there have sometimes been occasions when students have refused to take on board my advice, or have become very defensive when I have given them my frank feedback. I can remember one student I was supervising, who for reasons best known to himself wrote an individual chapter of his dissertation which was about three times longer than the amount I had recommended. As I recall, in terms of its word count, the length of that individual chapter was close to what the entire dissertation should have been. When I pointed out this rather obvious shortcoming, the student wasn't particularly defensive, but he did seem surprised that my feedback on what he had done was negative; I think he had misguidedly thought I would be pleased that he had written so much more than was required. Another student decided to depart from my advice to structure her dissertation around six main chapters and handed in a piece of work which was actually divided into 12 very fragmented chapters. Not surprisingly, this submission failed and the student ultimately left the university without a Master's degree. Such problems can usually be avoided. Remember that the role of your supervisor is to give you the benefit of their extensive professional experience and academic expertise; if you are to gain from this, then you need to be respectful of their recommendations. Do always keep in mind that they are trying to help you after all.

f. *Enjoy the supervisory experience and try to learn as much as you can*

Having the chance to work closely with an experienced academic for a period of six or more months has the potential to be a very fulfilling experience, especially if you are thinking of continuing in academia and going on to complete a PhD. Some of my former Masters' students have been sufficiently inspired to enrol on doctorates in the same subject area and in a few cases, I have either worked with them again as their supervisor, or I have served as one of their final examiners. If you are planning a career in academia, working closely with your supervisor and learning from their expertise will also give you a taste of what you yourself can expect to be doing once you start working in the field.

Check Your Understanding: Independent Task 7.4

An MA Applied Linguistics student has been assigned a supervisor from a different academic unit in the home school. The student does not know her supervisor and has not yet had the opportunity to work with her. From their very first meeting, the student feels that the chemistry between them is not going to be very good: she finds the supervisor's communication style to be very abrasive and she also feels that the supervisor doesn't really have a very deep understanding of her chosen subject area.

What should this student do? How might the issues be resolved?

A suggested answer to this task has been provided on page 169.

Suggested Answers to Independent Tasks

Task 7.1a

There are several ways in which this dissertation proposal could be modified so that it becomes more academically credible. If the student is keen to explore attitudes to Communicative Language Teaching, then one possibility could be for the student to investigate the extent to which teachers employ CLT techniques and approaches in their classrooms. This could then be contrasted with the same teachers' claimed attitudes and beliefs towards using CLT. One way of approaching such a research project would be to begin by carrying out a qualitative survey of teachers' opinions. For example, a target group of teachers might be screened using semi-structured interviews in which the researcher asked them to share their views on CLT and the extent to which they are willing to employ CLT activities in their classes. The second stage of this research would then involve a series of classroom observations when the researcher watches the same teachers in action and notes what they do. When comparing the data from the interviews and the data from the classroom observations, the researcher might discover some similarities or discrepancies between the teachers' stated beliefs and their actual practices. There is already quite a lot of literature on how well teachers' beliefs do or don't match with their actual practices, so this research topic would potentially be adding something to the existing knowledge pool.

Task 7.1b

The first port of call would be to carry out keyword searches in several of the mainstream journals. Step-by-step detail on how to go about doing this was provided for you in Chapter 3. As I outlined there, as soon as a relevant article is located, you should go to the references list/bibliography and look at which sources were consulted then try to locate the most recent and relevant of those for yourself. By following this 'stepping stone' approach, you will very soon ascertain what literature on your topic is available.

Searching in the university catalogue might also uncover individual academic monographs and book chapters, but these should be your secondary focus. In the first instance, you should be searching in the relevant academic journals as these will provide you with the sources that are the most up to date.

Task 7.1c

There are several ways in which this topic might be tweaked to give it greater academic credibility and make it more 'do-able'. As I discussed in the chapter, it is not really ontologically possible to say with any degree of certainty that one methodology is any better or worse than another because there are simply too many other variables which would need to be considered. However, this does not mean that aspects of different methodological approaches cannot be usefully investigated. The key issue here is to ensure that the research questions are valid ones. In this particular case, if the student was interested in doing some kind of comparison between GTM and CLT, one approach could be to investigate teachers' beliefs and practices with regard to these methodologies, as I have already outlined under 7.1a. Another possibility could be to look at a range of published ELT course books and evaluate to what extent the proposed activities reflect GTM or CLT pedagogic principles. For example, most modern ELT textbooks claim to take a communicative approach but then the design of their content sometimes contradicts this.

In both of these suggested research projects, naturally the methodological approaches would need to match with what was being investigated, e.g., probably qualitative interviews followed by observations in the case of methodological beliefs vs. practices, then a comparative quantitative linguistic analysis for the textbooks.

166 *Planning Your Dissertation*

Task 7.1d

Applying the acid test of the question listed under Step 5 to this dissertation proposal would result in the following:

1. Is my topic *relevant* for an MA TESOL/Applied Linguistics? Is it *academically credible*? **[Yes. The topic is certainly relevant and the questions are academically credible]**
2. Is there *literature* available on my topic? Has anybody else already looked at it? Will my research *add anything* to the existing field? **[Yes. There is some limited literature on the role that qualifications might be expected to play in EAP, e.g., Pennington, 1992; Krzanowski, 2001; Sharpling, 2002; Bell, 2016, 2023; Campion, 2016; Lowton, 2020. The proposed research would add to the existing knowledge]**
3. Is the research itself 'do-able'? Can my proposed question(s) actually *be answered*? **[Yes. RQ1 is perhaps the most definitively answerable question. RQ2 and RQ3 are by nature more open to interpretation but they are valid questions for exploration nonetheless]**
4. Are there any *logistical constraints* around my topic and question(s)? **[Access will need to be granted to a suitable pool of EAP employers; some care will need to be taken over how these research participants are selected to ensure there is a representative spread. Access will also be needed to a suitable group of practising EAP teachers in order to investigate RQs 2 and 3]**
5. Are there any *ethical constraints* around my topic and question(s)? **[No, not really. All the participants will almost certainly need to be anonymised to protect their identity and there will be the usual considerations around privacy and data storage, but beyond this, there should be no significant ethical barriers]**
6. *How* will I go about investigating my topic and answering my question(s)? Which specific *paradigms* and *research methods* will I use? **[A series of semi-structured qualitative interviews with a selection of EAP recruiters such as Heads of Departments etc., then interviews and/or questionnaires with a selection of EAP teachers. The most likely ontological research paradigm will be qualitative but if sufficient participants can be recruited, then a quantitative survey could also be possible. The study would lend itself well to mixed methods in this regard]**

Task 7.1e

This student has violated almost all of the academic recommendations I have made in this chapter. His first mistake was not to have started working on his dissertation immediately. As soon as the proposal was formally approved, he should have been mapping out a dissertation completion timeline and getting started on all of the necessary wider reading for his Literature Review. The student's second mistake was to approach things so linearly, assuming that he would have enough time to finish all of the Semester 2 coursework first before starting his dissertation. As I have advised in this chapter, he should have recognised the need for multi-tasking right from the outset. Mistake number three was the decision to give himself a two-week holiday at the end of May. This was a particularly risky thing to do and shows a complete disregard of priorities. When you are writing up your dissertation, that task must become your top priority and you simply cannot afford to take any time off until the work has been completed.

The other issues that the student faces are arguably all knock-on effects from his initial poor management of time. For example, he should have been aware that once the academic year finishes, staff are likely to start leaving and university operations such as the convening of Ethics Committees will gradually close down. This means that if changes are needed, adequate administrative time needs to be factored in to allow them to be properly managed. The same principle applies when it comes to gathering research data. The student was hoping to interview academic staff but he neglected to consider the times when they would be willing and available, or what he should do as a Plan B if it turned out that for some reason he was unable to gain access to them.

In sum, all of the problems this student now faces were easily avoidable if he had paid more careful attention to what the process of completing a dissertation would actually require of him.

Task 7.2a

i. A researcher wants to look at how a group of High School students have performed on one particular section of an ELT placement test. **[Primarily quantitative. A qualitative dimension could be brought in if the researcher wanted to get the test-takers' views on what they found difficult/easy]**

168 *Planning Your Dissertation*

ii. A researcher wants to better understand teachers' beliefs about how to teach reading. **[Primarily qualitative, although a quantitative dimension could also be brought in depending on the scale of the investigation]**

iii. A researcher is interested in whether non-native English teachers face hiring discrimination compared to native English speakers. **[Most likely qualitative, although again, this topic could also be approached from a quantitative perspective if the researcher was comparing large-scale hiring practices, e.g., a statistical comparison of the total number of NESTs and NNESTs recruited by a range of institutions over an extended time period]**

iv. A researcher wants to investigate the frequency of specific grammatical forms in scientific reports. **[Purely quantitative]**

v. A researcher wants to investigate whether English language teachers are more likely to favour MA TESOL or MA Applied Linguistics in their choice of qualifications. **[Primarily qualitative, though a quantitative dimension could be brought in depending on the scale of the investigation]**

vi. A researcher wants to investigate the academic and socio-cultural adjustment problems faced by Chinese first year students at an EMI institution. **[Qualitative would be the most obvious choice here as the researcher will need to understand the students' feelings and experiences, but this topic could also be approached from a quantitative perspective, e.g., with the large-scale use of questionnaires]**

Task 7.2b

i. A researcher wants to better understand teachers' beliefs about how to teach reading. **[Mixed methods could be used here by employing questionnaires, semi-structured interviews and classroom observations]**

ii. A researcher is interested in whether non-native English teachers face hiring discrimination compared to native English speakers. **[A mixed-methods approach in this case might involve the large-scale statistical analysis of published hiring data contrasted with the findings from qualitative interviews]**

iii. A researcher wants to investigate whether English language teachers are more likely to favour MA TESOL or MA Applied Linguistics in their choice of qualifications. [**Similar to iii above, a mixed-methods approach here might involve the large-scale statistical analysis of different teachers' profiles coupled with qualitative interviews. A quantitative dimension could also be brought in by using questionnaires**]

iv. A researcher wants to investigate the academic and socio-cultural adjustment problems faced by Chinese first year students at an EMI institution. [**As in (v) above, a mixed-methods approach in this case would probably involve a mix of questionnaires and interviews. If there was sufficient time and the opportunity to do so, the researcher might also decide to build in an observation component in which the students were shadowed during their daily academic interactions. However, for a research project on the scale of an MA dissertation, longitudinal fieldwork of this nature would probably not be so practical**]

Task 7.3a

This proposal shows some promise as a potential dissertation topic but there are a few areas that still need to be tightened up. For example, the proposed research questions and research methodology could be looked at a little more closely. The need for both quantitative and qualitative approaches is not entirely clear. RQ4 seems to presuppose that formulaic sequences *are* in fact an important feature of how IELTS writing is judged and that test-takers therefore need to know about them, but this is not a given. It appears that the stated purpose of RQ3 is to ascertain the extent to which this is the case. Depending on the results for this question, it may well be that RQ3 then cancels out the need to investigate RQ4. Ontological and epistemological aspects like these would benefit from a closer consideration.

Task 7.4

It is not uncommon for students to think that they're not going to get on very well with their supervisor, especially if they have been assigned someone they haven't worked closely with before, or already got to know well. The key thing in situations like this though is to give all parties a fair chance. The lack of direct specialist knowledge is not in itself so surprising or unreasonable. Not every student will have the opportunity to work with someone who is an acknowledged expert in their chosen area but all supervisors will be knowledgeable about TESOL/Applied Linguistics in general and will be able to advise students on matters to do with research. *Not* having someone who specialises directly in your particular topic can actually sometimes turn out to be an advantage, as they will then be more objective and much less likely to try and mould your ideas to fit in with their own.

It would be rather extreme to change supervisor after just one meeting (unless there was an extremely compelling reason for doing so) and most universities would probably recommend that in the first instance, the student (and supervisor) should just monitor how things go. First impressions are not always accurate and in time, the student might well find that her attitude towards the supervisor will change. After a series of meetings, however, if the student still felt that things were not working, then she should certainly discuss the matter with the MA programme director and formally request that her supervisor be re-assigned. This would be well within her rights and most programme directors would be sympathetic to such requests and do their best to help.

Additional Resources for Further Reading

Dörnyei, Z. (2007). *Research Methods in Applied Linguistics: Quantitative, Qualitative and Mixed Methodologies.* Oxford University Press.

Paltridge, B. & Phakiti, A. (Eds.) (2015). *Research Methods in Applied Linguistics.* Bloomsbury.

Phakiti, A. (2003) *Experimental Research Methods in Language Learning.* Bloomsbury.

Woodrow, L. (2020). *Doing a Master's Dissertation in TESOL and Applied Linguistics.* Routledge.

Chapter References

Bell, D.E. (2016). Practitioners, pedagogies, and professionalism in English for Academic Purposes (EAP): The development of a contested field. Unpublished PhD diss., University of Nottingham, UK.

Bell, D.E. (2023). *English for Academic Purposes: Perspectives on the Past, Present & Future.* Channel View Publications.

Brown, J.D. & Rodgers, T.S. (2002). *Doing Second Language Research.* Oxford University Press.

Campion, G. (2016). 'The learning never ends': Exploring teachers' views on the transition from General English to EAP. *Journal of English for Academic Purposes, 23,* 59–70.

Creswell, J.W. (1998). *Qualitative Inquiry and Research Design.* Sage.

Dörnyei, Z. (2007). *Research Methods in Applied Linguistics.* Oxford.

Flick, U. (2009). *An Introduction to Qualitative Research* (4th ed.). Sage.
Krzanowski, M. (2001). S/he holds the Trinity/UCLES Diploma: Are they ready to teach EAP? www.baleap.org.uk/pims/pimreports/2001/bath/krzanowski.htm Litosseliti, L. (Ed.) (2018). *Research Methods in Linguistics* (2nd ed.). Bloomsbury.
Lowton, R. (2020). The (T)EAP of the iceberg: The role of qualifications in teaching English for academic purposes. MA TESOL diss., University of Nottingham Ningbo China.
McKay, S.L. (2006). *Researching Second Language Classrooms*. Lawrence Erlbaum.
Miles, M.B. & Huberman, M.A. (1994). *Qualitative Data Analysis*. Sage.
Paltridge, B. & Phakiti, A. (2015). *Research Methods in Applied Linguistics*. Bloomsbury.
Pennington, M.C. (1992). Second class or economy? The status of the English language teaching profession in tertiary education. *Prospect, 7*(3), 7–19.
Rasinger, S.M. (2013). *Quantitative Research in Linguistics* (2nd ed.). Bloomsbury.
Rose, H., McKinley, J. & Briggs Baffoe-Djan, J. (2020). *Data Collection Research Methods in Applied Linguistics*. Bloomsbury.
Schwandt, T. A. (2001). *Dictionary of Qualitative Inquiry* (2nd ed.). Sage.
Sharpling, G. (2002). Learning to teach English for academic purposes: Some current training and development issues. *ELTED, 6*, 82–94.
Silvermann, D. (2010). *Doing Qualitative Research* (3rd ed.). Sage.

8 Writing Up Your Dissertation Part I

Introduction

This chapter begins by looking at the overall structure of a Masters' dissertation. It suggests some target word counts and examines the different rhetorical role which each chapter should play. It then focuses in some detail on the different aspects involved in writing up the first three chapters of your dissertation: the Introduction chapter, the Literature Review chapter and the Methodology chapter.

Additional resources for your further reading are listed on page 208.

8.1 Dissertation Structure and Length

As you learned in the previous chapter, a Masters' dissertation usually represents a piece of independent academic writing of around 15,000 words. For a text of this length to be understood, it is important for it to be based on a clear structure, so that the writer's ideas flow logically and the reader can follow all the different claims and arguments. Traditionally speaking, most Masters' dissertations typically consist of six individual chapters. These are outlined in the box below, along with an indication in square parenthesis of the approximate word counts which are representative of each different stage:

'Standard' Master's Dissertation Structure and Target Wordcounts

Acknowledgements [60–100]
Abstract [250–300]
CHAPTER 1: Introduction [1,000–1,150]
CHAPTER 2: Literature Review [3,500–4,000]
CHAPTER 3: Methodology [1,500–1,600]
CHAPTER 4: Results [2,000–2,150]
CHAPTER 5: Discussion [3,000–3,150]
CHAPTER 6: Conclusion [1,000–1,100]
References [700–850]
Appendices [450–600]

However, as I have commented at different points throughout this book, you can and should expect to find slight variations from institution to institution. Some universities, for example, do not include the references and the appendix in the final word count whereas others insist that the final word count must represent absolutely everything. Make sure that you check with your course tutors what the official expectations on this are in your own case and then carefully stick to whatever they tell you. Submitting a dissertation which is significantly over (or under) the stipulated word count will usually attract a penalty and end up costing you marks. This can sometimes make a difference to your final degree classification, so it is very important indeed to get this detail right. It would certainly be a great shame for your final result to drop from a Distinction to a Merit, or from a Merit to a Pass, just because you failed to follow the regulations. That being said, there is no need for you to get *overly* hung-up on numbers. The word counts I have listed above are still just suggestions and there will always be some variance between individual dissertations. If you end up writing a little bit more or a little bit less for one section, for example, that is fine; it just means that in order to compensate, you will then need to write a little bit less or a little bit more somewhere else. It *is* very important to keep a good balance between the different chapters though, as this does affect the final quality of your work and could cost you marks. It would look odd, for instance, if the Literature Review and Discussion chapters were noticeably very short, as these are usually the longest chapters in the entire dissertation. Similarly, you must not be tempted to leave any chapters out, as this would also make the final dissertation look strange. On this point, I was once marking a dissertation which had started well and was generally looking quite credible, but then to my considerable surprise, I discovered that there was no Methodology chapter. Either by accident or design, the student had somehow managed to leave this part out. In this particular case, the dissertation was therefore ultimately classified as a fail.

While we are considering the overall dissertation structure, a very common problem I encounter is that students sometimes decide (or are advised by their supervisors) to combine their Results and Discussion into just one chapter. This practice is very much open to debate. My personal advice to students is that it is usually better to keep their Results and Discussion chapters *separate*, as this then helps to keep the writing more balanced and focused. As I will discuss below, the rhetorical purpose of these two chapters is actually quite different. From my experience of marking Masters' student work, if the Results and Discussion are combined into a single chapter, then there can often be a danger that the proper rhetorical purpose for each ends up getting confused or lost. In *some* circumstances (e.g., it might be that your Literature Review chapter has needed to be a little longer than usual, in which case the word count of your remaining chapters would have to be reduced as a result) it *may* become advisable for the Results and Discussion chapters to be combined, but for the most

174 *Writing Up Your Dissertation Part I*

part, I myself think that it is a better and much safer academic practice for beginner-level dissertation writers to keep them separate.

8.1.1 Rhetorical Purpose

Each chapter of your dissertation should have its own very clear rhetorical purpose. This becomes especially important when the markers evaluate the quality of your dissertation as a whole. For you to be awarded high marks, as I have described above, a good sense of balance needs to have been maintained between the different chapters throughout the dissertation, not only in terms of their word count but also with regard to the specific information they include and the way in which those details are then presented and discussed.

Check Your Understanding: Independent Task 8.1a

Match descriptions (a)–(j) with their appropriate locations in a dissertation.

a. Where you present your findings.
b. Where you list all the works you have cited.
c. Where you give thanks to all the different people who have helped and supported you.
d. Where you discuss what other researchers have written about your topic and how your own work fits into this.
e. Where you provide a brief overview of the entire dissertation.
f. Where you consider the wider implications of your findings and what they might mean for the field; where you make any recommendations.
g. Where you explain what your dissertation will be about, why you chose this topic, what your specific research questions are and why they are worthy of investigation.
h. Where you include documentation such as a copy of your ethics approval form or samples of your data analysis.
i. Where you discuss and provide a rationale for the particular ontological paradigms and research methodologies you have chosen; where you describe the specific procedures you have followed.
j. Where you critically evaluate your findings; where you consider how your findings compare with what other researchers have found.

A suggested answer to this task has been provided on page 201.

Failing to have a clearly identifiable rhetorical purpose can be a very common reason why dissertations lose marks, so it is important for you to develop a good understanding of how this principle works. When I am reading my students' work, I often find that different sections of their dissertations turn out to have been misplaced and this then spoils the overall rhetorical flow. For instance, a student might have included a highly detailed discussion of their methodology in Chapter 1, when it would have been more appropriate for this to have been included in Chapter 3. Similarly, and as I have already discussed above, when students decide to combine Chapters 4 and 5, it can then inadvertently lead to a sense of rhetorical confusion and ineffective presentation of their Results, Discussion and Conclusion.

While there is most certainly more than just one way to write a successful dissertation, and I would not wish for any of my advice here to become overly prescriptive, nor to be taken as immutably cast in stone, some care *does* need to be taken over these structural and rhetorical dimensions. From my experience as an MA TESOL course director, getting these aspects right can make all the difference between being awarded a pass and a fail, or a high grade and just an average grade.

Check Your Understanding: Independent Task 8.1b

Look at the following excerpts from a student dissertation. Based on what you have learned above about rhetorical purpose, which specific chapter or section do you think each excerpt is most likely to belong to? [note that apart from Bell, 2022 and Lowton, 2020, the other academic citations here are entirely fictional]

a. Bell (2022) has argued that discussions of methodology and pedagogy remain significantly under-represented within the pages of JEAP.
b. The question of practitioner identity and status in EAP has therefore become an important issue for the field and is worthy of more detailed investigation.
c. Each interviewee agreed that their entry to TESOL had been almost entirely unplanned and was largely serendipitous.
d. I decided from the outset that a qualitative approach would best serve my needs.
e. Based on my findings from this research, it seems clear that more attention needs to be paid to raising novice teachers' awareness of their pedagogic values and beliefs. A closer focus on this could very easily be built into existing pre-service training programmes.

f. Writing this dissertation has not been easy for me and would not have been possible without the help and support of various people behind the scenes.
g. Although it might seem from their initial responses that the first three teachers did not see much value in their pre-service training, a finding supported by Chan (2017) and Wu (2021), it later transpired that their views on this were in fact much less clear-cut. Two of the teachers – 'Jenny' and 'Freda' – went on to praise the guidance they had received from mentors.
h. My abiding interest in conversation analysis is thus grounded in both academic and practical concerns, and has served as a catalyst for this present study.
i. Bell, D.E. (2022). Methodology in EAP: Why is it largely still an overlooked issue? Journal of English for Academic Purposes, 55, 101073.
j. Gerunds represented the most frequently used grammatical form (n = 42) closely followed by instances of the Simple Past tense (n = 36).
k. As Lowton (2020) points out, although it has undoubtedly achieved a great deal for UK EAP, BALEAP still has several blind spots. Earlier authors (notably Ding & Bruce, 2017) have also been very critical of BALEAP's shortcomings.
l. One clear recommendation is that schools should invest in more technical training for their staff.
m. Detailed below is a sample of the participant consent form.

A suggested answer to this task has been provided on page 202.

8.1.2 The Importance of Effective Signposting

As I discussed in Chapter 4, a key feature of good academic writing is that it will make effective use of signposting language. This becomes especially important in the case of a dissertation because if adequate structural signposting devices are absent, then the sheer length of the work makes it all the more difficult for the reader to digest and follow.

When you are preparing each chapter of your dissertation, you can apply effective signposting principles in several ways. The first and perhaps most obvious means of signposting for your reader is to use appropriate headings and sub-headings to help break up your text. On this note, it is worth remembering that each chapter of your dissertation should begin on a clean page with the chapter heading itself neatly centred and clearly labelled in a distinctive typeface and noticeable font size so that it stands out.

The next way in which you should apply signposting techniques is in your chapter openings and closings. In this regard, it can be very helpful at the beginning and end of each chapter to include a short sub-section in which you outline the different content that the chapter will cover/has covered. If you wish, in the case of each chapter's opening section, this can also be complemented by a numbered contents list detailing the different chapter sub-headings. The underlying purpose behind each of these techniques is to provide optimum clarity for your reader. The same principles apply here as they do for any other type of academic submission: the easier it is for someone to read your work and follow its argumentation and structure, then the more likely it becomes that you will be awarded a good grade.

Check Your Understanding: Independent Task 8.1c

Chapter 1 serves as the general introduction to your dissertation. At the very beginning of this chapter though, based on the signposting principles I have discussed above, you will still need to begin with a short descriptive overview of what the chapter itself is going to be focusing on.

Imagine that you are writing the dissertation from the previous chapter on the role of qualifications in EAP (see page 144).

Draft a short introductory paragraph in which you explain that the chapter will cover:

- A brief overview of the role of qualifications in EAP
- The questions you intend to investigate
- Why you feel this topic is important and your reasons for choosing it
- An overview of how the rest of your dissertation will be structured

Present this work as if it is the opening to a real dissertation, i.e., type your answer on a clean page and try to use white space well with appropriate typefaces and formatting.

A suggested answer to this task has been provided on page 203.

8.2 Writing Chapter 1: The Introduction

Based on what has been discussed so far, if you already know your topic and research questions, you should now be ready to tackle the writing up of the first chapter of your dissertation. As I explained in Chapter 7 though,

178 *Writing Up Your Dissertation Part I*

most writers do not in fact begin their dissertation writing with Chapter 1. Given that this is a fairly short chapter and relatively easy to write, its completion usually gets left to later. If you are reading this book in the same order that you are writing your dissertation chapters, then depending on your starting point, at this juncture you may wish to turn to a different section. You will be able to find the relevant guidance either in this chapter or the next. If you *have* decided to start your writing from Chapter 1 though, then by all means read on.

The example below provides an illustrative snapshot of what the opening page of an MA TESOL dissertation Chapter 1 *might* look like:

CHAPTER 1: INTRODUCTION

    1.1   *A Personal Career Journey*
    1.2   *My Specific Research Questions*
    1.3   *The Nature of This Research*
    1.4   *Dissertation Overview*

The main purpose of this opening chapter is to set the professional context for my research, and to explain my reasoning behind the particular questions which this dissertation attempts to answer.

I begin by describing aspects of my career journey to date, and reflect on how these have influenced and guided my current thinking, particularly with regard to those areas of English for Academic Purposes (EAP) which I believe warrant further investigation.

I then outline the specific questions which this dissertation will address, and situate the significance of these within the wider context of EAP today.

I close the chapter by describing the nature of my research in more detail, and then provide a brief overview of what will be covered in each of the chapters which follow.

It is worth drawing your attention to several key features here. First of all, note the way in which the chapter heading has been presented and the effective use of white space. Also, note the numbered contents summary, which allows the reader to see at a glance what the chapter will cover and under which sections each discussion will appear. Just as you were asked to practice in Independent Task 8.1b, the chapter then provides a short introduction in which the forthcoming content of the chapter is clearly signposted. A specific feature worth noticing here, particularly if English is

Writing Up Your Dissertation Part I

not your first language, is that this introductory signposting is written using *the Present Simple tense*. This temporal positioning aspect of academic writing becomes very important in a dissertation, and in striking the right tone you will be required to use different tenses at different times. I will be returning to this point in later sections, but for now it is simply worth noting that when presenting the different dissertation chapters, this is a feature of academic writing you will need to develop a degree of personal sensitivity for.

Having stated above that signposting is an important feature of academic writing it is now worth unpacking this a little further and examining some of the core language that is used in the signposting process. Being able to draw on a variety of appropriate verbs can be a very helpful stylistic device when writing the openings to your dissertation chapters.

Some Useful Verb Forms

Discuss	The main purpose of this chapter is…
Outline	
Reflect on	I begin by…
Provide an overview of	I then reflect on…
Highlight	I outline…
Consider	I close the chapter by…
Conclude	I provide an overview of…
Close	

Check Your Understanding: Independent Task 8.2a

Look back at the sample Chapter 1 opening on page 178. If you own this book, you may wish to underline or use a coloured highlighter to identify each instance of when the writer uses a signposting verb form. If you are borrowing the book from a library, make a list of these features on a separate piece of paper or on your computer.

A suggested answer to this task has been provided on page 204.

Now that we have examined how to signpost the general structure of the chapter for the reader, let us look at how an example opening section might begin:

1.1 A Personal Career Journey

My professional career involvement within the field of English Language Teaching (ELT) now spans some 12 years. By far the largest portion of this period, at least eight consecutive years, has been spent employed in the sub-field of English for Specific Purposes (ESP), with a particular focus on teaching English for Academic Purposes (EAP), the area with which this dissertation is most directly concerned.

As both a researcher and an EAP practitioner, I am interested in understanding how and why people decide to begin careers in EAP; the different routes which they follow in gaining entry to the profession; the trajectories which their careers typically then take; the ways in which EAP practitioners understand, develop and profess their professional expertise; and finally, the ways in which institutions offering EAP courses might most effectively establish and maintain appropriate professional standards. Underpinning each of these areas is an interest in how EAP as an academic discipline has developed and continues to develop, and the effect that this has had on the work of those directly involved in EAP teaching. My research interests are thus firmly grounded in, and informed by, the real-world, everyday concerns which confront EAP practitioners and their managers as they attempt to carry out their daily duties in the academic workplace.

As before, it is worth me drawing your attention to several features here. Note how the writer provides relevant background information on why the dissertation topic was selected. Note also how the writer foregrounds the context against which the research questions will later be formulated. A final point worth mentioning is the frequent use of the personal pronoun 'I'. As I discussed in Chapter 6, remember that it is now an acceptable feature of modern academic writing to use the First Person pronoun. This becomes particularly relevant when you are writing your dissertation Chapter 1.

Look at how this example chapter continues:

1.2 My Specific Research Questions

This dissertation seeks to investigate two particular questions in relation to the field of EAP:

> - *How has the pedagogic field of EAP changed over time?*
> - *How has the work of EAP practitioners developed alongside this?*
>
> As I have already described, my now extensive involvement in English Language Teaching (ELT), the last eight years of which having been spent in university contexts, has given me a strong and abiding interest, both personal and professional, in EAP. While the main focus of this interest most probably originally came from my 'chalk-face' perspectives as a classroom-based EAP practitioner, in more recent years, possibly due to the various changes in my workplace roles, it has expanded to cover the perspectives of those responsible for setting up and then managing EAP programmes. I strongly believe that my research questions are highly relevant to the perspectives from each of these different camps.

There are several interesting features in this section. Once again, the writer uses a numbered sub-heading to introduce the main topic and to provide a clear break with the focus of the previous section.

As before, there is explicit signposting of the writer's intentions using the Present Simple tense – 'seeks to investigate' – and the research questions are very clearly presented using italics, bullet points and a sensible use of white space. The writer then provides a clear justification for why those particular research questions were chosen and why they are of personal professional interest. As in the previous section, the writer draws extensively on First Person pronoun usage throughout.

It is also normal in the Introduction chapter of a dissertation to say a little about how the research will be conducted. This discussion only needs to be *brief*, however, as the main emphasis on methodological matters will take place in Chapter 3. For now, the reader only needs to be given a very general flavour of how the research has been approached. Look at how this has been handled in the example below:

> **1.3 The Nature of the Research**
>
> Spanning more than four different decades – from the 1960s through to the present day – my research has been built around a series of in-depth, open-ended interviews with 12 internationally recognised academics who have been actively involved in the teaching of ESP/EAP, and whose names are now synonymous with particular aspects of the field's development.

> In choosing this qualitative form of research methodology and in adopting this particular approach over others, my intention has been to capture a broad range of professional narratives from those who have historically been involved in the shaping of EAP and the mapping of its territory. I hope to demonstrate how the field itself has been structured by the agency of those key individuals most committed to it.

In this section, it is worth noting the mix of different verb tenses that the writer uses. Whereas in the introductory signposting section, *all* the action was taking place in the Present Simple tense, now the writer's perspective oscillates between the Present Perfect – 'my research has been built around'; 'my intention has been' – and looking towards the future – 'I hope to demonstrate'. As I have commented above, when you are writing up your dissertation, you will need to be sensitive to how you should pitch these different temporal perspectives.

In the final part of Chapter 1, it can be helpful to provide your reader with a brief overview of how the rest of the dissertation will be structured. Look at an example of this below:

> **1.4 Dissertation Overview**
>
> This dissertation has been divided into six chapters. Having now attempted in this opening chapter to set the scene for my research interests, and to explain how these have grown alongside my personal career trajectory, Chapter 2 presents a comprehensive review of the relevant academic literature. This chapter draws principally on the following themes:
>
> i. The emergence of EAP, its early history, the reasons for its subsequent development and the ways in which it differs from mainstream ELT.
> ii. Key themes, trends and developments in the history of EAP.
> iii. The impact of all of the above on the work of EAP practitioners.
>
> Chapter 3 focuses on my research methodology and provides a rationale for the various methodological decisions which I have taken during the course of the study. I also examine the ontological paradigms which have underpinned my approach and discuss some of the limitations of these. Towards the end of the chapter, I discuss ethical considerations and also some aspects of my own reflexivity.
>
> Chapter 4 reports on....

As I outlined in Section 8.1, the Introduction chapter to a dissertation is usually quite short and typically falls within a word count range of 1,000–1,150 words. The sample excerpts I have provided above together add up to 853 words, representing roughly 75% of the target amount. Only a few more details would therefore need to be added. Before closing, the writer might also decide to add a line or two to summarise the chapter content and provide a preview of what will come next. This particular Chapter 1 could then be considered complete.

Check Your Understanding: Independent Task 8.2b

Based on what you have now learned about how to write the Introduction chapter, answer True (T) or False (F) to questions (i)–(v):

i. One of the rhetorical purposes of Chapter 1 is to explain why you chose your topic and why it is worthy of investigation.
ii. Another rhetorical purpose of Chapter 1 is to explain your results.
iii. Providing an overview of your topic in Chapter 1 is not necessary because you already did this in the abstract.
iv. Chapter 1 should be written using the Simple Past tense throughout to reflect that your research has been completed.
v. Signposting language is especially important in Chapter 1 because you are introducing the reader to your dissertation.

A suggested answer to this task has been provided on page 204.

8.3 Writing Chapter 2: The Literature Review

As I outlined in Section 8.1, for most MA TESOL/Applied Linguistics students, the Literature Review typically represents the longest chapter in their entire dissertation. For this reason, I usually advise my students to begin their writing-up process with this chapter. Apart from anything else, I find that the sheer scale of the undertaking can be helpful in encouraging good writing habits and getting writers into a steady production flow. Another good reason for starting your dissertation work with the Literature Review is because of the significant time it usually takes when carrying out a detailed literature search. Tracking down hard-to-find sources may require inter-library loans, or you might find yourself waiting for core texts to be returned because other students or researchers are already using them. All of these things can eat into your valuable time, so it is absolutely vital to plan ahead.

One of the earliest considerations you will need to face when conducting your Literature Review comes in deciding exactly which literature needs to be covered. This matter is not always as simple as it may first sound.

A common weakness that I find in many of our MA student dissertations is that their Literature Reviews are not sufficiently relevant to the topic they were investigating, or the coverage itself is too shallow in its focus and either too broad or too narrow in its scope. A good Literature Review needs to cover ground that is relevant to both the dissertation topic *and* the specific research questions that are being investigated. Writers need to be discerning, therefore, in choosing what to focus on and what to leave out. It is *not* just a matter of cataloguing anything and everything that has ever been written about a given subject area. This point particularly needs to be kept in mind if writers choose to follow a historical approach to the Literature Review, as I will discuss below.

When first deciding what the overall scope of your Literature Review chapter should be, it can be helpful to identify a series of relevant sub-topics or themes. Look at how this has been handled in the sample dissertation below:

Title:

- Perceptions of Expertise: What constitutes a 'good' EAP teacher?

Research Questions:

- What are the key features of successful EAP teachers?
- How might these be measured and evaluated?
- Is expertise in ELT the same as expertise in EAP?

Likely Sub-Topics

- Definition & Scope of English for Academic Purposes
- Studies of Expertise in General
- Studies of Expertise in Teaching & English Language Teaching (ELT)
- Professional Standards & Benchmarking in ELT
- Differences between ELT and EAP
- Expertise in EAP Contexts

There are several features worth commenting on here. A preliminary point is that in a dissertation examining perceptions of expertise in teaching EAP, readers would probably first expect to see some definitions of those opening two concepts, i.e., 'expertise' and 'EAP'. In the case of EAP, this would mean a discussion of what EAP is, where it came from and how it is being defined and positioned for the purposes of this particular dissertation. In the case of expertise, as a means of providing some relevant background, there would probably first need to be some coverage of how expertise has been conceptualised in other areas. In the example above, all of this is encompassed by bullet points one and two. It is important to stress, however, that the *depth* of coverage in each of these sections would not entirely be the same. The section on EAP, for example, would probably only run to a couple of hundred words. The section on expertise in general would also not be very much longer, as the rhetorical purpose here is simply to set the overall context and show that the writer is aware of how expertise has been approached and conceptualised historically. The start of the following section on expertise in teaching would not need to be very long either, as this is not the main focus of the dissertation. Here, the writer would simply need to show some critical awareness of how the construct of expertise in teaching has been framed and investigated by previous researchers. However, the latter half of this section *is* likely to be a little longer, as the topic of studies of expertise in ELT is obviously much more directly relevant to the dissertation. The same can be said of the subsequent section on professional standards and benchmarking; a detailed discussion of how ELT sets its standards would be considered highly pertinent to this investigation, as this ties in closely with concepts of expertise. The final two sections of the chapter are likely to be the most detailed and therefore the lengthiest, as they are dealing more explicitly with the specifics of the research questions. One of the rhetorical purposes of these latter sections, especially the final one, is to convince the reader that there has been a research gap and to suggest how the dissertation will try to address such a deficit. I will be returning to examine this concept of the research gap again below.

It should be evident from the above that when looking at the overall rhetorical structure, a Literature Review chapter thus progresses in a sort of inverted triangle format, starting quite generally but gradually becoming more specific. An indication of this overall structure and some target word counts for each specific section is provided for your reference below:

CHAPTER 2: LITERATURE REVIEW

2.1 Definition & Scope of English for Academic Purposes [175–200]
2.2 Studies of Expertise in General [200–250]
2.3 Studies of Expertise in Teaching & English Language Teaching (ELT) [400–600]
2.4 Professional Standards & Benchmarking in ELT [450–500]
2.5 Differences between ELT and EAP [1,025–1,150]
2.6 Expertise in EAP Contexts [1,250–1,300]

Check Your Understanding: Independent Task 8.3a

Look at the sample dissertation title and research questions below. If you were going to write on this subject, what sub-topics would you include in your Literature Review?

TITLE

Addressing Chinese Undergraduate Student Needs: A Case Study of an EMI University

RESEARCH QUESTIONS

What are Chinese undergraduate students' needs in an EMI environment?
Do perspectives of their needs differ between stakeholders?
How, and to what extent, are their needs ultimately met?
A suggested answer to this task has been provided on page 205.

As I have suggested for the Introduction chapter, it can be good practice to open your Literature Review with a brief overview of how the chapter will be structured and a synopsis of the main themes. An example of this type of writing is provided in the box below:

> The main aim of this chapter is to provide a critical survey of what the relevant academic literature has identified as being the key issues and developments in EAP during the period since its birth until the present day.
>
> The chapter begins by defining the scope and parameters of EAP as an academic discipline and then moves to a discussion of the various factors which have generally been considered as responsible for EAP's emergence and subsequent growth. The key features which make EAP distinct from other forms of English Language Teaching are then considered, before the chapter turns to specific developments and themes in the course and conduct of EAP's history. For ease of reference, these different stages of EAP's historical development have been categorised and grouped under three particular chronological timeframes: the early days, 1960s-1970s; the middle period,

> 1980s-1990s, and finally the modern period, from the year 2000 until the present day.
>
> Within each timeframe, the specific developments themselves are dealt with under a series of individually named headings and sub-headings.

Check Your Understanding: Independent Task 8.3b

Look back at the Literature Review sub-topics you generated for Independent Task 8.3a. Using the example above as a guide, draft a similar chapter opening in which you discuss what your Literature Review will cover when discussing Chinese undergraduate student needs in EMI contexts.

A suggested answer to this task has been provided on page 205.

When it comes to the wider underlying rhetorical structure of a Literature Review, writers have several options open to them. As Paltridge and Phakiti (2015, p. 262) have very helpfully pointed out, three models are particularly common: a *historical* approach, a *contrastive* approach and an *aspect-by-aspect* approach. It is worth us briefly considering how these approaches might differ.

In the case of the *historical* approach, as the name suggests, writers typically provide a chronological survey of the relevant literature, which starts in the past and ends in the present. However, this is not to suggest that anything goes. As I have suggested above, writers do still need to be discerning about what they include and what they leave out. When conducting an historical style Literature Review, writers need to be able to identify what the seminal texts have been and how these represent particular landmarks in our understanding of a given topic. The closing sections of Literature Review chapters which have been written following the historical style usually then include a clear statement of where the perceived research gap is and how it will be filled.

In a *contrastive* approach, instead of working through the literature chronologically, the writer selects different competing perspectives on a topic and does some critical comparing and contrasting. This process is then used to provide a justification and rationale for the present study. An *aspect-by-aspect* approach to the Literature Review shares some similarities with the contrastive approach in that it involves a detailed discussion of different features relevant to the topic, but the main difference here is that there will not necessarily be such an explicit rhetorical sense of comparing

188 *Writing Up Your Dissertation Part I*

and contrasting. Writers simply choose the aspects they feel to be most relevant to their topic. The aspect-by-aspect approach is therefore somewhat more subjective in that it remains rather more dependent than the other two approaches on what the writer chooses to select. However, it should always be kept in mind that all three of these approaches have some areas of overlap and it is not uncommon to find Literature Reviews which choose to draw on particular dimensions of them all.

> **Check Your Understanding: Independent Task 8.3c**
>
> Gather together a selection of previous MA TESOL/Applied Linguistics dissertations (these are usually deposited in the university library, or may be held by your School or Faculty office) and look at how the different Literature Review chapters have been written.
>
> In each case, can you identify which rhetorical style the writer was following?

If you are reviewing the literature on a topic which has evidently attracted a lot of attention from researchers and can therefore be approached from a range of angles, it is important to make it clear to your reader exactly which aspects your review will mainly be focusing on. Look at how this has been handled below in an excerpt from a real Masters' dissertation titled 'Academic & Socio-cultural Adjustment Difficulties of Chinese International Students in Britain' (Bell, 2003):

> In the past four decades, the question of the difficulties that non-native speaker students (NNES) face when studying in English native speaker environments (ENSE) has received a considerable amount of attention. However, it also has to be said that the vast majority of these works have concerned themselves with students studying in Australia, Canada or the United States; to date, there has been relatively little such research carried out on students in the United Kingdom. Furthermore, while there have been research studies that have focused explicitly on African students (e.g., Pruitt, 1978), South-east Asian students (e.g., Maxwell et al., 2000), Malaysian students (e.g., Tafarodi & Smith, 2001) and Japanese students (e.g., Toyokawa & Toyokawa, 2002), there are currently relatively few papers which deal explicitly with mainland Chinese students (some notable exceptions to this rule being Weidong, 1996; Meder et al., 1998; Ma,

2001) and those which *do* have tended not to focus specifically on undergraduates, nor on any particular subject discipline (though see Ma, 2001).

When reviewing the literature, it also soon becomes very clear that the topic of international students studying in English-speaking environments is a multi-faceted affair and one which can be approached from a range of different angles. For example, quite a number of researchers (notably Ward & Kennedy, 1994; Ward, 1996; Berry, 1997; Lazarus, 1997; Schönpflug, 1997; Piontkowski et al., 2000; Ma 2001) who have concerned themselves specifically with the process of acculturation (notably Furnham & Bochner, 1986; Schram & Lauver, 1988; Ward & Kennedy, 1992; Alwright, 1996; Ryan & Twibell, 2000) have predominantly focused on identifying the different factors which can combine to cause international students problems and, through these, have examined the broader issue of culture shock. Others still (e.g., notably Berry & Annis, 1974; Berry & Kim, 1988; Ward & Kennedy, 1993; Leong & Chou, 1996) have preferred to explore the psychological effects of overseas study on mental health and have therefore considered issues relating to international student support and counselling.

In order to keep this review within manageable borders, the discussion which follows will limit itself to what the literature has had to say about the different types of academic and socio-cultural difficulties experienced by Chinese international students and to what extent these can be attributed to differences in cultural values and norms.

There are a few things worth commenting on here. Note the definitive opening statement in which the writer makes it clear that the broad topic under discussion has already attracted considerable attention. Note also how the writer then justifies this claim by outlining the countries in which the main research has predominated (Australia, Canada and the United States); the different nationalities which have typically been studied (Africans, South-east Asians, Malaysians, Japanese); and the specific subject areas which have most commonly attracted attention from researchers (acculturation; culture shock; international student support and counselling). In rhetorical terms, this information has been deliberately positioned to show the specific research gap which the dissertation then aims to investigate and fill (the academic and socio-cultural difficulties of *Chinese* international students in the *UK*).

As I have discussed above, other dissertations may choose to follow a slightly different modus operandi. In the case of the dissertation topic from Independent Task 8.3a, for example, the writer might begin by discussing how the topic of needs analysis first started to attract attention, before moving on to select particular dimensions for more critical comparison. This style of writing would therefore be blending aspects of the historical approach and the contrastive approach. Look at how this has been handled below:

2.1 Needs Analysis: An Important but Contested Construct

It could be argued that practitioner and research interest in needs first became prominent in the late 1970s with the publication of John Munby's seminal text, *Communicative Syllabus Design* (1978) and also a chapter by Ron Mackay, which appeared in a collection he co-edited with Alan Mountford that same year, 'English for Specific Purposes' (1978).

However, these early conceptualisations of needs principally tended to focus on identifying the types of language that ESP/EAP learners would be most likely to encounter. As such, the emphasis was therefore very clearly on linguistic needs as determined by the target situation. For Hutchinson and Waters (1987, p. 55), such needs can be called 'necessities' in that they represent what it is believed the learner needs to know in order to function in a given context. As Hutchinson and Waters went on to argue though, *only* focusing on such target situation needs can present a distorted picture. From their perspective, a more comprehensive analysis of needs must also take into account the learners' 'lacks' and 'wants' (pp. 55–56). It must be said that this more inclusive view of needs analysis has generally found favour and continues to dominate the discussions post-Millennium. As Ken Hyland (2006) has pointed out:

> Needs is actually an umbrella term that embraces many aspects, incorporating learners' goals and backgrounds, their language proficiencies, their reasons for taking the course, their teaching and learning preferences, and the situations they will need to communicate in.
>
> (p. 73)

As Hyland's definition shows, needs analysis is clearly a multi-faceted affair, which needs to take into account a number of different dimensions. This is particularly true in the case of ESP and EAP. As Diane Belcher (2006) has proposed, 'it is probably no exaggeration to say that needs assessment is seen in ESP as the foundation on which all other decisions are, or should be, made' (p. 135). More recently, these

> views have been echoed by Laurence Anthony (2018), who has no hesitation in identifying needs analysis as one of the four main pillars of ESP (p. 46). From all of the above, there can be little doubt that needs analysis occupies an important place in the historical development of ESP and EAP.

In this example, it is worth noting how the writer uses the literature as supporting evidence for the stance that understanding needs is an important feature of ESP and EAP. By critically contrasting different researchers' views of needs (Munby; Mackay; Hutchinson and Waters; Hyland), the writer is simultaneously not only reviewing the literature but also using it to bolster a particular line of argument. Critical and evaluative use of the literature like this is very different to mere description. A common weakness I often find in some of my own Masters' students' writing is that their Literature Review chapters can have the tendency to turn into a lengthy catalogue of 'he said, she said', with no real sense of any critical engagement or evaluation. A good Literature Review needs to do much more than this. When you are reviewing the academic literature at Masters' level, you need to go beyond mere description and *critically engage* with the different ideas and claims you are reporting. Your own stance on the issues you are discussing should therefore be evident throughout.

As I have already mentioned, at the end of each dissertation chapter, it can be helpful to include a brief summary of what was covered and also a preview of what will come next. In the case of Literature Review chapters, this dimension is especially useful because it serves to highlight the research gap and why this needs to be filled. Look at how this has been handled in the example below:

> This chapter has provided a critical overview of how the topic of academic and socio-cultural difficulties of NNES students has been treated by the international academic literature. As I hope to have shown, although some student nationalities and their learning contexts have attracted significant attention from researchers, to date there has been relatively little focus on the experience faced by mainland Chinese.
>
> In the following chapter, I will discuss the specific methodological mechanisms by which my research has sought to address this deficit.

One final point worth making about the Literature Review concerns the nature of the literature itself. As I had advised in Chapter 3 of this book, as a general rule of thumb, whenever you draw on academic sources, it is very important indeed that the works you are citing are as recent as possible. In the specific case of a Literature Review, this means that while you might begin by going back a few decades and making mention of certain seminal texts, by the end of the chapter, your writing <u>must</u> aim to bring things fully up to date. If you look back at the example dissertation from 2003 examining the academic and socio-cultural adjustment difficulties of Chinese undergraduates in the UK, you will see that many of the cited sources there had been published just a year or two before. Failing to draw on sufficiently recent sources is a very common weakness in student dissertations and this can prove costly in terms of final marks. When you are compiling your Literature Review, keep in mind the 3R formula I proposed in Chapter 3 and constantly check that your sources are Relevant, Recent and Reliable.

8.4 Writing Chapter 3: The Methodology

If, as I have recommended, you have already thought very carefully about your choice of methodology at the dissertation proposal stage and can justify the different ontological and epistemological paradigms which your research represents, then in some ways, the Methodology chapter should be one of the easiest for you to write. After all, this is your opportunity to tell the reader exactly what you did and why, so as long as you are clear on those two aspects, and are able to draw on appropriate academic sources in your justification, then writing a good Methodology chapter should not necessarily present you with too much difficulty.

As with all the other chapters of your dissertation though, it is important to be clear from the outset on the different themes and topics that a good Methodology chapter should be expected to address. As I have already discussed, your target word count for the Methodology chapter should be in the region of 1,500–1,600 words, which in comparison to the Literature Review and Discussion chapters is actually not very much. It follows, therefore, that your writing here will need to be particularly focused and concise.

> **Check Your Understanding: Independent Task 8.4a**
>
> What are some of the different themes, sections and sub-sections which should be covered in the Methodology chapter? Make a list of all the points you think you might include.
> A suggested answer to this task has been provided on page 206.

Before I examine more specific dimensions of writing up the Methodology chapter, it is worth us revisiting some of the methodological considerations I touched on in Chapter 7.

8.4.1 Quantitative Forms of Research Methodology

As I have already discussed, research belonging to the quantitative paradigm is principally concerned with a positivist ontological outlook and as such, it seeks to objectively *quantify* aspects of whatever topic is under investigation. From a methodological standpoint, this means that quantitative approaches will usually rely on large samples and involve the application of statistical analysis. One of the typical ways in which quantitative research methodology is applied in TESOL/Applied Linguistics is with the use of large-scale surveys. Such surveys can take a variety of forms. For example, a TESOL researcher might be interested in gathering data from a target population of students on their preferred learning strategies. A large-scale survey of this nature could thus be conducted using questionnaires, which would typically require the respondents to give their answers based on a Likert scale; alternatively, it could be carried out by a series of structured interviews. What each of these cases has in common though is that in taking a *quantitative* approach to the methodology, the researcher would be using statistics to measure the reliability and validity of the responses. As part of this, the researcher would be interested in examining any differences between specific variables and also in drawing statistical comparisons between the answers given by the different respondents.

Two further forms of quantitative methodology commonly found in TESOL/Applied Linguistics are experimental research and correlational research. These are similar in that they are both principally concerned with the investigation of variables. For example, in the case of experimental research, variables such as types of classroom instruction or teacher behaviour can be quantitatively measured and tested for their effects on student learning. Correlational research, on the other hand, might look at sets of student grades or test scores and seek to investigate the relationship between different sets of variables and the extent to which causation might be at play. This kind of research becomes particularly relevant in quantitative studies on language testing and assessment because it can help to shed light on issues around test reliability and validity. Approaches to research on linguistic analysis may also be fundamentally quantitative in nature, such as frequency surveys of how often a particular verb form appears in certain genres of writing. Barber's famous study of linguistic features of scientific writing (1962) is a good example of this. In each of these cases, the recognisable stamp of quantitative methodology becomes evident in the need for statistically significant sample sizes and the core preoccupation with data reliability and validity.

8.4.2 Qualitative Forms of Research Methodology

In marked contrast to quantitative approaches, qualitative forms of research methodology are much less concerned with 'proving' claims based on statistical analysis. As I discussed in Chapter 7, qualitative research belongs to a constructivist ontological paradigm, which sees reality as being open to different sociological interpretations depending on the specific nature of the protagonists. It follows from this that qualitative research tends to be based on much smaller sample sizes, but is then *deeper* in terms of how the actual data are analysed and interpreted.

In the case of TESOL/Applied Linguistics, perhaps the most common manifestation of qualitative inquiry comes in the form of interviews and focus groups. While a series of highly structured interviews might form part of quantitative methodology (because in this case, the interviews would represent little more than face-to-face questionnaires) from a *qualitative* standpoint, the preference would be for interviews to be either completely unstructured or semi-structured, as these formats allow for the gathering of more detailed responses and therefore 'richer' data. A very typical line of qualitative inquiry in TESOL research, for example, concerns the investigation of teachers' values and beliefs. In research of this nature, a relatively small number of respondents might be invited to share their thoughts and experiences; the researcher would then analyse their responses, drawing out any key themes and looking for similarities and differences. Unlike in quantitative research, however, a qualitative approach would *not* be attempting to draw statistically relevant conclusions, or to make broad generalisations. In qualitative terms, the focus of the research would be more on trying to understand what the results might mean for that particular group of respondents in that particular context and at that particular time. Qualitative research thus tends to be much more subjective in nature than quantitative research, a point which continues to draw criticism from those of a more positivist ontological outlook.

Some other very common forms of qualitative methodology in TESOL/Applied Linguistics are the use of observation instruments, research diaries and personal narratives. In the case of observation, classrooms are not surprisingly the most typical research location, with researchers usually interested in observing the behaviour of teachers, learners or both. In qualitative research of this nature, the observer needs to devise a suitable observation tool, so that the action being observed can be faithfully captured. In making sense of what was observed, the observer will then also need to create a suitable analytic framework to assist with coding and categorisation. I will be returning to the matter of approaches to qualitative coding in a later section below.

> **Check Your Understanding: Independent Task 8.4b**
>
> Consider dissertation topics (i) to (iii) below. In each case, which methodological approaches do you think would be the most suitable?
>
> i. The researcher wants to investigate whether pre-teaching vocabulary has any impact on Primary School students' reading comprehension.

ii. The researcher wants to investigate EAP teachers' attitudes to being observed by their line managers.
iii. The researcher wants to investigate whether the move structures in academic abstracts differ between academic disciplines.

A suggested answer to this task has been provided on page 206.

As I have already suggested in the case of the Introduction and Literature Review chapters, the opening of your Methodology chapter should also provide an overview of how the chapter itself will be structured. Look at how this has been handled in the dissertation excerpt below:

> In this chapter, I provide an overview of the methodology which has underpinned my research for this dissertation. Throughout, I also critically reflect on the lessons which I have personally learned as a researcher from having now experienced such a process.
>
> I begin the chapter by revisiting my specific research questions, before moving to a discussion of why I consider a qualitative, interview-based approach to have been particularly appropriate as a means of suggesting some possible answers.
>
> I then discuss in detail the actual nature of my research sample: the participant selection criteria I used and my justification for choosing the specific research subjects which I did; the protocols I duly followed in terms of gaining access, receiving formal consent and respecting confidentiality; the structure and design of the interviews and my choice and sequencing of the individual interview questions; the piloting and quality control mechanisms I employed; the particular issues I encountered in the course and conduct of the interviews themselves; the approach I took to transcribing and coding the ensuing raw interview data; and finally, some of the ontological and epistemological considerations which guided my approaches throughout.
>
> As support for some of the methodology-related claims which I make in this chapter, I draw on several academic sources, but have been particularly guided by Brinkmann and Kvale (2015), Harding (2013), Seidman (2013) and Charmaz (2006).

As before, there are several features worth drawing your attention to here. First of all, note how the writer says he will revisit the dissertation research questions. The last time these were explicitly drawn attention to was most probably in Chapter 1, so it is important to show them again here, as this then provides an appropriate backdrop for the discussions which follow. The next feature worth noticing is that the writer promises to provide some discussion of why his chosen research methodology – a qualitative approach in this case – was selected. While a detailed examination of ontological and epistemological issues is not usually expected at the Masters' level and such a discussion would, in any case, be very much limited by the available word count for this chapter, it is nonetheless important to provide a *brief* discussion of why certain methodological paradigms were favoured over others. If you can do this, it demonstrates to your reader that your approach to the research has been purposeful and you have made *principled* choices. As I have already commented in this book, a common weakness in many of the student Masters' dissertations I read each year is that their Methodology chapters can appear to be completely arbitrary with approaches simply chosen at random. If you are able to demonstrate that some careful thought has been put into your methodological choices and that you have therefore taken a principled approach to your research, this will enhance the overall academic credibility of your work and you will almost certainly be awarded higher marks.

A further point worth mentioning is that the writer makes reference to what he himself has learned throughout the research process. This phenomenon is formally known as reflexivity. Including a reflexive dimension arguably becomes more critical at the doctoral level than at Masters, but there is no harm for Masters' students also to show some awareness of how this operates, as it helps to demonstrate their awareness of wider thinking and criticality. I will return to discuss in more detail how reflexive elements can be built into the Methodology chapter in a later section.

Two remaining points from this sample are also worthy of mention. The first is that in the third paragraph, the writer details all the different steps of the research process. As I started this section by stating, the Methodology chapter is your opportunity to explain to the reader exactly what you did and, more importantly, why. This dimension is squarely reflected in the list of points which the writer enumerates in paragraph 3. The second and final point is that the writer makes explicit mention of the sources he will draw on as evidence and support. As I have already explained, ideally speaking, all methodological claims in the dissertation will need to be supported with references to the relevant academic literature. In this example, the writer is quite explicit in drawing attention to four particular sources which he claims to have relied on for methodological guidance. Based on this early signposting, the reader can then expect to see further references to work by these authors later in the chapter.

8.4.3 Approaches to Data Coding

As I have already mentioned several times, in the Methodology chapter writers are fundamentally expected to explain *what* they did and *why*. In the case of ontological paradigms in general, this should be relatively straightforward and only a brief explanation is required, but when it comes to providing the finer details of the research project, such as *how* different dimensions were analysed and *why* certain results were obtained, it is important for the writer to provide sufficient information so that the overall validity and reliability of their methodology can be properly evaluated. A common weakness I often encounter in my own Masters' students' research writing is that there sometimes seems to be a cosmic leap from the research paradigm they say they have chosen, to the results they later describe, without due explanation of the intervening processes in-between. This is where a detailed and critical discussion of the steps which were employed in sorting and coding the data truly comes into its own.

If you have taken a quantitative approach to your research, a discussion of the coding process is likely to be statistical in nature with reference to lots of numerical data, i.e., how many people said something, how many instances of a certain dimension were present, or how frequently a given phenomenon occurred. If, on the other hand, your research has been *qualitative*, then the process has the potential to be a little more complicated. In a discussion of qualitative interview coding, for example, you will need to explain by which mechanisms you decided to sort and make sense of your data. There are many ways to approach qualitative coding and it is now far beyond the scope of this chapter to explore any of these in detail (for further guidance on this, readers may wish to consult a very useful chapter on data coding by Kathy Charmaz (2006). A full text on qualitative coding by Johnny Saldaňa (2016) also provides many useful insights. These resources are listed in full on page 208) but as an illustrative example of how coding and data analysis might be discussed, look at the two written excerpts in the boxes below:

3.2.4 Approaches to Coding and Data Analysis

My approach to the analysis of the data which have emerged from this study has been predominantly inductive in nature, and as such, owes much to the early principles of both phenomenology (Berger & Luckmann, 1966; Garfinkel, 1967; Giorgi, 1975) and grounded theory (Glaser & Strauss, 1967; Charmaz, 2006). As Harding (2013) has pointed out, when taking an inductive approach, '…the researcher approaches a subject without predetermined ideas of what they are looking for and seeks to generate "middle range" theory – somewhere between grand theory and a working hypothesis – based on their data' (p. 13).

These broad research principles have guided my decision-making throughout, from the ways in which I initially approached the interview transcripts, through to the specific techniques which were then employed in the thematic categorisation and coding of emerging patterns and trends. The specific processes which I followed and my justification for these will be discussed in further detail below.

In the excerpt above, the writer makes it clear from the outset which methodological principles his approach to data analysis will be based upon (phenomenology; grounded theory). Note how he is careful to cross-reference these with appropriate academic citations as justification. There is then some clear signposting for the reader in order to preview the information that will follow.

---

a. Analysis of the Interview Transcripts

Applying the principles of an inductive approach meant that it was important for me to go through each of my interview transcripts line by line, making a note of any points of interest as I went. This opening stage of data analysis was important in allowing me to build my understanding of each set of interview data as a whole.

A further outcome of this process was that it soon became apparent that the relevance of the interviewees' responses did not always stay in lockstep with the specific questions which had been asked of them. For example, when going through the data, I often found that comments which were of direct relevance to my questions had either been made earlier, i.e., before a given question had even been asked, or later, i.e., as additional information which had been supplied when responding to a different topic. This meant that the notes which had been created from my initial line-by-line readings constantly had to be re-visited. Understanding this recursive and cyclical aspect of the data analysis process was crucial in helping me to capture the full richness of what the interviewees had said.

Writing Up Your Dissertation Part I 199

In the second excerpt above, the writer is telling the reader exactly which methodological approach he took (he first read through each transcript line by line and made notes) and what he learned from this process (gathering all of the information relevant to his interview questions required a cyclical, recursive approach). Another feature particularly worth mentioning here is the temporal aspect of how this writing has been presented. Note how the writer is now writing *from a past tense perspective*. This can be contrasted with the temporal aspect and verb tenses which are used when writing the Introduction chapter, as I have detailed under Sub-section 8.2.

As a last piece of advice when you are describing your methodological processes in Chapter 3, I would suggest that you try at all times to put yourself into the shoes of the reader. Keep asking yourself, 'Are my explanations clear?'; 'Could somebody else now use my data and go through the same steps that I did and get the same or similar results?' Trying to see things from the reader's perspective should help you to stay focused and ensure that your explanations consistently make sense.

8.4.4 *Ethical Considerations*

Before the end of your Methodology chapter, it is a good idea to make some mention of ethical considerations and how you dealt with them. This section does not need to be hugely detailed, a couple of hundred words will more than suffice, but there is nonetheless quite a big difference between a 'good' discussion of ethical considerations and one which is merely run of the mill.

One of the most common weaknesses I come across in many of my Masters' students' discussions of ethics is that their writing in this section simply becomes a procedural description of what they did, i.e., they simply state the fact that they completed an ethics approval form and got their supervisor's approval. A proper discussion of ethical considerations needs to go beyond this. Merely explaining that you sought ethical approval is a procedural matter and nothing worth writing home about. A more appropriate section on ethics (and one which would undoubtedly attract a higher final grade from the markers) is a critical discussion in which *genuine* ethical concerns are considered and evaluated. For example, how was the privacy of the research participants protected? Why was this aspect important anyway? If (as is often the case in Masters' research) the research participants are personally known to the researcher, why should this issue matter and what effect might it have on the reliability of the final results? By engaging in questions such as these, a writer shows a *genuine* awareness of ethical concerns and the role which they play in the academic research process. In sum, while a discussion of ethical concerns is a common and expected feature of the Methodology chapter, in order to be awarded high marks, you will be expected to show some genuine critical engagement with what you have identified as relevant issues, rather than simply providing a bland description of mere procedures.

> ### Check Your Understanding: Independent Task 8.4c
>
> What might some of the underlying ethical considerations be in items (i) to (v) below?
>
> i. The researcher is basing her research on interviews with her MA TESOL classmates.
> ii. The researcher has distributed questionnaires to his own students.
> iii. The researcher wants to observe and video-record classes of Primary School children.
> iv. The researcher is basing her research on interviews with students from Faculties at the institution at which she is doing her Masters.
> v. The researcher wants to identify the research participants by their real name.
>
> A suggested answer to this task has been provided on page 207.

8.4.5 Reflexivity

As I have described above, reflexivity essentially refers to what you yourself have learned from a given process. When you are writing at the Masters' level, you won't necessarily need to have a named sub-heading representing this dimension, but there are still several ways and areas in which reflexive elements can be built into a dissertation.

Showing some awareness of your own subjectivity in interpreting the results could be one example of this, as could a discussion of your research limitations. If you decide to include a section on this latter aspect though, as with what I have advised above on ethics, do try to ensure that you identify *genuine* limitations and then discuss them in sufficient detail. A very common weakness that I find in many student dissertations is that the limitations section can often seem rather contrived. For example, there would be little point in you bluntly stating that only having included female interviewees is one of the limitations of your research, if this was something that you yourself had explicitly chosen to do from the outset. Reading something like this would probably invite a comment from the marker such as, 'So why didn't you think about this earlier and include some males in your sampling?'

Bona fide limitations tend to be things that are *genuinely* beyond your control, but which nonetheless may have had an impact on the reliability or validity of your research.

8.4.6 Some Closing Reminders

Before I close this chapter, it is worth highlighting a couple of final reminders. As I hope will now be evident, producing a successful Methodology chapter *first* requires you to be clear on why you have made the methodological choices that you have and, *second*, requires you to be able to write about those processes succinctly and with authority and clarity. This means that you must:

- *Own your topic in methodological terms*. Make principled decisions and ones which you know you can later justify. Nothing should ever have just happened by chance.
- *Put yourself into your reader's shoes*. Keep asking yourself if an outsider would be able to follow what you are trying to say.

I am acutely aware that this chapter has barely scratched the surface of all the different possible approaches to quantitative and qualitative research design. It is very important, therefore, that you read up on some of these areas in more detail. The most effective way to do this is to consult work which has been produced by those who are acknowledged experts in specific methodologies. The edited text below by Brian Paltridge and Aek Phakiti has an absolute wealth of information in this regard and is a truly excellent starting point:

Paltridge, B. & Phakiti, A. (Eds.) (2015). *Research Methods in Applied Linguistics. A Practical Resource*. Bloomsbury.

Further resources have been listed on pages 208–210.

> **Suggested Answers to Independent Tasks**
>
> **Task 8.1a**
>
> a. Where you present your findings. **[Chapter 4: Results]**
> b. Where you list all the works you have cited. **[References]**
> c. Where you give thanks to all the different people who have helped and supported you. **[Acknowledgements]**
> d. Where you discuss what other researchers have written about your topic and how your own work fits into this. **[Chapter 2: Literature Review]**
> e. Where you provide a brief overview of the entire dissertation. **[Abstract]**
> f. Where you consider the wider implications of your findings and what they might mean for the field; where you make any recommendations. **[Chapter 6: Conclusion]**

g. Where you explain what your dissertation will be about, why you chose this topic, what your specific research questions are and why they are worthy of investigation. **[Chapter 1: Introduction]**
h. Where you include documentation such as a copy of your ethics approval form or samples of your data analysis. **[Appendices]**
i. Where you discuss and provide a rationale for the particular ontological paradigms and research methodologies you have chosen; where you describe the specific procedures you have followed. **[Chapter 3: Methodology]**
j. Where you critically evaluate your findings; where you consider how your findings compare with what other researchers have found. **[Chapter 5: Discussion]**

Task 8.1b

a. Bell (2022) has argued that discussions of methodology and pedagogy remain significantly under-represented within the pages of JEAP. **[Chapter 2: Literature Review]**
b. The question of practitioner identity and status in EAP has therefore become an important issue for the field and is worthy of more detailed investigation. **[Chapter 1: Introduction]**
c. Each interviewee agreed that their entry to TESOL had been almost entirely unplanned and was largely serendipitous. **[Chapter 4: Results]**
d. I decided from the outset that a qualitative approach would best serve my needs. **[Chapter 3: Methodology]**
e. Based on my findings from this research, it seems clear that more attention needs to be paid to raising novice teachers' awareness of their pedagogic values and beliefs. A closer focus on this could very easily be built into existing pre-service training programmes. **[Chapter 6: Conclusion]**
f. Writing this dissertation has not been easy for me and would not have been possible without the help and support of various people behind the scenes. **[Acknowledgements]**
g. Although it might seem from their initial responses that the first three teachers did not see much value in their pre-service training, a finding supported by Chan (2017) and Wu (2021), it later transpired that their views on this were in fact much less clear-cut. Two of the teachers – 'Jenny' and 'Freda' – went on to praise the guidance they

had received from mentors. **[Chapter 4: Results; possibly also Chapter 5: Discussion]**
h. My abiding interest in conversation analysis is thus grounded in both academic and practical concerns, and has served as a catalyst for this present study. **[Chapter 1: Introduction]**
i. Bell, D.E. (2022). Methodology in EAP: Why is it largely still an overlooked issue? *Journal of English for Academic Purposes*, 55, 101073. **[References]**
j. Gerunds represented the most frequently used grammatical form (n = 42) closely followed by instances of the Simple Past tense (n = 36). **[Chapter 4: Results]**
k. As Lowton (2020) points out, although it has undoubtedly achieved a great deal for UK EAP, BALEAP still has several blind spots. Earlier authors (notably Ding & Bruce, 2017) have also been very critical of BALEAP's shortcomings. **[Chapter 2: Literature Review; possibly also Chapter 5: Discussion]**
l. One clear recommendation is that schools should invest in more technical training for their staff. **[Chapter 6: Conclusion]**
m. Detailed below is a sample of the participant consent form. **[Appendices]**

Task 8.1c

CHAPTER 1: Introduction

1.1 A Personal & Professional Journey
1.2 My Research Questions
1.3 The Role of Qualifications in TESOL & EAP
1.4 Structure of this Dissertation

INTRODUCTION

In this opening chapter, my intention is to set the wider context for my research, explain why I believe my chosen topic is worthy of investigation and provide readers with an overview of the specific questions I am expecting this dissertation to engage with.

The chapter begins by charting my personal transition from teaching General English to teaching EAP and discusses the important role that professional qualifications have played in this. As I intend to show, the development of qualifications in EAP has lagged far behind other areas of TESOL. It is my contention that this has several important ramifications for the continued development of EAP as an academic discipline.

The remainder of the chapter seeks to provide a structural preview of the dissertation as a whole.

****

1.1 A Personal & Professional Journey

Task 8.2a

CHAPTER 1: INTRODUCTION

1.1 A Personal Career Journey
1.2 My Specific Research Questions
1.3 The Nature of This Research
1.4 Dissertation Overview

The main purpose of this opening chapter is to set the professional context for my research, and to explain my reasoning behind the particular questions which this dissertation attempts to answer.

I begin by describing aspects of my career journey to date, and reflect on how these have influenced and guided my current thinking, particularly with regard to those areas of English for Academic Purposes (EAP) which I believe warrant further investigation.

I then outline the specific questions which this dissertation will address, and situate the significance of these within the wider context of EAP today.

I close the chapter by describing the nature of my research in more detail, and then provide a brief overview of what will be covered in each of the chapters which follow.

Task 8.2b

i. One of the rhetorical purposes of Chapter 1 is to explain why you chose your topic and why it is worthy of investigation. **[T]**
ii. Another rhetorical purpose of Chapter 1 is to explain your results. **[F]**
iii. Providing an overview of your topic in Chapter 1 is not necessary because you already did this in the abstract. **[F]**

iv. Chapter 1 should be written using the Simple Past tense throughout to reflect that your research has been completed. **[F]**
v. Signposting language is especially important in Chapter 1 because you are introducing the reader to your dissertation. **[T]**

Task 8.3a

The Literature Review would probably include:
An Overview of the Concept of Needs Analysis
(its historical development; the different ways in which needs have been conceptualised; different approaches to needs analysis; the way in which stakeholder perspectives may differ)
An Overview of How EMI Has Developed Globally
(its historical development; the specific challenges)
Literature on the Growth of EMI in China
(different challenges faced by students; how institutions have tried to address these challenges and the support mechanisms that have been put in place)

Task 8.3b

CHAPTER 2: Literature Review

The main aim of this chapter is to provide a critical survey of what the academic literature has identified as being key considerations around needs analysis and the concept of English Medium Instruction (EMI).

The chapter begins by discussing the emergence of needs analysis in the 1970s. It then charts some of the different milestones in needs analysis historical development since that early period up until the present day. As part of this discussion, the chapter also considers how needs may in fact be conceived of quite differently, depending on the specific perspectives of particular stakeholders.

The next section of the chapter turns its attention to English Medium Instruction (EMI) and considers how and why this form of academic delivery has emerged, along with some critical discussion of the specific challenges it has faced.

The final section of the chapter looks at EMI's development in the specific context of China and discusses the challenges that Chinese learners have typically encountered, some of the different things that institutions have done to address these and the specific support mechanisms which have been put in place.

Task 8.4a

The Methodology chapter should include:

A re-statement of what your specific research questions are.

Some discussion of your wider research paradigm and why this was chosen over others, e.g., did you take a positivist or interpretivist stance? Is your research qualitative, quantitative or mixed methods?

Some discussion of the specifics of your methodological approach, e.g., if you chose to carry out interviews, what kind of interviews were they? Why were these deemed appropriate? How did you choose the people in your sample? What criteria influenced those decisions?

Some discussion of how you analysed your data, e.g., an account of any coding procedures or statistical tools which were applied. Why these were deemed appropriate.

Some discussion of any ethical issues you had to consider, e.g., how you protected your research participants; how you accounted for any bias.

Some discussion of any limitations (this could also appear in the Conclusion chapter).

A *brief* discussion of what you yourself have learned from the methodological process (reflexivity).

Task 8.4b

i. The researcher could set up two student control groups. Both groups are then asked to read the same texts but one group is explicitly pre-taught vocabulary before they read while the other is not. The same measure(s) of comprehension checking would then be applied to each group. For example, students might be asked to complete a series of post-reading multiple choice questions to check how much of the text they could understand. The researcher would then measure the results to see if there was any appreciable difference between the different groups. This would primarily be taking a quantitative approach.

ii. The researcher could identify a group of EAP teachers and survey them using questionnaires, interviews or both (focus groups could also be an option here) to gather their opinions on classroom observation. Ideally, the researcher would want to target different categories of EAP teacher, e.g., those with little experience, those with middle-range experience and those with extensive experience, to see if there were any differences of opinion depending on the teachers' background. This research would primarily be qualitative in nature.

iii. The researcher could gather together an extensive corpus of academic abstracts from a representative spread of different disciplines. These could then be analysed using a concordance tool to identify any differences in the move structure. This research would be quantitative in nature.

Task 8.4c

i. If the research participants are personally known to the researcher, then there is always an inherent danger of some bias creeping into the data. Respondents might give the answers that they think the researcher most wants to hear. As the researcher is an 'insider', they might also react differently to how they ordinarily would if they were being interviewed by someone from the outside.

ii. The potential ethical issue here is very similar to the point described above with the added dimension of an unequal power distribution. If a lecturer chooses his/her own students for research, the students might worry even more about their answers. They might feel that if they are honest in their feedback, it would be judged negatively against them.

iii. Any research with minors would first require informed consent from parents and/or other care providers. Taking a video recording of young children is also potentially problematic in this case, as there are safeguarding issues to be considered around how the data would be stored and used. Who would have access? Why and for what purpose? How would the identity of the participants be adequately protected?

iv. This example overlaps with the potential ethical issues already discussed under (i) and (ii). There is also an added dimension in that full consent would first need to be sought from the institution/relevant gatekeepers in other Faculties. The research participants are also highly likely to have concerns about keeping their identity private and not allowing themselves to be identified in case of any institutional repercussions.

v. In most cases, there would be no need for participants to be identified by their real name. An exception, however, could be if the identification of the respondents was an important part of the research design. In the case of my own PhD work, for example, I expressly chose to interview famous people from the world of EAP/ELT and wanted to have them publicly go on record with their views, because they had played an important personal role in one or more aspects of EAP's historical development. In this case, there was a clear rationale for naming people but of course the individuals themselves had to give their full consent and were aware that their names would be used. In the case of my own research, anonymity was still offered as an option, but only two out of my 15 interviewees chose to take it. If researchers decide to use real names when publishing their research, then extra special care needs to be taken over how that data will be stored and later used.

Additional Resources for Further Reading

Paltridge, B. & Phakiti, A. (2015). *Research Methods in Applied Linguistics*. Bloomsbury.

Woodrow, L. (2020). *Doing a Master's Dissertation in TESOL and Applied Linguistics*. Routledge.

Chapter References

Alwright, D. (1996). Social and pedagogic pressures in the language classroom: The role of socialisation. In H. Coleman (Ed) *Society and the Language Classroom*. Cambridge University Press.

Anthony, L. (2018). *Introducing English for Specific Purposes*. Routledge.

Barber, C.L. (1962). Some measurable characteristics of modern scientific prose. Reprinted in J.M. Swales (1985) (Ed.) *Episodes in ESP* (pp. 3–14). Pergamon.

Belcher, D.D. (2006). English for Specific Purposes: teaching for perceived needs and imagined futures in the worlds of work, study and everyday life. *TESOL Quarterly*, 40(1), 133–156.

Bell, D.E. (2003). Academic & socio-cultural adjustment difficulties of Chinese international students in Britain. Unpublished Masters diss., University of Central Lancashire.

Bell, D.E. (2022). Methodology in EAP: Why is it largely still an overlooked issue? *Journal of English for Academic Purposes*, 55. https://doi.org/10.1016/j.jeap.2021.101073.

Berger, P.L. and Luckmann, T. (1966). *The Social Construction of Reality*. Doubleday.

Berry, J.W. (1997). Immigration, Acculturation and Adaptation. *Applied Psychology: an International Review*, 46, 5–34.

Berry, J.W. & Annis, R.C. (1974). Acculturative Stress. *Journal of Cross-cultural Psychology, 5,* 382–406.
Berry, J.W. & Kim, U. (1988). Acculturation and mental health. In P. Dasen, J.W. Berry & N. Sartorius (Eds.) *Health and Cross-cultural Psychology.* Sage.
Brinkman, S. & Kvale, S. (2015). *Interviews. Learning the Craft of Qualitative Research Interviewing.* (3rd ed.) Sage Publications.
Charmaz, K. (2006). *Constructing Grounded Theory.* Sage.
Furnham, A. & Bochner, S. (1982). Social difficulty in a foreign culture: An empirical analysis of culture shock. In S. Bochner (Ed.) *Cultures in Contact: Studies in Cross-cultural Interaction.* Pergamon.
Garfinkel, H. (1967). *Studies in Ethnomethodology.* Prentice Hall.
Giorgi, A. (1975). An application of phenomenological method in psychology. In A. Giorgi, C. Fischer and E. Murray (Eds.) *Duquesne Studies in Phenomenological Psychology* (Vol. 2, pp. 82–103). Duquesne University Press.
Glaser, B.G. & Strauss, A.M. (1967). *The Discovery of Grounded Theory: Strategies for Qualitative Research.* Aldine.
Harding, J. (2013). *Qualitative Data Analysis from Start to Finish.* Sage.
Hutchinson, T. & Waters, A. (1987) *English for Specific Purposes. A Learning-Centred Approach.* Cambridge University Press.
Hyland, K. (2006). English for specific purposes: Some influences and impacts. In J. Cummins & C. Davison (Eds.) *International Handbook of English Language Teaching* (pp. 379–390). Springer International Handbooks.
Lazarus, R.S. (1997). Acculturation Isn't Everything. *Applied Psychology: An International Review, 46,* 39–43.
Leong, F.T.L. & Chou, E.L. (1996). Counselling international students. In P.B. Pedersen, J.G. Draguns, W.J. Lonner & J.E. Trimble (Eds.), *Counselling Across Cultures* (4th ed.) Sage.
Lowton, R. (2020). The (T)EAP of the iceberg: The role of qualifications in teaching English for academic purposes. MA TESOL diss., University of Nottingham Ningbo China.
Ma, H. (2001). *How Do Chinese Business English Students Acculturate in the UK?* Unpublished Masters Dissertation. University of Central Lancashire.
Maxwell, G., Adam, M., Pooran, J. & Scott, B. (2000). Cultural diversity in learning: Developing effective learning for South East Asian hospitality management students. *Cross Cultural Management- An International Journal, 7,* 3–12.
Meder, B., De Meyer, I., Zhang, H., Lodge, M., Pitcher, J., Galloway, D., Matthews, W. & Tay, R. (1998). Voices of Asian Youth. www.ccc.govt.na/Reports/1998/VoicesofAsianYouth
Piontkowski, U., Florack, A., Hoekler, P. & Obdrzalek, P. (2000). Predicting acculturation attitudes of dominant and non-dominant groups. *International Journal of Intercultural Relations, 24,* 1–26.
Pruitt, F.J. (1978). The adaptation of African students to American society. *International Journal of Intercultural Relations, 2,* 90–118.
Ryan, M.E. & Twibell, R.S. (2000). Concerns, values, stress, coping, health and educational outcomes of college students who studied abroad. *International Journal of Intercultural Relations, 24,* 409–435.
Saldaňa, J. (2016). *The Coding Manual for Qualitative Researchers* (3rd ed.). Sage.
Schönpflug, U. (1997). Acculturation: Adaptation or development? *Applied Psychology: An International Review, 46,* 52–55.

Schram, J.L. & Lauver, P.J. (1988). Alienation in international students. *Journal of College Student Development, 29,* 146–150.

Seidman, I. (2013). *Interviewing as Qualitative Research.* Fourth Edition. Teachers College Press.

Tarafodi, R.W. & Smith, A.J. (2001). Individualism-collectivism and depressive sensitivity to life events: The case of Malaysian Sojourners. *International Journal of Intercultural Relations, 25,* 73-88.

Toyokawa, T. & Toyokawa, N. (2002). Extracurricular activities and the adjustment of Asian international students: A study of Japanese students. *International Journal of Intercultural Relations, 26,* 363–379.

Ward, C. (1996). Acculturation. In D. Landis & R. Bhagat (Eds.) *Handbook of Intercultural Training.* Sage.

Ward, C. & Kennedy, A. (1992). Locus of control, mood distrurbance and social difficulty during cross-cultural transitions. *International Journal of Intercultural Relations, 16,* 175–194.

Ward, C. & Kennedy, A. (1993). Psychological and socio-cultural adjustment during cross-cultural transitions: A comparison of secondary students at home and abroad. *International Journal of Psychology, 28,* 129–147.

Ward, C. & Kennedy, A. (1994). Acculturation strategies, psychological adjustment and socio-cultural competence during cross-cultural transitions. *International Journal of Intercultural Relations, 18,* 329–343.

Weidong, C. (1996). The language activities of some Chinese postgraduate students and visiting scholars in Britain. *Language Problems and Language Planning, 20,* 39–41.

9 Writing Up Your Dissertation Part II

Introduction

This penultimate chapter of this book turns its attention to writing up the final three parts of your dissertation: the Results, Discussion and Conclusion chapters. After examining some different approaches to each of these, the chapter returns to consider the dissertation as a whole and looks at issues such as how to craft an effective Abstract and Acknowledgements section, which documents should be included in the Appendices, and finally, how the completed dissertation should be most effectively formatted and presented. This chapter then closes with a detailed checklist of the specific issues you should be paying attention to when you proofread your work before submission.

Additional resources for your further reading are listed on page 243.

9.1 Writing Chapter 4: Results

As discussed in Chapter 8, I almost always advise my students to keep Chapters 4 and 5 of their dissertations distinct from one another, as from my experience as an MA supervisor and course director, I find that this then helps them to keep the writing more tightly focused on how each of those chapters should differ in terms of their underlying rhetorical structure and purpose. However, your own institution/supervisor might have a very different view on this practice, so as always, if you are in any doubt, it is best to seek local advice. All of that being said let me now examine some of the different aspects of how to approach the writing up of Chapter 4 in more detail.

As the name suggests, the main focus of Chapter 4 should be on sharing your results, sometimes also called your research findings. However, this is not necessarily as straightforward as it first might sound. For one thing, the *manner* in which your results should be presented is likely to differ depending on whether your research was quantitative, qualitative or mixed methods in nature. For another, the process of presenting your results involves the application of some criticality and is not just a matter of you idly

DOI: 10.4324/9781003269854-9

212 *Writing Up Your Dissertation Part II*

copying and pasting a succession of tables or interview transcripts: presenting your results effectively will *always* involve a certain degree of principled selection, careful structuring and critical synthesis.

As I have advised for every other chapter so far in the dissertation, Chapter 4 should open with a brief introduction to signpost for the reader, as clearly as possible, what the ensuing rhetorical structure and content of the chapter will be. An illustrative example of this is provided below:

CHAPTER 4: Results

Introduction

This chapter aims to present the main results of my research. Grouped and categorised school by school, in the sub-sections which follow, I will report on the responses teachers gave when asked to share their values and beliefs about approaches to teaching grammar. These findings will be presented under five specific headings:

i) Early Influences on Teaching Style
ii) The Role of Pre-Service Training
iii) The Role of In-Service Training
iv) Communities of Practice
v) Continuing Professional Development

As a cross-reference, the specific interview questions which each of these areas relate to are listed in the table below. For the purposes of further cross-referencing, a complete list of the interview questions has been included in the Appendices.

In terms of the temporal positioning of this chapter, note that after a broad opening statement in the Present tense, i.e., 'This chapter aims to present the main results of my research', the writer then switches to the Future Tense, i.e., 'I *will* report on...', 'These findings *will* be presented...'. Note also the inclusion of forward signposting in referencing a material which has been included in the Appendices, in this case, a complete list of the interview questions.

As I suggested earlier, it should be clear from the above that in deciding how to present these results, there has been a process of principled critical synthesis. The writer doesn't just blandly list every individual teacher's response to every individual interview question, he has instead evidently distilled what he thinks are the most important points and then tried to categorise them under appropriate headings. He also says that he will make it clear for the reader which interview questions he has matched against his chosen categories. All of this shows an awareness of how to structure research data for the readers' ease of understanding. A very common weakness I find when reading some of my own students' dissertations is that they often *neglect* to do this and simply present all of their results in a raw and uncritical state. As I have argued above, good presentation of results needs to be much more principled than this. I will be returning to look at the presentation of the results from this particular example in more detail in Sub-section 9.1.2.

9.1.1 *Presenting Quantitative Results*

When presenting their results based on a quantitative analysis, dissertation writers will typically tabulate aspects of the hard quantitative data they gathered as their supporting evidence.

Look at an example of how this might operate in the sample writing excerpt shown in the box below. The results in this case refer to a small-scale corpus analysis of how certain types of hedging devices are used in Applied Linguistics journal abstracts:

As I discussed in the previous chapter, the main aim of this study has been to carry out an investigation of academic hedging using a corpus of 30 different abstracts sampled from three journals in Applied Linguistics (10 abstracts randomly selected from each journal) for the year 2020.

Drawing on the specific typology of hedges proposed by Hyland (1998), I have used the freeware concordance tool AntConc 3.5.7 (Anthony, 2018) to chart the occurrence of hedging devices in relation to three specific categories: epistemic verbs, epistemic adjectives and epistemic adverbs.

The top 10 results under each of these categories are listed in Table 4.1:

Table 4.1 Comparison of the Top 10 Epistemic Verbs, Adjectives and Adverbs

Epistemic Verbs	Count	Epistemic Adj	Count	Epistemic Adv	Count
Raw frequency	125	Raw frequency	89	Raw frequency	137
Suggest	30	Theoretical	22	Significantly	30
Seem	22	Significant	20	Slightly	26
Indicate	18	Possible	14	Highly	23
Appear	16	Potential	12	Widely	19
Feel	12	Large	7	Probably	17
Tend to	10	Small	7	Primarily	9
Conclude	8	Little	2	Frequently	5
Claim	5	Common	2	Often	4
Predict	3	General	2	Closely	2
Think	1	Slight	1	Likely	2

> As this table shows, epistemic adverbs appeared as a hedging device with the greatest overall frequency (n = 137), followed by epistemic verbs (n = 125) and then epistemic adjectives (n = 89).
>
> Under epistemic adverbs, the lexical token 'significantly' was used by writers with the greatest frequency (n = 30), appearing in each of the abstracts sampled. This can be contrasted with writers' usage of the epistemic verb 'suggest' (n = 30) which also appeared in every abstract.

The main points to draw your attention here are how the writer clearly indicates the size of his sample (30 randomly selected abstracts) and then explains how the linguistic data were sorted and categorised. The contents of the table are then closely referenced, with the writer drawing explicit attention to the frequency data for epistemic adverbs, verbs and adjectives.

One common weakness that I find in many of my own students' dissertations when they carry out quantitative research is that their Results chapters can simply become a bewildering array of different numbers and tables. If you are going to present quantitative data, then remember that you must always 'unpack' it sufficiently and explain to the reader what everything means.

Check Your Understanding: Independent Task 9.1a

If your research belongs to the quantitative paradigm, then you will need to become familiar with a range of statistical tools and concepts used for measuring reliability and validity.

Write a short definition for each of the following:

i. Cronbach alpha coefficient
ii. t-Tests
iii. ANOVA (Analysis of Variance)
iv. Null hypothesis
v. Likert scale questionnaires
vi. Cohen's kappa
vii. MANOVA (Multivariate Analysis of Variance)
viii. Normal distribution
ix. Factor analysis
x. Chi-square test

A suggested answer to this task has been provided on page 241.

9.1.2 Presenting Qualitative Results

When presenting qualitative results, dissertation writers will also need to support their claims by drawing on detailed examples from their raw data, but now of course, it follows that such data will be qualitative in nature. This means that there will not be much, if indeed any, reference to the mechanisms for measuring statistical validity which I have discussed in the previous section. The data that are presented now are much more likely to be based on the presentation of text rather than numbers. In practice, this operates on very similar principles to those that govern effective academic writing in general, as I discussed in Chapter 5, whereby writers often provide evidence for their claims by including direct supporting quotations from the academic literature. The only difference here, of course, is that rather than you using quotations from others' research findings as your supporting evidence, this time you will be using quotations from your own. An illustrative example of how this might operate is provided for you in the box below. This material links back to the qualitative study of teachers' values and beliefs regarding pedagogic approaches to teaching grammar which I first shared under Section 9.1:

---

i) **Early Influences on Teaching Style**

When they were asked to comment on any early experiences which they felt had been formative in influencing their pedagogic values and beliefs, several of the teachers from Number 1 Middle School made mention of inspirational teachers they had encountered when they themselves were students:

> For the first year in High School I absolutely hated English, but then we got a new teacher – Miss Chang. I think it's fair to say that she has influenced me a lot. She taught us that learning a language should be about more than just passing an exam; it should be a tool for real-life communication. Until I met her, I think I'd approached English grammar kind of like maths, you know, just rote-learning formulas. Miss Chang made me realize that there should actually be a lot more to it than that. Language users have choices and different grammar can be used to convey different meanings. This is something I learned from her and something I now try to pass on to my own students.
>
> [JULIA]

> My first headmaster doubled up as an English teacher and he taught me all the way through Primary School. I think he's the one who first kindled my interest in foreign languages. I'd say he was quite rare for people of that time, in that he'd travelled quite extensively outside of China and could speak English well. He also knew some German and Russian and he used to tell us stories about the different cities he'd visited and the interesting people he'd met. When I think back, he was definitely an important influence on my later choice of career. We all wanted to grow up and be someone like him.
>
> [SIMON]
>
> I think I was very lucky because our school had been designated as what they termed an 'Experimental School'. This was a project where certain schools in the province were trialling the teaching of some subjects in English – I guess it was an early form of CLIL. Anyway, one of the outcomes of this special designation was that we got some foreign teachers in the school and they worked in tandem with the local Chinese. I was first taught Elementary Science in English by a guy from the UK. He'd already worked in China for many years – I think his wife was Chinese – but he was a great role-model to us for language learning. He showed us that English was a tool for *real* learning, not just something you did to pass an exam. This definitely changed my whole attitude to English, there's no question about it.
>
> [SANDRA]

There are various points of interest here. First of all, you should note how more than one teacher's views have been presented. The writer opened with the claim that *several* of the teachers he had interviewed had made mention of inspirational individuals from their past. In order to substantiate this claim, it follows that there then needs to be supporting evidence from *several* sources. It would look very odd, and would weaken the argument considerably, if the writer had only quoted an interview response from one teacher. It is often claimed in books on research methodology that when compared to quantitative data, qualitative data are especially 'thick' or 'rich', but of course this very much depends on what data exactly are being presented. If you have been able to gather very detailed responses from your interviewees, then the data you can draw on will indeed be very rich; if you have settled for just one-word answers to your interview questions, then it will be much less so. Do always try to keep this point in mind when you are carrying out qualitative research. When it comes to writing up your results, the richness of what you will be able to pull out will be

Writing Up Your Dissertation Part II 217

entirely dependent on the richness of what your research participants were first able to put in.

Another thing worth paying attention to in the example above is the temporal positioning of the data itself – note that the results are presented using the Simple Past tense, i.e., 'When they were asked to comment.... several of the teachers made mention of....'. When you are writing up your Results chapter, do bear in mind that you are reporting on events *which have already taken place*, so this needs to be very clearly reflected in your choice of verb tenses.

A final point worth noting in this example is the fact that the writer directly identifies exactly where his data have come from. He makes it clear that these quotes represent the views of three particular teachers at the Number 1 Middle School. The teachers have all been named (using pseudonyms of course) and it is therefore very easy for the reader to see who exactly said what. Close referencing of this nature makes the presentation of the results easier to follow and in so doing it also serves to give the work as a whole much greater academic credibility.

Check Your Understanding: Independent Task 9.1b

Some detailed excerpts from qualitative interview discussions with four teachers at the Number 1 Middle School (a fictional location and study) are listed below.

Use this material to write a paragraph in which you present results under the second sub-heading:

ii) The Role of Pre-Service Training.

> If I'm honest, I don't think my pre-service training had much of an impact on me at all. This is partly because of the way in which the training itself was presented, but also because I didn't have enough of a contextual peg at that time myself for things to really make sense. I mean, we learned all the different theories on language acquisition – you know, the usual stuff like behaviourism, cognitivism, social constructivism or whatever – but there was never any effort made to link any of this with what we would later experience in the classroom. I mean, I learned all of Krashen's hypotheses as if they were hard facts *[laughs]* but there was no attempt to map them onto what I would face with a class of 40 young learners.
>
> [VIVIAN]

> I'm probably a bit older than some of the other people you've been talking to here, so I think you have to remember that back when I was first thinking of becoming a teacher, high quality pre-service

training didn't really exist; not in the way that it does now anyway. I did English for my undergraduate degree and I think there was this assumption that just studying that subject would make you ready to be an English teacher *[laughs]*. There was no focus on classroom pedagogy or anything like that. We just learned who the main movers and shakers had been and what they had said about language learning. We certainly weren't taught to question those theories, think about how they might fit into our own worldview, or even consider whether or not they would work in China.

[BILL]

My pre-service training was almost non-existent. I used to go to lectures once or twice a week as part of my UG degree, but we weren't asked to think about what any of it meant or whether we believed in it. We just took notes on various 'facts', learned it by heart and then answered questions in the end of year exam. I don't think any of this had any great impact on what I now believe as a teacher. All of that came much later, after I'd got some experience.

[SANDRA]

Pre-service training? What's that? *[laughs]*. My university invited some teachers from one of the High Schools we were supposedly going to do an internship at to come and give us a series of talks, but it was a waste of time. I only went to the first lecture. It was so boring, I just skipped all the rest. We got a copy of the textbook they were using and the message was basically, 'All you need to do is follow this'. I don't think I learned anything at all.

[LISA]

A suggested answer to this task has been provided on page 242.

Before I close this section on the presentation of qualitative results, a couple more points are worth making. Firstly, you must always be careful to ensure that the results you present are a good match with the questions you were trying to answer. This applies not only in the sense of answers to the specific questions which you asked in your interviews, but also with regard to your wider research questions. I sometimes find with my own students' work that by the time they reach Chapter 4, it is as if they have forgotten what their dissertation had originally set out to answer. The way this issue most typically manifests itself can be seen in the presentation of data in which the links between the topic under investigation and the results which were ultimately gathered seem to lack any sense of coherence. If I use the dissertation above as an example of what I mean by this, when carrying out his interviews, the researcher's opening set of questions might well have explored how long the research participants had been teachers and what motivated them to make that career choice in the first place. This is all potentially useful *background* information which could later be critically evaluated as one of the variables for comparison in Chapter 5. However, there would be little point in providing a detailed overview of such data in Chapter 4, as it clearly bears no direct relevance to the dissertation's central research question, i.e., how do High School teachers construct their pedagogic values and beliefs about the teaching of grammar? When you are writing up the Results chapter, you must remain vigilant about issues like this and not fall into the trap of straying too far off topic. When sharing your findings in Chapter 4, always keep checking that there is still a clearly discernible relationship between the results you present and the broader research questions your dissertation was attempting to answer.

A second and closely related point to this is that there also needs to be a credible balance in the relative *weighting* of all the different results that you present. This becomes especially important if you have chosen a mixed-methods approach to your research and are drawing on both quantitative and qualitative findings. Again, providing a direct example may perhaps best illustrate the point I am trying to make. I sometimes come across student dissertations, for instance, in which the writers say they have employed *both* questionnaires and interviews as part of their data gathering. A prototype presentation of this nature might then have writers claiming that questionnaires were distributed to hundreds of participants followed by a series of qualitative interviews for purposes of data triangulation and to assist with the overall validity and reliability. So far, so good. However, such a claim would then fall flat on its face and lose all academic credibility, if it transpired that only one or two interviews had in fact been carried out. The lack of balance here should be glaringly obvious, but in recent years, I have seen enough such cases appearing in student dissertations to convince me that the point here evidently needs to be driven home:

If you decide to use more than one method of data collection, then make sure that both the *way* you do this and *also the results you later present* are adequately balanced. If you have decided to use both questionnaires and interviews, or interviews and classroom observations, then when you are presenting your results in Chapter 4, there needs to be a credible and well-balanced spread of the different data sets gathered from each.

As all of these issues clearly also have important ramifications for the data analysis, let me now switch focus and consider some of the things you will need to keep in mind when writing up the Discussion chapter.

9.2 Writing Chapter 5: Discussion

The first point which must be stressed when you are writing up your Discussion chapter, as I have repeatedly emphasised, is for you not to forget that there is quite a big difference in its rhetorical purpose. Whatever else you end up doing with it, Chapter 5 should definitely not just become a repeat of what you did in Chapter 4. Unfortunately though, from my experience of reading and marking hundreds and hundreds of student dissertations, more often than not, this is in fact exactly what typically *does* happen and lots of marks are needlessly lost as a result.

While Chapter 4 is all about the *sharing* of results, Chapter 5 is principally concerned with a critical discussion of what those results might *signify*. In other words, when you are writing up Chapter 5, you need to be looking below the surface of your findings and carrying out a critical analysis. The process of doing this will involve you in looking across your data set and doing some critical comparing and contrasting; you will also be checking to see if there are any emerging patterns or trends and then evaluating the wider significance of these. As I discussed in the previous section, the exact way you go about doing this is likely to differ somewhat depending on whether your chosen research paradigm was quantitative, qualitative or mixed methods, but in each of these cases, you will nevertheless always still be trying to see how your research results fit into the bigger academic picture. In this regard, links will often start to emerge between the points you raise in the Discussion chapter and the issues which you covered in the Literature Review. When you are writing up Chapter 5, it can be worth making such connections explicit. Your own research findings may well support or contradict what other investigators have found, for example, and as its name would suggest, Chapter 5 is of course the ideal place for detailed discussions of this nature to take place.

As I have suggested for each of the dissertation chapters so far, Chapter 5 should open with a brief introduction to signpost which content will be focused on. As I have already provided several examples of how such introductory signposting works, I will refrain from doing so again now. Instead, let us jump ahead and look at a short representative sample of some analytic writing which might appear a little later in the main Chapter 5 body. Once again, I will be using the example topic about the different factors which can influence teachers' values and beliefs in their pedagogic approaches to teaching grammar:

> When examining and coding the interview responses, several key themes became apparent to me. In their own way, it was clear that each of these had played an important role in forging my interviewees' attitudes and beliefs, both towards English Language Teaching

in general and their pedagogic approaches to grammar in particular. These will now be discussed in detail under the following sub-headings:

  i. The Influence of Early-Stage Individuals
 ii. Zeitgeist
iii. Demo Lessons & Regional Competitions
 iv. The Ethos of Different Institutions
  v. The Influence of Outsiders

5.1.1 The Influence of Early-Stage Individuals

A point which received frequent mention by respondents from across each of the three schools I surveyed was the influence of certain individuals at early stages in their development. These individuals ranged from homeroom teachers to school principals but what each of them had in common was their ability to motivate and inspire students:

> My first headmaster doubled up as an English teacher and he taught me all the way through Primary School... he's the one who first kindled my interest in foreign languages... he was definitely an important influence on my later choice of career. We all wanted to grow up and be someone like him.
> [SIMON]

> Miss Chang....influenced me a lot. She taught us that learning a language should be about more than just passing an exam; it should be a tool for real-life communication... This is something I learned from her and something I now try to pass on to my own students.
> [JULIA]

> I was lucky to be taught by Mr Wang – he was recognised as being the best English teacher in our school. He brought the subject alive. In his classes, grammar was never something to be afraid of...
> [TONY]

As discussed in Chapter 2, the importance of early role models in helping teachers to form their values and beliefs has been extensively flagged in the international academic literature (e.g., Izadinia, 2015; Pennington, 2015; Trent, 2013). It is worth noting that irrespective of the cultural context, the key ingredient here seems to be the ability

> for such role models to make their students see English as being about much more than just exams. As my interviewee Tony commented on his teacher Mr Wang, 'he brought the subject alive'. The dynamism of key individuals and their ability to help students personalise their learning are themes I will be returning to when I consider the influence of outsiders.
>
> Another key feature of early role models is …..

Several things are worth drawing your attention to in this sample excerpt. First of all, note how the key points which will be discussed have been clearly signposted for the reader using sub-headings. Note also how the writer continues to provide support for his claims by quoting directly from the raw interview data. However, unlike in Chapter 4, these results are then linked with some of the earlier points from Chapter 2 and are subjected to a more critical analysis. In identifying that a key ingredient of all role models appears to be their ability to raise English to a higher status than that of just an examination subject, the writer is going beyond mere description and is providing evidence of some critical analysis and reflection. This is the very essence of Chapter 5 and is what makes it rhetorically different from the style of writing found in Chapter 4. If we were to extend this example above, as evidenced by the statement 'Another key feature…', we could expect to see some further elaboration on the influence of early-stage individuals before the discussion switches to consider the role played by Zeitgeist and then the remaining three categories. As I have already stated, the Discussion chapter should represent some 3,000+ words of writing. In the case of this example, this would mean that in order to do them justice, each of the named sub-sections would need to be allocated around 500–600 words of critical discussion.

As suggested in Section 9.1.2, the Discussion chapter is the time when you will be looking critically at your results and considering the role which might be played by different variables. In the writing sample above, when discussing the issue of Zeitgeist, the writer might have looked at the responses from different categories of participants and concluded that different historical time periods had exerted their own specific influences. When interviewing the older teachers, for example, he might have noticed a particular pattern in their responses and then used this to draw a connection between their pedagogic approaches and the specific methodologies which were prevalent at that time. This could then be compared and contrasted with the responses from the younger teachers he had surveyed, who may have been exposed to completely different ideologies. The key point to take away from each of these examples is that when discussing your results, you will always need to look across your entire data set and consider *why* different answers may have been generated by different categories of respondents. Providing your readers with ample evidence of critical reflection of this nature lies at the very heart of Chapter 5.

9.3 Writing Chapter 6: Conclusion

Chapter 6 is the final chapter of your dissertation and the one in which everything needs to be pulled together and appropriately rounded off. Like Chapter 1, the Introduction, Chapter 6 is not particularly long. If you are writing your dissertation based on the 15k target word count I have suggested in this book, then Chapter 6 should usually represent around 1,000–1,100 words. As with all the other chapters, however, your Conclusion chapter is still expected to follow certain rhetorical conventions. It is worth us now considering what these are.

As I have advised throughout this book, Chapter 6 should first begin with some structural signposting, so that the readers know what to expect. Most typically, Conclusion chapters will then progress to include an explicit focus on the following:

- A brief summary of what the dissertation set out to accomplish
- Confirmation that the research questions were addressed and answered
- Some acknowledgement of the dissertation's strengths and limitations
- Recommendations for future action

9.3.1 A Note on Summarising

As I have indicated above, Conclusion chapters typically include a *brief* summary of what the dissertation has set out to accomplish and also provide some confirmation that the research questions have been adequately addressed and answered.

In the case of the summary, the operative word here is brief. A very common weakness that I find in many of the MA student dissertations I screen each year is that their Conclusion chapters can simply become a descriptive and highly tedious rehashing of all the things they have already explained. You should definitely try to avoid this. There is no need for you to provide a lengthy blow-by-blow narrative of absolutely everything you did and found. Such detail should have already been more than adequately covered in the preceding chapters. The main purpose of your summary is simply to reaffirm what you set out to investigate *as a contextual precursor to what you will then subsequently recommend*. The summary section itself can usually be captured in a few sentences, a concise paragraph or two at the very most. Look at an example of how such a summary and confirmation of the research context operates in the writing sample below:

> This dissertation has investigated some of the academic and socio-cultural adjustment difficulties non-native English speaker (NNES) students face when they carry out postgraduate taught studies in an English Medium of Instruction (EMI) environment. Framed as a small-scale qualitative case study of one specific EMI institution based in China, my research has sought answers to the following questions:
>
> - What academic and socio-cultural challenges do postgraduate NNES students encounter when joining an EMI institution for the first time? Are there any factors which can exacerbate or alleviate these challenges?
> - What coping strategies do NNES students typically employ and how aware are they of doing so?
> - What forms of academic and socio-cultural support for NNES are provided by the institution?
>
> As I hope to have shown from my discussions in the preceding chapters, there can be little doubt that NNES students do typically encounter some significant challenges when they join an EMI institution. In academic terms, these can range from the linguistic challenges caused by the heavy daily demands placed on NNES by speaking, listening, reading and writing in English through to a more general unfamiliarity with different academic expectations and the role in Western academia played by critical thinking. From a socio-cultural standpoint, the challenges can include a significant reduction in confidence and well-being, accompanied by a pervading sense of identity loss. Across both the academic and socio-cultural domains, my research findings suggest that the overall severity of the experience can be significantly lessened by factors such as the extent to which students are able to form peer support groups, whether they or their families have previously spent any time overseas and whether friendships can be made with native English speaker students (NES).

As I have already commented in my discussions around other dissertation chapters, writers must pay careful attention to the temporal aspect of how their work is presented. As it is describing a body of research which has already been completed, note that any summary which appears in the Conclusion chapter should typically be written from a Present Perfect tense perspective, i.e., 'This dissertation has investigated....'; 'My research has sought answers to…'; 'As I hope to have shown…'. However, when the writing moves to discuss the research findings, the choice of verb tense will then switch to the Simple Present tense, i.e., 'My research findings suggest that…'

9.3.2 Acknowledging Strengths and Limitations

As I briefly touched on in Chapter 8, some mention of your dissertation's strengths and limitations might conceivably appear in your Methodology chapter. However, it is also quite common to see a dedicated section on limitations appearing as part of the Conclusion. When discussing limitations, as I have already commented, a key thing to keep in mind is that you should only be drawing attention to *genuine* limitations; there is very little point in you making claims which are going to sound artificial or contrived. Doing so will only create a negative impression and your work will lose marks. If you have put adequate thought into your choice of research paradigm and the sampling of participants and have already provided a credible justification for these, then there should be no need to draw attention to things which were well within your control as a researcher. If you honestly felt that such points were serious impediments to the credibility and quality of your research, then you should have addressed them from the beginning. You will gain very little credit from the tutors marking your work in commenting on such pseudo-limitations. Conversely, you will not impress anyone very much either if you try to make grandiose claims about the strengths of your work but then these turn out to be either not very credible in academic terms or inadequately substantiated. When you identify and discuss the strengths and weaknesses of your work, you always need to put some careful thought into the claims that you make. Look at an example of how this might operate in the sample below:

5.3 Strengths & Limitations

As outlined in my introductory chapter, to date, the difficulties faced by non-native English speaker students in adjusting to EMI environments in their home countries have received relatively little attention in the academic literature. This has been particularly true of China, which is rather surprising given the significant expansion of EMI provision there in recent years. I would therefore posit that a primary strength of this research is that it has at least attempted to deal with this gap in the literature.

As discussed in Chapter 3, I believe another strength has been my specific choice of research methodology. Of the existing studies to

226 *Writing Up Your Dissertation Part II*

> date, most appear to have taken large-scale quantitative approaches to their data gathering. This has certainly resulted in some impressive statistics, but I would personally argue that if we are to *really* understand how non-native English speaker students feel, then we need to 'get inside their heads' and try to more deeply understand their lived-in experiences. I see the qualitative approaches I have taken in this dissertation as representing an honest attempt to do just that.
>
> However, I must also acknowledge, of course, that from some perspectives, the smaller scale nature of qualitative research can simultaneously be seen as a weakness and a limitation. Based, as they are, on a case study carried out at just one EMI institution, my research findings are clearly not going to be representative of the challenges every student in China faces when they encounter EMI and, as such, they cannot be generalised. The same study carried out at a different institution might well generate a completely contradictory set of results and of course this must always be kept in mind.
>
> A related and further limitation I must acknowledge in this regard is the fact that my research participants were all personal contacts. As I explained in Chapter 3, although I took all reasonable steps to reduce bias, I must recognise nonetheless that a certain degree of subjectivity in this study is perhaps unavoidable. My research participants were my former classmates after all and some of the challenges they recounted were already known to me personally. In this sense, I am unable to claim complete neutrality in my reportage of their experiences and must acknowledge that even at a subconscious level, my own subjective judgements are likely to have been creeping in.
>
> Such limitations notwithstanding, this dissertation does represent a genuine attempt to engage with a currently under-represented topic and I believe my research findings have highlighted several areas which require more detailed attention. I will therefore be making some specific recommendations for action on these in the following sub-section.

Note how the writer opens by justifying the choice of research topic and pointing out that the dissertation has attempted to fill a recognisable gap in the literature. Cross-referencing this claim with the comments in an earlier chapter makes it more plausible and strengthens its academic credibility. Note also the repeated justification for the choice of research methodology and how the research in this dissertation differs from previous studies. This is also a plausible claim and provides evidence of some critical awareness.

The limitations which the writer identifies here are broadly credible, although if a marker wanted to nit-pick about the choice of research participants, then the use of personal contacts might justifiably be challenged as one particular dimension of this research methodology which could have been avoided. For a Masters-level dissertation, however, I think most examiners would be unlikely to place too much negative emphasis on this. The fact that the researcher has shown some awareness of the issue as a potential limitation and has formally named it as such should be enough.

A final point worth noting here is how the writer closes the strengths and limitations discussion by signalling that this will lead to a section on specific recommendations. Logical structuring of this nature helps with the rhetorical flow and also adds to the overall sense of credibility.

9.3.3 Recommendations for Future Action

This section will arguably take up the largest portion of your Conclusion chapter. As I have already discussed, Chapter 4 should present the results of your research, Chapter 5 should then discuss what you think those results mean and evaluate their wider significance when they are contrasted with the work of others, but Chapter 6 should be taking a more global and pragmatic perspective, considering what your research findings mean for the field as a whole and what actions should now be taken as a consequence.

When you present and discuss such recommended actions though, do make sure that you provide sufficient depth and critical detail for them to be credible and taken seriously. A common problem I find in some of my own MA students' writing is that their concluding recommendations can often come across as being over-simplistic and unnecessarily trite. In the sample dissertation dealing with academic and socio-cultural adjustment difficulties of non-native English speaker students, for example, it would be far too basic if the closing recommendation was simply that universities need to do more to help. At best, writing something like this would be construed as stating the obvious. In order to have any gravitas and credibility, recommendations need to include significantly more detail than this and be much more critical in their scope. In this case, instead of just saying that universities should do more to help, the writer would instead need to be exploring what exactly such help might constitute, how it might be implemented and how any barriers to its implementation could be overcome. All of this would allow for a much 'meatier' discussion. In showing some critical awareness of such finer details, the writer would be heightening the overall sense of credibility. When you make your final recommendations, always take full ownership of what you are saying and demonstrate that you have adequately thought things through.

A related point worth drawing your attention to here is that there is no need for you to include a default statement that 'more research on this topic is needed' unless you can demonstrate in some detail that this is genuinely the case. As with my earlier comment on the danger of including contrived limitations, a weakness that I often come across in students' work is the automatic claim that further research is necessary. In my experience, such claims tend to be overused to the point that they cease to have any real meaning. If you *genuinely* think that your chosen research topic would benefit from further study, then you should aim to provide sufficient supporting detail to make such a claim plausible.

A final point to make on the writing up of Chapter 6 is that as with any piece of extended academic prose, your writing should not just appear to run out of steam and suddenly stop. The same as when you conclude an academic essay, you will need to find a way of tying everything together so that your work builds momentum and reaches a suitable ending. As I have suggested in the structural overview listed under Section 9.3, this is one of the reasons why I advise my students to discuss any limitations of their research *before* they make their final recommendations, as doing so allows them to end their dissertation on an upbeat note. Clearly, you do not want your final sentences of the dissertation to be emphasising weaknesses and recommending that further research is needed, as this will only serve to weaken your credibility and detract from the readers' overall impression. When you close your dissertation, do try to keep this point in mind. The Conclusion chapter is the culmination of many months of hard work after all, so you should try to build on this in the gravity and academic credibility of your ending.

Two sample closing sections from MA TESOL dissertations have been provided for your reference below. In each case, pay attention to how the writers have:

- Summed up in a few words what their dissertations had focused on
- Closed with specific recommendations

TOPIC: Academic & Socio-Cultural Adjustment Difficulties of NNES Students in EMI Environments: A Case Study

As I hope to have shown, the significant rise in EMI provision necessitates a closer look at the academic and socio-cultural difficulties faced by non-native English speaker students. While there can be no easy answers to the problems such students face across these domains, from my own perspective, institutions hoping to increase their student retention rates and raise their international rankings would be well-advised to monitor their support mechanisms and keep their eyes very firmly on the student satisfaction ball.

> TOPIC: Are Mainstream UK TESOL Qualifications Fit for Purpose in EAP?
> This dissertation has critically evaluated the suitability of mainstream UK TESOL qualifications in preparing teachers for the delivery of classes in EAP. I have argued that while such TESOL qualifications evidently play a role in developing generic ELT pedagogic abilities and raising teachers' awareness of classroom management, much more explicit attention needs to be paid to the specific knowledge and skills required in EAP contexts. As a means of achieving this, I have suggested three possible mechanisms: the creation of a universally recognised postgraduate qualification in TEAP to be managed and administered by BALEAP; the creation of a suite of postgraduate qualifications to be established by individual universities but then placed under the QAA oversight of the Higher Education Academy; or the addition of TEAP-specific pathways to all existing TESOL qualifications which candidates must then complete in order to be considered qualified in EAP. It remains to be seen if any of these recommendations will ever come to pass. However, at the very least, I hope that those in positions of leadership in EAP will begin to acknowledge that problems around qualifications exist and that some form of action does therefore need to be taken.

Check Your Understanding: Independent Task 9.3

Source a selection of different MA TESOL/Applied Linguistics dissertations (your School or Faculty office may have a repository of these, or you can search in the university library) and in each case, look critically at the sections in which the writers discuss their research strengths and limitations.

Based on the points that have been covered in this chapter, how well have they handled these aspects? Comment on any areas that you think might need some improvement.

9.4 Beginnings: Acknowledgements and Abstracts

Although it might seem a little odd for me to be discussing the *beginnings* of a dissertation in a section immediately following a discussion of the conclusion, the fact of the matter is that during the dissertation production process, although they will physically appear at the front, the Acknowledgements and Abstract sections are usually among the last things you will write. There are, of course, some very good reasons for this. Let us first consider the Abstract.

As discussed in Chapter 8, in terms of its rhetorical purpose, the Abstract is intended to provide readers with a brief overview of the dissertation as a whole. It would therefore be quite difficult for you to write this in its entirety before the dissertation had been completed. Ideally speaking, by the time you come to write your Abstract, you will be looking down on your dissertation as if from a bird's eye perspective. You will know which topic you chose to investigate, why this was relevant, the particular research questions you sought to answer and how you went about doing so, the specific results you obtained and what those results might be expected to mean when they are positioned within wider academic contexts.

One immediate consequence of the points outlined above is that Abstracts are expected to follow a particular style and rhetorical structure. From a genre analysis perspective, this means that they can be broken down into a series of different moves. Look at an example of how this might typically operate below:

	Abstract	
1	The role of qualifications in UK-based EAP is an area which has to date received relatively little attention from researchers. For the most part, EAP as a discipline has not yet established widely recognised qualifications of its own, but has instead chosen to rely on the more generic qualifications found in TESOL and Applied Linguistics. This state of affairs is problematic on several counts.	*Lines 1–3* **SETTING A CONTEXT** *Lines 3–8* **IDENTIFYING A PROBLEM**
5		
10	Drawing on qualitative data gathered from a series of semi-structured interviews with veteran EAP recruiters representing a cross-section of British universities, this study aims to present a much more auspicious account of the worth of EAP-specific qualifications to both EAP practitioners and the discipline as a whole.	*Lines 9–14* **DESCRIBING THE RESEARCH FOCUS & METHODOLOGICAL APPROACH**
15	The findings cast some doubt on the efficacy of General ELT qualifications for EAP and suggest a greatly enlarged role for EAP-specific qualifications	*Lines 15–21* **DETAILING FINDINGS**

20 24	as the discipline continues to move forward. While questions remain around the form such qualifications might take, and the most appropriate regulatory bodies for their accreditation, this study recommends the adoption of employment-based Masters' programmes as representing the best way forward for preparing EAP practitioners and raising EAP's symbolic capital.	*Lines 21–24* **MAKING RECOMMENDATIONS**

Abstract sample adapted with permission from Lowton, R. (2020). The (T)EAP of the iceberg: The role of qualifications in teaching English for academic purposes. Unpublished MA TESOL diss., University of Nottingham Ningbo China (UNNC).

In this particular example, there are five distinct moves which the Abstract follows. However, note that these moves themselves do not necessarily have to correspond with paragraphs and that it is perfectly possible to have different moves taking place within very close proximity of one another, as indeed is the case in this example with moves 1 and 2. Note also that some moves may be optional and can be present or not present depending on the nature of the study. Not *every* Abstract will necessarily include a Making Recommendations move, for example; in some dissertations, the Abstract will instead simply close with a more detailed unpacking of the findings. There are no absolute rights or wrongs with this – everything will depend on the nature of the research and the specific research questions which have been investigated. The example above is a useful starting point, however, and can be drawn upon as a general guiding framework for when you come to craft an Abstract of your own.

Check Your Understanding: Independent Task 9.4a

Look at the selection of different MA TESOL/Applied Linguistics dissertations you sourced for the previous Independent task. In each individual case, look at how the Abstract has been written.

Do the writers always follow the same five-move structure I have suggested here, or do they do anything different?

In contrast with the Abstract, the Acknowledgements section of a dissertation generally allows writers a much greater degree of personal freedom in what they want to say. This is not to suggest that absolutely anything goes, however, and as with other genres of writing, the Acknowledgements section usually also follows a fairly predictable rhetorical structure.

For most of us, producing a Masters' dissertation represents a significant academic and professional milestone. When writing the Acknowledgements section, it is therefore worth thinking carefully about all the different people who have helped and supported you along the way. This is your opportunity to say a public thank you, after all, and to signal your appreciation and gratitude. Look at the prototype Acknowledgements section below:

Acknowledgements

Writing this dissertation would not have been possible unless I had received the help and gracious support of several people 'behind the scenes'. First and foremost, I must give grateful thanks to my supervisor, Professor Jane Fisher. A tremendous source of personal inspiration, she has guided me at every stage of the research process and provided invaluable feedback on my various chapter drafts. I will remain forever in her debt.

I must also thank the many teachers and students who gave so freely of their time and agreed to be observed and interviewed. Without their open cooperation and trust, it is clear that this research project could never have been completed.

Finally, I wish to thank my loving husband John and our two children Sam and Kylie. Thank you for giving me the much needed time at evenings and weekends, and for always being there to cheer me up on the occasions when things were tough.

I hope this work will make you proud.

It should come as no great surprise that the student's supervisor is appearing first on the thank you list. If you have worked closely with your supervisor and received their detailed feedback and guidance on your work, then it is to be expected that you will make mention of this in your Acknowledgements.

It is also fairly standard practice to acknowledge your gratitude to the people who agreed to take part in your research. Without their help and cooperation, after all, the dissertation could never have got off the ground.

Most writers tend to close their Acknowledgements section with some mention of the more personal support they might have received from spouses, significant others, wider family members and friends. Writing a Masters' dissertation involves a huge commitment of time which might otherwise have been spent with loved ones, so it is both proper and courteous for you to acknowledge this.

As a final comment on the Acknowledgements section, something I have started to notice in the dissertations I have marked in recent years is a propensity for students to thank their pets. There is nothing necessarily wrong with this, and if you genuinely feel that your cat or dog has been a source of massive inspiration to you, then so be it. It does begin to look a little odd, however, to see students pledging their gratitude to a pet at the very top of the thank you list and then neglecting to make any mention of their supervisor, or their research participants. Most supervisors are not so thin-skinned that they will lie awake at night weeping if they are not acknowledged, but saying thank you to your pet kitten and then forgetting to express your gratitude to your supervisor is, at best, a violation of the expected conventions of the Acknowledgements genre and, at worst, simply rude. My own advice to students on this matter is to approach the Acknowledgements section of your dissertation as you would any other piece of important academic writing: take it seriously, always consider your audience and strive to present yourself well.

Check Your Understanding: Independent Task 9.4b

Drawing on the advice and examples which have been provided in this chapter, try to craft a dissertation Abstract and Acknowledgements section of your own.

9.5 Endings: Appendices

While the Abstract and Acknowledgements sections constitute an essential feature of dissertations and will *always* need to be present, the Appendices tend to be a rhetorically somewhat greyer area and there is usually a degree of flexibility when it comes to what should or should not be included. As with the stylistic differences I discussed when reporting results, the kinds of documents which might appear in the Appendices have a lot to do with whether the research was quantitative, qualitative or mixed methods in nature. In the case of highly quantitative research, Appendices often contain detailed tables, graphs and charts. On this point, however, some care needs to be taken in deciding what should be included in the main body of the dissertation and what is more appropriately put into the Appendices. If readers are forced to keep turning to the end of the dissertation to check key information, it will disrupt their concentration flow and make the dissertation as a whole significantly harder to follow. Researchers do, therefore, need to exercise some judgement over what results to include directly in the text and what to append. Some of this also comes down to my earlier point about the need for synthesis. As I have already explained, when you present your results, it is not simply a case of you cutting and pasting reams and reams of data; at all times, there needs to be some careful thought put into how your data can best be presented for easy comprehension.

If the research has been qualitative in nature, then the documents which would typically appear in the Appendices include lists of interview questions, sample transcripts and examples of how you carried out your coding. Again though, some care needs to be taken in how these documents are presented. There would be no need, for example, to include *full* interview transcripts, as this would likely run to tens of thousands of words and would cause you to exceed the dissertation word count. A short excerpt from one transcribed interview, however, would be perfectly acceptable and would provide your readers with a useful example of how the interview transcription as a whole had been carried out. The same goes for examples of coding procedures.

Beyond the methodology-specific documentation already mentioned, Appendices also usually include information which can be seen as common to *all* dissertations, irrespective of the favoured research paradigm. Examples of this type of paperwork include documentation such as ethics approvals, participant information sheets and participant consent forms. Including documentation of this nature serves to show the reader that you have followed the appropriate academic processes when carrying out your research. While you would be unlikely to *fail* your dissertation for not including documented proof that you had sought and successfully been granted research ethics approval, if such paperwork was absent, it would still very likely be something that the markers would pick up and comment on. This then might also result in you losing some marks. I therefore usually advise all my own students that *as a minimum*, their Appendices should always aim to include copies of signed ethics approvals, sample participant information sheets and sample participant consent forms. This at least then covers all the expected administrative bases and ticks the right logistical boxes.

If keeping within the overall dissertation word count is becoming an issue, it is also worth remembering that the documents included in the Appendices can always be inserted as JPEG files or screenshots. This can be especially useful when sharing textually dense documentation such as excerpts from interview transcripts, or when providing detailed examples of qualitative coding procedures.

Check Your Understanding: Independent Task 9.5

Based on the advice which has been provided in this chapter, decide whether statements (i) to (v) are True (T) or False (F):

i. It is good practice to include copies of your ethics approval, participant information sheet and participant consent form in the Appendices.

ii. If your research was qualitative, you should include full transcripts of all interviews in the Appendices.
iii. If your research was quantitative, there is no need for you to include anything in the Appendices.
iv. It can be helpful to include samples of any coding procedures in the Appendices.
v. You should include signed consent forms from *every* participant who took part in your research in the Appendices.

A suggested answer to this task has been provided on page 243.

9.6 Final Considerations

Once the entire dissertation has been written, you then have some important decisions to make about how its final form will be presented. This stage should not be underestimated, as sloppy presentation or poor attention to detail can significantly mar what might otherwise be judged as perfectly respectable work. There is a common saying in English that 'First impressions count' and this is certainly true when it comes to the reading and grading of Masters' dissertations. If your work creates a poor first impression, then there will very likely be a significant price to be paid when it comes to the award of your final mark. It is therefore really very important indeed to spend some time and effort in getting things right and to present your work in the most effective and attractive way possible.

Effective presentation of a dissertation begins by considering its visual layout and the writer's choice of fonts. As I commented in the previous chapter, modern word-processing software offers us a massive range of different font styles, but when it comes to presenting your dissertation, less is almost always more. Resist the temptation to go for fancy, flamboyant typefaces and instead choose a font type for your writing which is going to be easy on the readers' eye. Some fonts are clearly better than others in this regard and it is worth experimenting with a selection of different font styles until you find the one that you think looks the best. One way of doing this is to copy a random paragraph from your dissertation and then create a separate MS Word document in which you paste several versions of that paragraph using a different font each time. If you then put these different versions next to one another, it should be easy for you to see which font offers the greatest clarity and looks the most attractive. The *size* of the font is also an important consideration here and it is well worth comparing a few alternatives. In most cases, 12-point font is likely to be your go-to size for the text in the main dissertation body, but some fonts can look better when they are presented as 10-point, 11-point or even 13-point. The key thing here is to experiment until you find what you think is the best fit. Remember also to leave adequate spacing between the lines of your text. Look at an example of how this comparative selection process might operate in the box below:

Some Examples of Different Fonts and Sizes

Once the entire dissertation has been written, you then have some important decisions to make about how its final form will be presented. This stage should not be underestimated, as sloppy presentation or poor attention to detail can significantly mar what might otherwise be judged as perfectly respectable work. Choosing the correct font style and size for your dissertation is therefore an important consideration.

Bookman Old Style 10

Once the entire dissertation has been written, you then have some important decisions to make about how its final form will be presented. This stage should not be underestimated, as sloppy presentation or poor attention to detail can significantly mar what might otherwise be judged as perfectly respectable work. Choosing the correct font style and size for your dissertation is therefore an important consideration.

Times New Roman 11

Once the entire dissertation has been written, you then have some important decisions to make about how its final form will be presented. This stage should not be underestimated, as sloppy presentation or poor attention to detail can significantly mar what might otherwise be judged as perfectly respectable work. Choosing the correct font style and size for your dissertation is therefore an important consideration.

Calibri 12

Once the entire dissertation has been written, you then have some important decisions to make about how its final form will be presented. This stage should not be underestimated, as sloppy presentation or poor attention to detail can significantly mar what might otherwise be judged as perfectly respectable work. Choosing the correct font style and size for your dissertation is therefore an important consideration.

Candara 13

Once you have decided on which font style and size to use for the writing in the main dissertation body, you will need to reach a decision on how you will present the chapter headings, section headings and sub-headings. Once again, some care needs to be taken over this and you may well need to experiment with a few different styles until you find the one that you think looks the best. In the first instance, I advise my own students that all chapter headings should begin on a clean page and should be presented in a format and font size which stands out significantly from the main text. There would be very little point, for example, in you writing everything using the same font size. The reader should always be able to discern a clear difference between the chapter headings, the section headings and the sub-headings. Whichever style is chosen for this, the mode of presentation you follow should remain consistent throughout the entire dissertation.

An illustrative example of this principle being put into practice is provided below:

CHAPTER 1: Introduction
[Size 24 BOLD CAPITALS + bold sentence style]

In this opening chapter I outline blah blah blurbel blurbel waffle waffle blah blah blah [Size 12]

1.1 Reasons for Choosing This Topic [Size 15 bold sentence style]

Blurbel blurbel blah blah blah.....[Size 12]

1.1.1 The Rise of Translanguaging [Size 14 italics sentence style]

Blurbel blurbel blah blah blah.....[Size 12]

Note the very obvious difference in font sizes and stylistic formats between the chapter heading, the main text, the heading and the sub-heading. Note also the system of numbering. As I discussed in Chapter 4, a point worth mentioning here is that you should be careful not to overdo the use of headings and sub-headings, as this can make your work look too fragmented and bitty. I often see student dissertations which include sub-heading after sub-heading, which in turn results in them being forced to use very clumsy numbering (e.g., 1.1.1, 1.1.2, 1.1.3 followed by 1.1.1.1, 1.1.1.2 then 1.1.1.1a, 1.1.1.1b etc.). As a rule of thumb, I would suggest that this practice should be avoided. If you are thinking carefully about how to structure your work and going into sufficient detail on each point that you include, then it should not really be necessary for you to go beyond just one numbered category of sub-headings, such as the 1.1.1, 1.1.2, 1.1.3 format I have suggested above. My advice here is always to use headings and sub-headings both judiciously and sparingly. Try to ensure that each time you use a sub-heading, there are at least a couple of hundred words of text before you introduce the next one.

Beyond the effective use of headings and sub-headings, you will also need to develop some sensitivity for textual layout and the role of white space. This becomes especially important if you decide to include diagrams, graphs or tables in the body of your writing. I often see student work in which tables or other graphics have been crammed onto the page which usually then means that there is insufficient spacing left between the table boundary, the table descriptor and the main dissertation text. Try not to do this. Learn to use white space judiciously so that the text remains easy to read. By the same token, of course, don't end up going overboard on the white space, so that you are left with huge gaps. I often find myself reading student dissertations in which inexplicable blanks suddenly occur in the written text with paragraphs appearing fragmented and disconnected. Formatting glitches of this nature can very easily be avoided and if for some strange reason they are missed during the writing process, then they should certainly be picked up at the proofreading stage, more of which below. For now though, do simply try to keep in mind what I have said already about the importance of first impressions. If you are sloppy in the presentation of your work, then you will definitely lose marks and your final grade will come down accordingly. From my own perspective, there is absolutely no excuse for students throwing away marks so needlessly, but as an MA dissertation marker, I must also say that I never cease to be surprised by how frequently these fundamental issues occur.

Check Your Understanding: Independent Task 9.6

Create an appropriate layout for an opening chapter page of your dissertation based on the points that have been covered in this chapter.
   Make sure that you:

- Choose an appropriate font
- Use different font sizes for the chapter heading, section headings, sub-headings and main text
- Create an appropriate numbering system for all sub-headings
- Space everything out well

9.7 Proofreading

As I have stressed throughout this book, academic writing is a highly cyclical, recursive process which will involve you in a process of checking, polishing, re-writing and then checking again. Even the most successful writers go through this cycle and you should most certainly not expect to write something perfectly the first time; you <u>must</u> get yourself into the habit of constantly revising, pruning and refining.

Even when you have got your writing into what you think is a final acceptable state though, you will still need to read through everything at least two or three times more to PROOFREAD and make sure that you haven't missed anything. One of the problems which *all* writers face is that after working on the same piece of text over many drafts, they can effectively become blind to their own writing. This means that they stop noticing spelling mistakes, formatting glitches and other stylistic errors. To help offset such textual blindness, it can be a useful strategy to put your writing down for a day or two and then come back to it to proofread with 'fresh eyes' later. If you do this, you may well find that you suddenly start to notice things which you had previously missed. This is especially true if you are writing your dissertation with English as a foreign or second language. If this is you, then your proofreading task will become even more critical, as apart from needing to be vigilant about standard proofreading issues such as checking the general layout and formatting, you will also need to be on the lookout for any problems with grammar, academic style, spelling and choice of lexis.

A general checklist of some of the different things which *all* proofreaders should be looking for has been presented for you below:

1. Formatting and General Layout
    Check that
    - ❑ You have been consistent throughout in your choice of font types and font sizes
    - ❑ You have been consistent throughout in your spacing and there are no areas which look unnecessarily cramped, or which have inexplicable gaps
    - ❑ You have labelled all tables, charts and graphs appropriately
    - ❑ You have justified your text so that the right-hand margins all fall neatly into line
    - ❑ You have started each individual chapter of the dissertation on a clean page
    - ❑ You have included page numbers
    - ❑ You have included a cover page with the dissertation title, your name, student ID and final word count clearly stated
2. Structure and Overall Content
    Check that:
    - ❑ You have included an Acknowledgements section in which you give thanks and show due respect to all the people who have helped you

- ❏ You have included an Abstract in which you provide an overview of your dissertation as a whole
- ❏ You have included a Table of Contents and that the page numbers you have listed there do in fact match up with the actual numbers on each page
- ❏ You have included an Introduction, a Literature Review, a Methodology chapter, a Results chapter, a Discussion chapter, a Conclusion chapter, a References list and Appendices
- ❏ You have stated clearly what your research questions were and there is a clear match between what you say you were investigating and the results you have presented
- ❏ You have kept within the overall target word count
- ❏ You have also maintained an appropriate balance in the word count of each chapter
- ❏ You have included sample copies of any ethics approvals, participant information sheets and participant consent forms in the Appendices

3. Writing Style

   Check that:
   - ❏ You have been consistent in including a short introduction at the start of each chapter
   - ❏ You have used signposting language to help guide the reader and signal the direction of your writing throughout
   - ❏ You have used appropriate verb tenses and temporal positioning for each chapter
   - ❏ You have adequately supported all of your claims with hard evidence, either from the wider academic literature or from your own research data
   - ❏ You have avoided making unsubstantiated sweeping generalisations
   - ❏ You have drawn as far as possible on recent academic sources

4. Use of Language

   Check that:
   - ❏ You have used appropriate academic language throughout
   - ❏ You have spelled and cited all authors' names correctly
   - ❏ You have used your own words, paraphrased appropriately and not committed plagiarism
   - ❏ You have spelled all words correctly
   - ❏ You have used correct grammar and punctuation throughout
   - ❏ You have included publication dates and page numbers for all direct quotations
   - ❏ You have listed all the sources you cited in the dissertation body in the References list
   - ❏ You have formatted your References list appropriately following the required stylistic academic conventions, e.g., sources presented in ascending academic order with publication dates and authors'

names clearly listed; book titles in italics; exact page numbers listed for all journal articles and book chapters etc.

If, after carefully going through all of the above, your answer for each item on the checklist is an honest 'yes', then you can be confident that you have done all that you possibly could have done and that you are now in fact ready to submit your dissertation.

Some institutions require their students to submit both an electronic and a printed/bound hard copy of the dissertation. Check what the specific requirements are with your supervisor or course director and make sure that you follow their guidelines to the letter. When submitting your work as an electronic file, it can sometimes be a good idea to save MS Word documents as an rtf (rich text format) file type. This can help to prevent the document formatting from becoming mangled in electronic transit. This is especially true if you are using a foreign language version of MS software, which may or may not be fully compatible with the recognised institutional systems.

Unless you still have some outstanding pieces of work to complete as resubmissions for the taught modules, submitting your dissertation should represent the final furlough of your MA TESOL/Applied Linguistics academic journey. Assuming that your work is awarded a pass, your composite grade will be calculated and confirmed at a formal examination board and all being well, you will have successfully achieved the award of Masters.

Well done!

At this stage, once the initial euphoria wears off, the question then facing many students becomes 'What next?' As a newly minted MA TESOL/Applied Linguistics graduate, there will now be a range of options open to you. In the following and final chapter of this book, I will be considering what some of these might be and advising you on how best to take full advantage of them.

Suggested Answers to Independent Tasks

Task 9.1a

i. **Cronbach alpha coefficient** measures the internal consistency or reliability of a set of survey items. Cronbach's Alpha: Definition, Calculations & Example - Statistics By Jim

ii. **t-Tests** compare the mean scores of two samples An Introduction to t-Tests | Definitions, Formula and Examples (scribbr.com)

iii. **ANOVA (Analysis of Variance)** splits an observed variability within a data set into two parts: systematic factors and random factors. Analysis of Variance (ANOVA) Explanation, Formula, and Applications (investopedia.com)

iv. **Null hypothesis** refers to a theory based on insufficient evidence which requires further testing to prove whether the observed data are true or false. Null Hypothesis – Overview, How It Works, Example (corporatefinanceinstitute.com)
v. **Likert scale questionnaires** are questionnaires which have been designed using questions in which the possible answers need to be ranked on a numbered scale, typically representing a rating across five different points, e.g., 1 = NEVER; 2 = RARELY; 3 = SOMETIMES; 4 = OFTEN; 5 = ALWAYS Likert Scale Surveys—Definitions, Examples & How-tos | Typeform
vi. **Cohen's kappa** refers to a statistic used to measure the level of agreement between two raters or judges Cohen's Kappa Statistic: Definition & Example–Statology
vii. **MANOVA (Multivariate Analysis of Variance)** is an extension of ANOVA. MANOVA takes into account multiple continuous dependent variables MANOVA–Statistics Solutions
viii. **Normal distribution** is when many random variables are represented on a symmetrical Bell-shaped graph Normal Distribution | Examples, Formulas, & Uses (scribbr.com)
ix. **Factor analysis** is used to identify a small number of factors which can be used to represent relationships among sets of inter-related variables. Lesson 12: Factor Analysis | STAT 505 (psu.edu)
x. **Chi-square test** is a procedure for observing the difference between observed and expected data. Chi-Square (X^2) Tests | Types, Formula & Examples (scribbr.com)

Task 9.1b

> *ii) The Role of Pre-Service Training.*
>
> When they were asked about the role of pre-service training, the interviewees indicated that it had either not been in existence, or it had not been particularly useful:
>
> When I was first thinking of becoming a teacher, high-quality pre-service training didn't really exist; not in the way that it does now anyway [Bill]
>
> My pre-service training was almost non-existent [Sandra]

> Pre-service training? What's that?... I don't think I learned anything at all [Lisa]
>
> I don't think my pre-service training had much of an impact on me at all.... [Vivian]
>
> As in interviewee Vivian's case, when pre-service training *was* available, part of the reason for it not being especially useful was because it was presented to the participants when they were insufficiently prepared for it to make much sense. As Vivian explained, 'I didn't have enough of a contextual peg at that time myself for things to really make sense'. Closely allied to this, a related problem was that the participants were not encouraged to think critically about the input they received or make links between theory and practice. As Bill explained, 'We certainly weren't taught to question those theories, think about how they might fit into our own worldview, or even consider whether or not they would even work in China'. This was echoed by Sandra, 'I used to go to lectures once or twice a week... but we weren't asked to think about what any of it meant or whether we believed in it.... I don't think any of this had any great impact on what I now believe as a teacher'.
>
> From these comments, it seems clear that pre-service training did not play a very influential role in helping to form the participants' values and beliefs.

Task 9.5

i. True
ii. False
iii. False
iv. True
v. False

Additional Resources for Further Reading

Brown, J.D. (1991a). Statistics as a foreign language - Part 1: What to look for in reading statistical language studies. *TESOL Quarterly* 25(4), 569–586.

Brown, J.D. (1991b). Statistics as a foreign language - Part 2: More things to consider in reading statistical language studies. *TESOL Quarterly,* 26(4), 629–664.

Dörnyei, Z. (2007). *Research Methods in Applied Linguistics: Quantitative, Qualitative and Mixed Methodologies.* Oxford University Press.

Larson-Hall, J. (2010). *A Guide to Doing Statistics in Second Language Research Using SPSS*. Routledge.

Lowie, W. & Seton, B. (2013). *Essential Statistics for Applied Linguistics*. Palgrave Macmillan.

Paltridge, B. & Phakiti, A. (Eds.) (2015). *Research Methods in Applied Linguistics*. Bloomsbury.

Woodrow, L. (2014). *Writing about Quantitative Research in Applied Linguistics*. Palgrave Macmillan.

Woodrow, L. (2020). *Doing a Master's Dissertation in TESOL and Applied Linguistics*. Routledge.

Chapter References

Anthony, L. (2018). *Introducing English for Specific Purposes*. Routledge.

Hyland, K. (1998). *Hedging in Scientific Research Articles*. John Benjamins.

Izadinia, M. (2015). A closer look at the role of mentor teachers in shaping pre-service teachers' professional identity. *Teaching and Teacher Education*, 52, 1–10.

Lowton, R. (2020). The (T)EAP of the iceberg: The role of qualifications in teaching English for academic purposes. Unpublished MA TESOL diss., University of Nottingham Ningbo China.

Pennington, M. C. (2015). Teacher identity in TESOL: A frames perspective. In Y. L. Cheung, S. B. Said, K. Park (Eds.) *Teacher Identity and Development in Applied Linguistics: Current Trends and Perspectives* (pp. 16–30). Routledge.

Trent, J. (2013). From learner to teacher: practice, language, and identity in a teaching practicum. *Asia-Pacific Journal of Teacher Education*, 41(4), 426–440.

10 Life Beyond Your Masters

Introduction

This final chapter considers some of the different options that will be open to you after the successful completion of your Masters. My consideration of these options has been grouped under three broad headings: going on to further study, going back to work and engaging in continuing professional development. Following some detailed discussion on different aspects of each, this chapter closes with some general advice on how you can best avoid a few of the most common next step/career pitfalls.

Additional resources for your further reading are listed on page 266.

10.1 Going on to Further Study

Some students finish their Masters and feel sufficiently motivated and inspired by the journey to want to keep right on studying. For others, the experience of doing a Masters may have convinced them that further academic study would be the last thing on Earth they should ever consider.

If you belong to this second category, then you might want to skip ahead at this point and start reading again from Section 10.2. If you find yourself in the first category though and you are curious about the possibilities around further study, then the next three sub-sections are for you.

If you are seriously contemplating further study, then naturally the first question you will need to answer is what specific form that study should take. For most people, the next rung up on the academic ladder from a Masters is most typically a doctorate, although depending on their personal circumstances and professional profile, some may instead deliberately decide to choose other qualifications, as I will discuss in Sub-section 10.1.2.

If you are thinking of doing a doctorate, then you may be surprised to learn that nowadays there are in fact two quite different qualifications you could study towards: the traditional and probably most widely known Doctor of Philosophy, which carries the title of PhD, or the slightly less well-known Doctor of Education, also sometimes known as a professional

DOI: 10.4324/9781003269854-10

doctorate, which carries the title of EdD. Each of these qualifications will be discussed in more detail in the following sub-sections.

10.1.1 Doing a PhD or an EdD

Lots of my Masters' students over the years have expressed an interest in doing a PhD. Surprisingly few of them though have had much of an idea of what doing a PhD actually entails, so it is worth me saying a little here about what the process involves and how you should go about approaching it.

When students tell me that they want to do a PhD, my first question back is always, 'Why?' Doing a PhD will take up *at least* four years of your life, for some people significantly longer, so it is important to be clear from the outset what your motivations are. If you have absolutely no intention of working in academia, then I would definitely query your purpose and ask you to articulate how exactly you think a PhD will be useful. While it is true that some people choose to follow a doctorate purely out of personal interest, or for the vanity of later being able to call themselves 'Dr', for most, doctoral study usually represents the gateway to a career as an academic. I will approach the remainder of this discussion from that perspective and with that kind of person in mind.

Perhaps the first point to be made aware of is that unlike Masters' programmes, PhDs do not usually have any required taught components. This means that rather than being told exactly what and when you should study, you will have complete academic freedom to explore topics of your own devising. In many ways this can be both a blessing and a curse. The freedom to focus on a research area that you yourself are genuinely interested in is, of course, absolutely wonderful and something to be treasured, but it also means that you will need to be highly disciplined about managing your time and making sure that your studies stay on track.

In this regard, coming up with a viable PhD topic in the first place often seems to be the biggest challenge for most of my students. Putting yourself through a process similar to what I outlined in Chapter 7 (see pages 141–144) when I was sharing my advice on how to choose a suitable MA dissertation topic can be helpful here, as many of the same principles will apply. The bottom line though is to try to choose an area in which you are genuinely interested and want to learn more.

Once you have an idea of your topic and the research questions you would like to answer, the next stage is to turn this into a formal proposal. Some institutions provide their applicants with templates for doing this, but many leave the process wide open and you will need to be able to devise an appropriately structured doctoral research proposal all by yourself. Space now precludes a detailed discussion of how exactly you should go about doing this, but there are lots of resources you can draw on for help. Several such texts are listed for your reference on page 266.

While you are busy drawing up your formal research proposal, you also need to be thinking about where you want to study and who you might like to have as your supervisor. Supervision at the PhD level is essentially just a larger and longer-scale version of what happens at Masters, albeit with the very important difference that this time, you yourself will have much more agency over who your supervisor is likely to be. When you are researching your PhD topic, therefore, you should always be on the lookout for potential supervisors. As part of your wider academic reading, you will undoubtedly come across the names of various academics, that have been research active in your chosen area, and these will probably form the first entries on your potential supervisor shortlist. Choosing to do your PhD under the guidance of someone that is already a recognised expert in your field obviously makes a lot of sense and most people do generally try to go down that route. This means that before you formally submit a PhD proposal to a given institution, it makes good strategic sense to get in touch with the person(s) you think might make a good supervisor. This does not have to be an elaborately worded affair, a politely worded email will usually suffice, but as with any kind of application, do pay due diligence to what you are doing and make sure that what you are writing makes sense. I get requests for PhD supervision almost on a daily basis, but some of them instantly end up falling into the junk mail category. There is clearly very little point, for example, in you writing to a professor and saying that you share their research interests and would like to work with them as a doctoral student, then going on to talk about a research topic which has absolutely nothing to do with that professor's area of professional expertise. Such poorly thought out approaches will do you no favours whatsoever and will probably just result in your immediate rejection, so my advice in this regard would be to think carefully before you decide to contact anyone.

Assuming that you have been able to put together a well-crafted proposal and have identified a suitable supervisor who is amenable to working with you, then the next step is to make your formal application. Institutions tend to have different entry points when it comes to doctoral study, so once again, you will need to do your homework and check all the deadlines and make sure that you are clear on what paperwork is required from you. This becomes especially important if you are thinking of applying for a scholarship, as beyond the submission of your formal proposal, you will probably also be required to supply transcripts of your Masters' grades and letters of support from several referees.

Once your application has been formally accepted and your supervisor(s) confirmed, your doctoral journey can then begin. Most Western institutions offering doctorates operate on a system of primary and secondary supervision. This means that you will be assigned a Primary Supervisor, who will be your main point of contact, and also a Secondary Supervisor, who more typically gets involved in things later, often serving as a second pair of eyes when you actually start to produce your writing. As soon as your PhD registration has been formally confirmed, you will usually be invited to a preliminary meeting with your Primary Supervisor. This will be to discuss your research proposal in more detail and essentially get you started on your PhD. In the first year of doctoral study, the main emphasis tends to be on refining your research questions, drafting your proposed methodology and completing a comprehensive literature review. Your supervisor(s) will be on hand to guide you through this process, but as I have commented above, you yourself will always need to be highly disciplined about managing your time, ensuring that individual milestones are achieved and that everything stays on track.

At the end of your first year, you will typically be required to go through what is known as CoRS (Confirmation of Research Status). This entails the submission of an extended piece of writing usually around 10–15k words in length in which you can show the progress you have made. Following the submission of your CoRS paper, you will then take part in a mini viva (an oral examination) with an internal examiner, who will judge the overall quality of your work and then make a decision on whether or not you are fit to continue with your studies. Most students manage to pass their CoRS viva with the recommendation to make minor revisions and continue, but a small number sadly do end up falling by the wayside at this stage and are advised that the work they have produced does not meet doctoral standards. As with the writing of your Masters' dissertation, preparation and good time management here will be key factors. As soon as your PhD registration begins, you need to be aware that the clock is now ticking and therefore start working towards the submission of your CoRS paper. Your supervisor(s) will be there to guide you with this, but as I have already commented, you will be expected to take your own agency.

All of the things I have said above can also be applied to studying for an EdD, but with a few important differences. The first big difference is that unlike a traditional PhD, an EdD qualification is usually a mix of coursework and research. This means that on a four-year full-time programme, the first two years will be spent attending classes and doing coursework assignments and it is only during the final two years when you will be engaging in your independent research. EdD students will still need to go through a CoRS process, although this usually takes place at the end of Year 2 or later, rather than Year 1.

Another important difference between PhDs and EdDs is the sheer scale of the final submission. PhD theses typically represent a total word count of around 80k, whereas EdDs are typically much shorter and fall in the 50–55k word range. A further difference here comes in the nature of the intellectual focus. As a principally academic enterprise, PhD theses may or may not have a practical element to them. EdD theses on the other hand tend to be more typically involved with real-world educational issues. This often makes them a more popular choice with teachers, who may choose to do an EdD thesis based around an aspect of their own classroom practice while continuing to work part-time.

When deciding which type of doctoral programme to choose, you need to be realistic about your personal context and profile. If you are confident about your research abilities, know exactly what you want to study and feel that you can manage an 80k thesis, then registering for a traditional PhD will probably be your best choice. If, on the other hand, you feel that you would prefer to go through a more scaffolded process and your research interests are more practice-based than theoretical, then you might be better suited to an EdD. That said, EdDs are generally still not as widely available as PhDs, so logistical factors might also play an important role. As ever, it pays to do your homework and ask around before making your final decision. Either qualification is recognised as a doctorate and will give you the academic title of 'Dr', so it largely just comes down to what you think will be the best fit with your personal circumstances.

10.1.2 Doing Other Qualifications

As I have mentioned above, not everybody goes on to further academic study in the form of a doctorate. After completing their Masters, depending on their personal circumstances, some students may decide to do a less-advanced qualification, either because they want to change career direction, or more commonly, because they want to do something that is more professional practice-based rather than purely academic in focus. Two particularly good examples of such practical qualifications are the Trinity College Diploma in English Language Teaching and the Cambridge Diploma in English Language Teaching to Adults (DELTA).

If you started your English Language Teaching career in the UK, or were based in a location which was following the British qualification system, then there is a good chance that you may well have completed either the Trinity College Diploma or the DELTA *before* you started your Masters. This would certainly be representative of the traditional British-style ELT career progression canon. Based on this career pathway, entry routes into English Language Teaching most typically start right after undergraduate study with the successful completion of a one-month intensive certificate course such as the Cambridge Certificate in English Language Teaching (CELTA) or its equivalent qualification offered by Trinity College. Such courses are seen as entry-level qualifications to the TESOL profession and usually involve at least 120 hours of classroom-based instruction, a considerable chunk of which represents observed and assessed classroom teaching practice. Although such courses have been subjected to quite a lot of criticism over the years (e.g., see Ferguson & Donno, 2003; Stanley & Murray, 2013) it must nevertheless be acknowledged that they do generally offer anyone interested in English Language Teaching a recognised career route into the profession. After completing a CELTA or Trinity College

Certificate, most newly minted teachers usually then go off to get their first teaching job. Traditionally speaking, for those geographically based in the UK anyway, this would most typically involve a one- or two-year stint of being based overseas, teaching English in either a state-run or private language school. Times and traditions continue to change, but if I go back some 35 years and look at the development of my own career in English Language Teaching, this was, broadly speaking, the route I followed myself. After graduating from my four-year undergraduate honours degree in Modern Languages and getting qualified in TEFL (Teaching English as a Foreign Language), my first proper full-time teaching job was as an English language foreign teaching assistant at a Junior High School in Japan.

Some teachers complete their CELTA or equivalent qualification, teach overseas for a few years, then decide that a career in ELT is in fact not for them. Others, however, decide to remain in the profession and want to get themselves better qualified, in which case the next rung up on the qualification ladder is most typically one of the Diplomas. By this stage, teachers are likely to have around three or more years' teaching experience (many Diploma course providers insist on a minimum of three years full-time experience from their applicants) and are typically looking to move up into a more senior role.

Core strengths of both the DELTA and Trinity College Diplomas are the very strong emphasis that each places on observed and assessed classroom teaching ability. Teachers who have successfully gone through these programmes are undoubtedly technically very competent in the classroom and it must be said that this is where such Diploma qualifications generally part company with Masters. Although *some* Masters' programmes in TESOL/Applied Linguistics may include a practical teaching component (see my discussion of this in Chapter 6), most around the world still do not, which means that their focus is therefore much more theoretical in nature. This means that although some students successfully complete a Masters, they may later come to realise that if they seriously want to continue in a teaching career, they will need to work on improving their practical classroom delivery. In this regard, if you do not yet have one under your belt already, deciding to do a DELTA or Trinity College Diploma can sometimes represent a smart post-Masters strategic career developmental move.

If I think of the MA TESOL and MA Applied Linguistics programmes in my current institution, both of which are generally quite happy to accept students without any formal teaching experience, everything else being equal, someone successfully graduating from either of these programmes might still find it quite difficult to secure a well-paid teaching position outside of China because their lack of practical teaching experience would generally count against them. If this sounds like you, then in situations like these, deciding to do a DELTA or Trinity College Diploma can serve to cover an important gap in your professional armour and will definitely open up much wider career possibilities. If you are geographically based in the UK, a variety of

Life Beyond Your Masters 251

nationwide organisations offer the DELTA or Trinity College Diploma, so by searching online, you should be able to find a course provider fairly easily. If you are based outside of the UK, professional organisations such as International House now routinely offer DELTA qualifications at different locations overseas, so it is definitely worth checking to see what the options are in your own country. For some, investing in a DELTA or Trinity College Diploma might thus represent a more practical and affordable option than immediately starting a PhD, and over the years, this is a path which several of my previous MA graduate students have indeed successfully followed.

Beyond internationally recognised qualifications such as the Trinity College Diploma and DELTA, there are, of course, several country-specific qualifications which you might decide to do after completing your Masters. This will largely depend on your future career plans. If you are hoping to find a teaching position in a specific educational sector, then your country may formally require you to complete a recognised local qualification before you can be considered to have reached Qualified Teacher Status.

Alternatively, of course, you may not be thinking of a career in teaching at all. I will therefore be considering the various other work-based options that an MA TESOL or MA Applied Linguistics can offer you in the sections and sub-sections which follow.

10.2 Going Back to Work

As with deciding whether or not to progress to further study, going back to work after completing an MA TESOL/Applied Linguistics is likely to differ considerably from person to person, depending on the vagaries of their individual circumstances. Some people may simply return to the same job that they were doing pre-MA; indeed, I have had quite a few students over the years whose employers had sponsored their Masters on the understanding that they would be returning to work at the same institution immediately afterwards. For others, as I briefly explored in Chapter 1, the motivation for doing an MA in the first place may have been to improve their overall employment prospects and secure a more senior or better paid position. In such cases, the post-MA world will now literally be at their fingertips and they may find themselves faced with a bewildering array of different possibilities.

Whatever the specifics of your personal circumstances, if you are returning to (or first properly joining) the workplace after completing your Masters, there are still a few things worth bearing in mind, so that you will be able to gain the best competitive advantage. These will be discussed under the following sub-sections.

10.2.1 *Updating Your CV*

The very first thing you must do after successfully completing your MA TESOL/Applied Linguistics is to acknowledge your newly qualified status by updating your CV. The most basic way of doing this is simply to add a line or two to the qualifications section in which you explain where and when your Masters was completed. However, as with most things in life, you have the choice here of doing this in a bland unremarkable manner, or of doing it in such a way which maximises the potential impact. Given that you have just spent what was no doubt an extremely challenging and stressful year or more working on your Masters, my own advice here would be to aim for the latter. Think very carefully, therefore, about what exactly your experience of postgraduate study entailed. How can you present this in the best possible light, and what specific details might you want to draw a potential employer's attention to? If you served as a representative on a staff-student liaison committee, for example, then clearly this would be something well worth mentioning. Similarly, what about some of those different taught modules that you completed? If you scored particularly highly in certain areas, this would certainly merit highlighting on your CV. And what about the finer details of your dissertation topic? These might also be worthy of sharing with a wider audience. If you were applying for a job and the recruiting manager turned out to share your interest in a specific area of TESOL/Applied Linguistics, then this could make all the difference between you being hired and rejected. In sum, my advice is that you should always try to *maximise* rather than *minimise* the potential employment benefits from having now successfully completed your Masters.

Bearing this point in mind, compare the two CV listings below and decide which one you think looks best:

SAMPLE 1
2021–2022   University of Newtown
             MA TESOL

SAMPLE 2
2021–2022   University of Newtown
             MA TESOL
             Awarded with Merit
             Distinction grades in:
             Principles of Course Design [78]
             Approaches to English for Specific Purposes [73]
             Materials Writing & Evaluation [73]
             My dissertation – 'Understanding Needs Analysis in EMI Contexts' – represented a case study of approaches to needs analysis at an EMI institution in China and achieved a pass with **High Merit** [68]

Hopefully it should be clear to you that Sample 2 is better. This is because it supplies more detail and presents the CV writer in a much more positive light. Job markets these days are becoming ever more competitive, so as I have suggested above, when you are preparing your CV, always think very carefully about how to most effectively highlight and promote your personal achievements.

Check Your Understanding: Independent Task 10.2a

If you have now completed your MA and know your different grades, update your CV based on the principles that have been covered above.

10.2.2 Jobs Using TESOL and Applied Linguistics

Having now worked in various aspects of English Language Teaching for most of my professional life, one thing which continues to keep me genuinely interested in TESOL and Applied Linguistics in general is the sheer breadth and diversity of opportunities in the field.

I do not know this for certain, as I have no personal experience of working in either of the following areas, but if you are employed as a bank manager or the director of a retail outlet, I suspect that your opportunities for career diversification are probably quite limited. You might have the chance to move location or company, but the day-to-day nuts and bolts of your job role are still quite likely to remain the same. This is expressly *not* the case in TESOL/Applied Linguistics, which offers its qualified practitioners a truly diverse spectrum of possibilities.

The Independent Task 10.2b below asks you to consider what some of these might be.

Check Your Understanding: Independent Task 10.2b

In the very first chapter of this book, we looked at the core skill area of mind-mapping and I suggested that this can be a very useful means of gathering key information and brainstorming.

Create a mind map which captures as many different career opportunities in TESOL/Applied Linguistics as you can think of.

HINT: do not just limit yourself to jobs involving teaching.

A suggested answer to this task has been provided on page 264.

10.2.3 The Traditional Job Search vs. the Creative Job Search

When most people think of getting a job, their approach tends to be highly traditional in nature. They simply wait for when suitable positions are advertised and then they try to apply for them. This is all perfectly fine, but keeping a few core principles in mind can make the process significantly smoother and ultimately more successful.

The first of these core principles is to be systematic and organised in your approaches. If you are actively looking for a job, then the more planning and organisation you can carry out in advance, the better. As I suggested in Section 10.2.1, for example, as soon as you know that you are going to be entering the job market, you need to make sure that you have an updated version of your CV ready to go. You also need to make sure that you have a well-crafted cover letter template, which outlines why you are interested in a given role, your main areas of expertise, your availability and finally your contact details.

As you go through the process of applying for different jobs, the content and ordering of both CVs and cover letters can – and I would personally argue should – be slightly tweaked, so that they better match the specific requirements of the post you are applying for. In the various management roles I have held in my career, recruitment has always been a key component and over the years, I have screened literally tens of thousands of applicants. Even if someone's experience and credentials look quite good, I would venture from my personal experience that it can be a significant turn off if it seems evident that the applicant has simply been 'stick-bombing' and that the same application materials have very clearly been sent out in exactly the same format many times before and to multiple recipients. On occasion, I have even received applications in which some of the key names, job titles and other important details are wrong and have remained entirely unchanged. Needless to say, such sloppy applications have gone straight into the rejection pile. Always remember that first impressions count and when you are applying for a job, that very first stage is in fact absolutely crucial. There is very little point in you being knocked out of the running simply because you were unable to craft an appropriate covering letter or get the name of the institution you are applying to right. Rather than sending out the same old material each time, take some time to craft your covering letters so that they always address the specific concerns of the job you have chosen. At the very least, this will show the recruiter that you have genuinely looked at their job advertisement and have thought carefully about what you are doing.

Another core principle I try to pass on to my students about their job applications is that they should also aim to be systematic in their record keeping. In other words, they should always know where they have applied and when, what the job was, who the contact person was, what the outcome was etc. To help me do this when I am applying for jobs myself, I usually create an Excel spreadsheet in which I can easily keep track of all such relevant details. If you learn to be similarly systematic in your approach, it will allow you to keep very close tabs on all your job hunting activity and this can be helpful. Over a period of time, you might notice from your records, for example, that the same institution has a very high staff turnover rate and constantly seems to be hiring. This may not be a very auspicious sign in terms of the working environment and you could then use such information to help inform whether or not you might see yourself working there. I will be discussing some other uses of spreadsheets as an integral part of the wider job search process under Section 10.2.5.

The traditional job search probably accounts for the largest sector of the job market. However, it would be a mistake to assume that this is the *only* way in which finding gainful employment operates. As a newly minted MA TESOL/Applied Linguistics graduate, there are also some rather more creative approaches you could try. These will now be considered below.

If you have an entrepreneurial mindset, it can sometimes be possible to generate jobs which have never been formally advertised. I like to term this, 'the creative job search'. In the case of TESOL, particularly in the domain of teaching English for Specific Purposes (ESP), it is perfectly possible for you to generate opportunities for yourself by doing a critical evaluation of where there might be some gaps in the market and then thinking of how you could best position yourself to fill them. To illustrate exactly what I mean by this, I will share a personal example.

Many years ago when I was based in the UK, the whole country was facing an acute shortage of qualified doctors and nurses. One outcome of this shortage was that the UK government at the time decided to draft in large numbers of medical personnel from overseas. As a result, hospitals suddenly saw an influx of doctors and nurses from parts of Europe and geographical locations even further afield such as Latin America. For example, my own city at that time experienced an upsurge in medical staff from Venezuela. The UK government's decision to solve the medical staffing crisis by drawing on qualified and experienced professionals from outside of Britain was, on the face of it, a reasonable enough idea, but there was one rather major flaw – it turned out that many of the incoming doctors and nurses had poor English skills and found it very difficult indeed to cope with the demands of practising medicine in their new English-only environments. Watching this situation develop as an outsider, given my professional expertise at the time in ESP and my particular interest in teaching English for Medical Purposes, it struck me that there might be some opportunities for creative job searching. In time, I duly set up a series of meetings with the staff of various hospitals in my region, presented myself as a freelance ESP training provider and as I had anticipated, before long, I had secured several classes of very highly motivated students. A few years later I went through a very similar experience when Britain was experiencing a nationwide catastrophe across its rural farming communities thanks to the outbreak of foot and mouth disease. By then I was already employed full-time in a university post, so my time for other work was limited, but just out of personal rather than financial interest, I still found myself doing some private ESP training with a small group of Spanish-speaking veterinary staff.

The lessons to be learned from these two examples will hopefully be clear. If you are prepared to think creatively, there is no reason why you should not be able to use your TESOL/Applied Linguistics skills to find well-paid freelance or independent consultancy work. As the world continues to become ever more international in its outlook, the opportunities for what I am terming creative job searching have expanded enormously and are continuing to do so. In my current location of China, for example, almost all of the international hotel chains require their staff to speak English in order to deal with overseas guests, but the reality is that there are actually very few formally provided training opportunities. For an entrepreneurially minded TESOL/Applied Linguistics professional, a situation like this represents a potentially lucrative and professionally fulfilling opportunity, and some of my previous graduates have gone on to establish language consultancy careers in such areas. Beyond the international hotels, hospitals, airports and private companies also represent potentially highly fruitful avenues for exploration and there are sure to be others worth investigating too. The underlying principle in each location remains the same, even if the specific contexts are different.

Check Your Understanding: Independent Task 10.2c

When I share my suggestions about creative job searching with my MA students, their most typical reaction is that they lack personal confidence and do not know how to 'break in' to such potential but largely hidden employment markets. These are valid concerns, so it is worth you also now critically reflecting on how you might get around such barriers.

If you wanted to set yourself up as freelance trainer or consultant, what are some of the different things you should do to break in? Should you just 'cold call' or are there more subtle and effective approaches you could take?

A suggested answer to this task has been provided on page 265.

10.2.4 *Working in the Higher Education Sector*

Many graduates in TESOL/Applied Linguistics will hope to find work in universities and colleges. As I discussed in Chapter 1, a common reason for doing a Masters in the first place is to open the door to better paid employment and it must be said that working in the Higher Education sector does often represent the top-end of jobs in English Language Teaching.

In the specific case of the UK, a common route into university-based teaching for TESOL/Applied Linguistics graduates is to apply for short-term employment on summer pre-sessional programmes. Most universities across the UK offer such programmes in English for Academic Purposes (EAP) and these can represent a very solid opportunity for people to cut their teeth on teaching in Higher Education while making good money and gaining valuable experience. The 'pre-sessional season' as I am fond of calling it typically runs from as early as April through to as late as October, with most of the work falling in the summer months of June, July and August. Institutions normally start hiring their pre-sessional teaching staff in the Spring and then recruitment typically continues throughout the summer months until all the posts have been filled. Registering your contact details with a typical UK higher educational recruitment website such as www.jobs.ac.uk will allow you to see exactly which institutions are hiring when. This now links back to the point I was making earlier about the effective use of spreadsheets. If you start your pre-sessional job search early in the Spring – say late February to March – and create a spreadsheet for yourself, this can then be populated with the details of all the different institutions as and when they start advertising, so that you can see at a glance who is offering what, the rates of pay and the different terms and conditions. Every institution tends to position its pre-sessional teaching slightly differently in order to attract sufficient numbers of staff. Some institutions may even offer their teachers subsidised housing as part of the overall package. This can be handy if you need to travel to a different location. The key learning point here is to shop around and compare all the different options on offer. This is where an effective spreadsheet comes into its own. If you are systematic in your planning and can target the right institutions, there is no reason why you should not be able to secure well-paid EAP teaching work for at least three months or more right through the summer. An added advantage here is that universities often then retain the best and brightest of their pre-sessional teachers for additional hourly paid teaching during the normal academic year on in-sessional programmes. The pre-sessional season can thus offer teachers a route into EAP as a profession and many of the now well-known people in EAP started their higher educational careers in this way. If you aspire to teach English in a university setting, once you have your Masters under your belt, working as a hired gun on pre-sessionals and later in-sessionals can be a very good way of getting your foot in the door. I will be returning to consider other aspects of careers in EAP under Section 10.3.3.

> **Check Your Understanding: Independent Task 10.2d**
>
> If you have never worked in EAP before, a typical interview question you might be asked would be to describe some of the differences between teaching General English and teaching EAP.
>
> What would your response be if you were asked such a question? Make a list of the ways in which EAP differs from General English in terms of Reading, Writing, Speaking and Listening.
>
> A suggested answer to this task has been provided on page 265.

10.3 Continuing Professional Development

Although the various aspects of going on to further study which I discussed under Section 10.1 would naturally and quite legitimately be counted as continuing professional development, I also wanted to include a separate section, which could examine the role of post-Masters' CPD in somewhat broader terms. Several of these areas are covered in my recommendations below.

10.3.1 Publishing Your Dissertation

If you have been able to write a good quality dissertation and your work has been awarded a high grade from the academics who have evaluated it, then you should definitely think about some of the opportunities in publishing. Do bear in mind here that this does not necessarily have to mean you publishing your entire dissertation; you might instead be able to focus on specific aspects of your work to help you write two or three separate papers. If you are planning to follow a teaching career in academia, then getting yourself into this publishing mindset as early as possible will certainly stand you in very good stead for the future.

When it comes to publishing your work, look at a range of journals and try to find the one which represents the best fit in terms of its theme, readership and impact factor. Some journals are harder to get into than others and you will need to be prepared to face the possibility of several rejections. However, as any research-active academic will tell you, you need to develop a thick skin about such things and you must persevere. You certainly should not give up easily.

When preparing to turn your dissertation into an academic journal publication, you will undoubtedly need to make several changes. For one thing, you will need to scale down the overall size. As I have discussed in this book, most Masters' dissertations fall into the 12–15k word count range, but as you will know already from your wider reading, most academic journal articles only tend to represent 5–8k words. This means that you will need to be selective with your material and re-write certain sections so that they become a better fit with journal requirements. This should not be all that difficult to do, as you already have a basis from which to work. Remember that in the bigger picture, the process of turning your dissertation into an academic article will also help you to become a better academic writer. A list of some of the main journals for TESOL/Applied Linguistics has been included for your reference on pages 267–268.

10.3.2 Presenting at Conferences

Closely linked with the suggestion of publishing your dissertation, or using some of its content to help you write other academic papers, is the idea that you should also try to present at academic conferences. This becomes especially important if you are intending to work in academia. Long before doing my own Masters, I was lucky in that I had worked with some colleagues who were already presenting and publishing their work and they had actively encouraged me to do the same. This meant that by the time I came to do my dissertation, going to international TESOL/Applied Linguistics events and presenting my work was already a normal and accepted part of my professional life. If you have never attended or presented at a conference before though, I can appreciate that it will probably seem very daunting. Many of my MA students over the years have told me that they do not consider themselves highly enough to participate in such events. However, as I have always advised them, you should try not to think like this. Everybody needs to start somewhere and if the work has been done well, then the findings from your own research are going to be just as valid and potentially as interesting for others as the work from internationally established 'big name' professors. I therefore advise all my Masters' students to be on the lookout for appropriate conferences and to push themselves to attend and submit papers. The professional organisations listed on page 269 each hold annual events and if you subscribe to some of their mailing lists, you will learn whenever their conferences and symposia are being publicised. As I will discuss in the following section, going to conferences and similar events represents an excellent opportunity for professional networking and learning more about the field. Attending a good conference and mingling with like-minded professionals can be an exceptionally invigorating experience which will give you new ideas and help you to feel part of a wider professional community. This holds true whichever sector of TESOL/Applied Linguistics you find yourself working in, i.e., you must not think that conferences are only for academics and those working at universities. International organisations such as IATEFL and TESOL have professional interest groups spanning almost every imaginable facet of the TESOL/Applied Linguistics profession and there are often sub-chapters which have been established in different countries too. As part of your continuing professional development, you should definitely aim to avail yourself of all such opportunities.

10.3.3 Finding Your Professional Niche

If you are serious about developing a career in TESOL or Applied Linguistics, then at some point, you will need to start thinking quite carefully about the direction in which you want your career to travel. If you are planning to work in the higher educational side of these disciplines, as I considered above under Section 10.2.4, then one decision you will probably need to make quite early on is whether you want your main emphasis to be on teaching or on research, as each of these tends to lead to slightly different career tracks.

Traditionally speaking, almost all university lecturers used to be engaged in research, as this was usually seen as a core expectation of their job. However, in more recent years, teaching-only contracts have started to become more common. If you know in advance that your professional interests are more aligned with the teaching side of things, then you may well find yourself employed under those explicit terms and conditions. Although there is still the broad expectation that they will engage in scholarly activity, staff recruited on such teaching-only contracts not surprisingly find themselves with quite high teaching hours. As a result, they are usually not formally required to engage in any research. This stands in very marked contrast to staff employed on R&T (Research and Teaching) contracts, whose annual performance will be evaluated not only on the quality of their teaching, but also on the volume and quality of their individual research outputs.

At this juncture, it is worth remembering that most full-time academic positions these days will require you to have a doctorate, irrespective of whether you are on a teaching-only or on a research and teaching contract. However, as I have already discussed above, it must also be said that many MA TESOL/Applied Linguistics graduates without a PhD do still end up working in universities as teachers of English for Academic Purposes (EAP). At the time of writing, it is still perfectly possible to find well-paid employment of this nature without having completed a doctorate, especially if you are prepared to work internationally. In my current location of China, for example, the opportunities in EAP are continuing to grow, as more and more Western universities choose to invest in educational partnerships with Chinese institutions. For many MA TESOL/Applied Linguistics graduates, the employment boom in these areas can represent very good career development opportunities and earning potential indeed, although there can also be some hidden downsides, as I have discussed elsewhere (e.g., see Bell, 2018, 2021, 2023) and as I will touch on briefly under Section 10.4.

Not all MA TESOL/Applied Linguistics graduates will choose to work in universities of course. As you probably identified in the mind-mapping exercise, after completing their Masters, some people may prefer to work in the primary, secondary or commercial educational sectors. This does not mean that they should not still be thinking about identifying their professional niche though. While the teaching vs. research dichotomy is unlikely to exist in the primary and secondary environment, the more typical binary in those contexts will be on teaching vs. administration, and once again, it is worth you thinking carefully about where your main passion and career development ambitions lie. For some, a qualification such as an MA TESOL/Applied Linguistics can undoubtedly represent a ticket to bigger and better things in terms of a career in administration and management. Over the years, some of my previous students have gone on to work in the primary or secondary sectors as school principals or members of senior management teams. As I have suggested throughout this section of the chapter though, rather than just drifting into such positions, it is worth thinking more strategically about which direction you would most like your career to develop towards. If you are particularly interested in developing your career as a manager or senior educational administrator, then do the necessary institutional homework and find out exactly what your options are and how you can best position yourself to take full advantage of them.

The final point I would like to make about finding your professional niche is to stress the importance of professional networking. Whichever employment sector you end up working in, learning to network effectively and building connections with others from your field is becoming ever more vital. Creating a public-facing profile for yourself using social media such as LinkedIn or similar professional networking platforms can often lead you to very good opportunities, as can becoming a member of international organisations such as AAAL (American Association for Applied Linguistics), BAAL (British Association for Applied Linguistics), TESOL (Teaching English to Speakers of Other Languages), AILA (International Association of Applied Linguistics), IATEFL (International Association of Teachers of English as a Foreign Language), EuroSLA (European Second Language Association) and BALEAP (British Association of Lecturers in English for Academic Purposes), or getting involved with fellowship schemes such as those offered by the HEA (Higher Education Academy) or RSA (Royal Society of Arts).

Further details on these organisations and a list of their websites has been included for your reference on page 269.

10.4 Closing Thoughts

In this closing chapter, I have tried to provide a broad overview of some of the different opportunities which will await you after completing an MA TESOL/Applied Linguistics. As I hope to have shown, both degrees can offer their holders a wide range of choices, whether this is in terms of going on to further study or in finding gainful employment. Successfully completing an MA TESOL/Applied Linguistics will undoubtedly open many doors for you which might otherwise have remained closed.

This is not to suggest, however, that the picture for MA graduates is uniformly rosy. As with all walks of life, there can also be some potential pitfalls along the way. In this final section of the book, I therefore feel it is worth me saying a little about what some of those pitfalls might be and how they can best be avoided.

I started this chapter by discussing the possibilities around returning to further study, so perhaps the first pitfall I should flag is the danger of starting a PhD or EdD, but then not successfully completing it. Many more people around the world pay for and enrol on doctoral programmes than those who actually go on to complete them. As I discussed under Section 10.1.1, if you are seriously thinking of going on to do a doctorate, then you need to be realistic about the considerable demands that this will make on you, not only in the academic sense, but also in terms of your finances, your time and your ongoing quality of life in general. Whichever way one chooses to look at it, doctoral study represents a significant investment and will involve some personal sacrifices to be made in each of the above, so the decision to enrol on a PhD or EdD should never be taken lightly. Over the years, I have had a small number of students who enthusiastically embarked on a doctorate only to find some time later that the demands of the journey were simply too challenging for them and/or couldn't realistically be reconciled with their personal financial situations or their bigger picture life plans. Such students typically then ended up dropping out, which, if I am brutally frank, meant that they had essentially wasted several years of their time, and also to some extent mine. Do try not to let yourself become one of these cases. Before you embark on a doctoral journey, be fully aware of what it will require of you and be absolutely honest with yourself about the realities of your situation. Sometimes enthusiasm and a personal or parental pipe dream are not enough – you also need to look very hard at your logistical realities, whether these be financial, temporal, geographical or familial, and make sure that there is an adequate match.

The next potential pitfall I would like to flag is rather more occluded, which in many ways makes it all the more invidious. Having now spent some three and a half decades of my life working as an international educator in English Language Teaching, I think I am in a good position to comment on both the positive aspects of ELT as a career choice and also its downsides. Looking back at the many teachers I have encountered over the years, particularly those based outside of their own country, one definite downside of TESOL can be the propensity it creates for people to drift. The international nature of TESOL makes it relatively easy to find jobs anywhere in the world, and of course for most people, this is usually one of the initial main attractions. After a decade or more in the field, most seasoned TESOL professionals will be able to show a range of international locations on their CV and this is generally presented as a positive. However, simultaneously, there can also be some hidden pitfalls here, which it is worth bearing in mind from the outset. One very common complaint is that becoming an expatriate and travelling from country to country as an itinerant TESOL professional can leave you feeling exceptionally out of touch with your own country and culture. Many people I have worked with over the years have found themselves in this position and some even get to the point when they feel that they no longer have a home. They might not be all that happy being based in the Middle East, South America or Asia, but then they also no longer feel any great connection with the UK, America, Australia or wherever they originally came from. This can be especially true for those who have married cross-culturally and have raised their families overseas. The sense of dislocation and loss of cultural identity in such cases can be acute. Many of these stories end happily, of course, and I am certainly not trying to dissuade anyone from becoming an expatriate or living their life in a country other than their own, but it is definitely worth keeping in mind that there is also a potentially darker side.

Closely related to the propensity for drift and a sense of cultural dislocation, another potential pitfall of choosing international TESOL as a career is that unless you are careful to plan ahead, it can leave you in a financially weaker position later. When they are working overseas, most TESOL professionals are not covered by pension plans. This makes it all the more important for them to plan ahead. For someone in their twenties or thirties, retirement might seem like a very long time off, but the reality is that the years soon flash by and if you have not been making financial provision for the future, it can be very easy indeed to find yourself left in a highly vulnerable position. Salaries which seemed attractive in one's twenties and thirties are much less likely to be attractive in their fifties and sixties, so it is extremely important to keep one eye on the financial future. The more savvy TESOL professionals I have worked with over the years have been well aware of this and have been careful to pay some of their earnings into private pension plans or make other kinds of longer-term investments. Some of the less financially savvy have found themselves at retirement age with an impressive list of international work locations on their CV but then little else to show for it and no financial means of returning to their country of origin. For me, the moral of the story here is to always think ahead and try to have a bigger picture plan. Nobody can account for everything down to the last detail – as John Lennon famously once said, 'Life is what happens when you're busy making other plans' – but in the case of international TESOL careers in particular, I would advise that it is especially important to keep your eye on this longer-term ball.

The final point I would like to make before I close this section and indeed finish this book is that learning and professional development should be seen as a lifelong process. This means that you will need to keep a close eye on your knowledge, skills and qualifications and always be prepared to upgrade them if you start to notice any gaps or weaknesses. This can be especially true if you are an MA TESOL/Applied Linguistics graduate working in the field of English for Academic Purposes (EAP). While there are still many well-paid international opportunities in teaching EAP for those only holding a Masters, it must also be said that the expectation that *all* academics in Higher Education should have a doctoral qualification is continuing to rise. The danger of working in Higher Education and *not* having the title 'Dr' is that you can very easily find yourself being discriminated against in terms of professional status, job conditions and potential career progression. I have discussed this at length elsewhere (e.g., see Bell, 2021, 2023) so I will not go into more detail here, but if you are an MA TESOL/Applied Linguistics graduate embarking on a career in teaching EAP, then my strong advice would be that you should definitely be planning at some point to invest in a doctorate. Although it may seem like an awful lot of work, doing so will only serve to cement your job stability, raise your professional status and open up your wider career options.

This essentially now brings us to the close of the extended MA TESOL/Applied Linguistics journey I have tried to outline in this book. I hope you have found what I have had to say useful and that in working through the different chapters and independent study materials you have learned some new knowledge and developed some new skills. It strikes me that if there has been one recurrent theme running throughout almost every chapter, then it is the importance of being adequately prepared. Whether you are writing an essay, preparing to teach a demo class, researching for your dissertation or looking at your future career development, remember that careful planning and preparation will always be the key.

I sincerely wish for your continued success.

Utrinque Paratus
(Motto of the British Army Parachute Regiment: Ready for Anything)

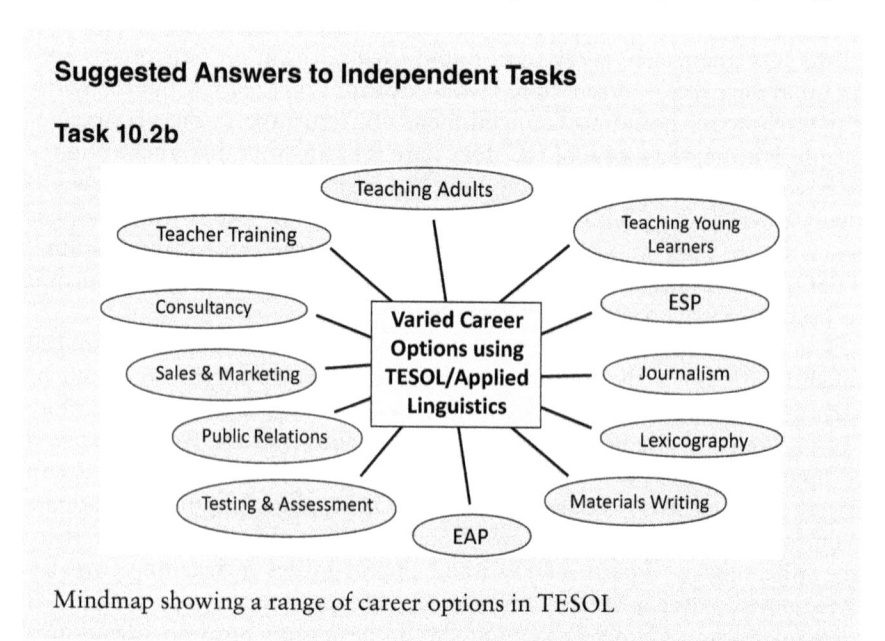

Suggested Answers to Independent Tasks

Task 10.2b

Varied Career Options using TESOL/Applied Linguistics:
- Teaching Adults
- Teaching Young Learners
- ESP
- Journalism
- Lexicography
- Materials Writing
- EAP
- Testing & Assessment
- Public Relations
- Sales & Marketing
- Consultancy
- Teacher Training

Mindmap showing a range of career options in TESOL

Task 10.2c

'Cold-calling' is arguably the least effective approach, unless you know that a certain person or organisation has a particular need, which you are confident you can fill, and more importantly, that you have made sure you are talking to the main decision maker(s). It is usually far more effective to do your initial groundwork by building relevant connections and connections. Attending business lunches and other events organised by local Chambers of Commerce or similar organisations can be a good way to make connections and meet relevant people. Offering to give talks and do training taster sessions can be another useful way of getting your name out there and building a reputation. It can take some time to become recognised and established as a freelance trainer or consultant, but once you are, then it usually becomes significantly easier to find additional business opportunities.

Task 10.2d

The way in which the four skills are encountered in EAP will be quite different to the usages and contexts traditionally found in General English:

Table 1 Table showing differences between General English and EAP

	General English	EAP
Reading	Novels, magazine articles, poetry; brochures and timetables; daily functional reading and also reading for pleasure	Journal articles; books; websites; historical references; emails; reading for specific academic contexts
Writing	Narratives, letters, email; text messages; daily functional writing	Essays; reports; dissertations; theses; emails; writing for specific academic contexts
Speaking	Introductions, sharing personal information, asking for directions; making bookings and reservations etc... daily functional speaking	Seminars and group discussions; oral presentations; meetings with supervisors; meetings with administrators; oral defences; speaking in specific academic contexts
Listening	Conversations; stories, TV or radio programmes; daily functional listening and listening for pleasure	Lectures; seminars; oral defences; listening in specific academic contexts

Additional Resources for Further Reading

Bell, D.E. (2023). *English for Academic Purposes: Perspectives on the Past, Present and Future.* Channel Publications.

Bolles, R.N. (2018). *What Color Is Your Parachute?: A Practical Manual for Job Hunters and Career Changers.* Ten Speed Press.

Downes, C. (2008). *Cambridge English for Job Hunting.* Cambridge University Press.

Jegede, F. (2021). *Doing a PhD in the Social Sciences: A Student's Guide to Post-Graduate Research and Writing.* Taylor & Francis.

Vick, J.M. & Furlong, J.S. (2008). *The Academic Job Search Handbook.* University of Pennsylvania Press.

Chapter References

Bell, D.E. (2018). The practice of EAP in Australia: A rose by any other name? In L.T. Wong & W.L.H. Wong (Eds.) *Teaching and Learning English for Academic Purposes. Current Research and Practices* (pp. 161–177). Nova Science Publishers Inc.

Bell, D.E. (2021). Accounting for the troubled status of English language teachers in Higher Education. *Teaching in Higher Education.* https://doi.org/10.1080/13562517.2021.1935848.

Ferguson, G. & Donno, S. (2003). One-month teacher training courses: time for a change? *ELT Journal, 57*(1), 26–33.

Stanley, P. & Murray, N. (2013). 'Qualified'? A framework for comparing ELT teacher preparation courses. *Australian Review of Applied Linguistics, 36*(1), 102–115.

A List of Common Journals for TESOL and Applied Linguistics

Ampersand | Journal | ScienceDirect.com by Elsevier

Annual Review of Applied Linguistics | Cambridge Core

Applied Linguistics | Oxford Academic (oup.com)

Assessing Writing | Journal | ScienceDirect.com by Elsevier

Assessment & Evaluation in Higher Education | Taylor & Francis Online (tandfonline.com)

Australian Review of Applied Linguistics (benjamins.com)

Home | English Language Teaching | CCSE (ccsenet.org)

ELT Journal | Oxford Academic (oup.com)

English for Specific Purposes | Journal | ScienceDirect.com by Elsevier

Folio | MATSDA Materials Development Association

Higher Education Quarterly – Wiley Online Library

International Journal of English for Academic Purposes: Research and Practice Home (liverpooluniversitypress.co.uk)

International Journal of English Language Teaching (IJELT) – EA Journals

JALT Journal | JALT Publications (jalt-publications.org)

Journal of Academic Language and Learning (aall.org.au)

Journal of Applied Linguistics (equinoxpub.com)

Journal of English for Academic Purposes | ScienceDirect.com by Elsevier

Journal of English Language Teaching and Applied Linguistics (JELTAL) (neliti.com)

Journal of Further and Higher Education | Taylor & Francis Online (tandfonline.com)

Journal of Pragmatics | ScienceDirect.com by Elsevier

Journal of Second Language Writing | ScienceDirect.com by Elsevier

Language Assessment Quarterly | Taylor & Francis Online (tandfonline.com)

Language and Education | Taylor & Francis Online (tandfonline.com)

Language Teaching | All issues | Cambridge Core

Language Teaching Research: SAGE Journals (sagepub.com)

Linguistics and Education | Journal | ScienceDirect.com by Elsevier

Home | MET (modernenglishteacher.com)

ReCALL | Cambridge Core

RELC Journal: SAGE Journals (sagepub.com)

Research Methods in Applied Linguistics | Journal | ScienceDirect.com by Elsevier

System | Journal | ScienceDirect.com by Elsevier

Teaching in Higher Education | Taylor & Francis Online (tandfonline.com)

TESL Canada Journal

TESL-EJ | http://www.tesl-ej.org

TESOL Quarterly – Wiley Online Library

The Language Teacher | JALT Publications (jalt-publications.org)

The Modern Language Journal – Wiley Online Library

A List of Useful Professional Organisations

AAAL
Home (aaal.org)

AALL
https://aall.org.au

AILA
Welcome – AILA

BAAL
British Association for Applied Linguistics – BAAL

BALEAP
https://www.baleap.org/

EuroSLA
EuroSLA – European Second Language Association

IATEFL
https://www.iatefl.org/

ILTA
International Language Testing Association (iltaonline.com)

JALT
About Us | NPO The Japan Association for Language Teaching (JALT)

JOBS AC UK
Jobs | Job Search | Job Vacancies on jobs.ac.uk

MATSDA
MATSDA Materials Development Association

MELTA
::: Malaysian English Language Teaching Association (MELTA) :::

TESOL
https://careers.tesol.org/
https://www.tesol.org/enhance-your-career/career-development/beginning-your-career/finding-a-job-in-tesol

Index

'3R formula' for assessing the validity of sources 50–51

academic: arguments 85; conventions 70; essays 93–103; etiquette 27; lexis 83; listening 40–47; literacy support 18; misconduct 51–52; reading 4; sources 48; speaking 27; style 70, 83; support 18; writing 79–92
accessing resources 48
alliteration (as a linguistic device) 106
APA referencing style 70
appeals to nature (as a linguistic device) 106
appropriacy of academic sources 5, 14–17, 50–51
aspect-by-aspect approach to writing a literature review 187–188
attendance policies 3–4
avoiding generalisations 81

bibliographies 67
Boolean keyword searches 16

CELTA (Cambridge Certificate in English Language Teaching) 249–251
cheating in exams 52
choosing academic sources 48–51
choosing a dissertation topic 140–151
citations 59–66
classroom contact hours 3
clear structuring in academic writing 79–81, 85, 88
coding qualitative data 197–198
coherent argumentation 85–90
collusion 53
'compare & contrast' type essays 93
conceptualisations of lessons 128–129
constructivism (as an ontological paradigm) 155–156, 193–194

continuing professional development 258–261, 267–269
contrastive approach to writing a literature review 187
core modules & elective modules 2
correlational research 193
counselling service 18
coursework assignments 13
the creative job search 255
credit ratings on masters programmes 3
critical evaluation of theories 120–122, 135
'critically evaluate' type essays 103
critical reflection 134–135
critical thinking skills 122
CV writing 251–253
cyclical nature of academic writing 14

DELTA (Diploma in English Language Teaching to Adults) 249–251
Deviant Spelling in Brand Names (as a linguistic device) 106
different 'ingredients' in lessons 130
direct quotations 59–65
discourse markers in lectures 40–41
'discussing a quotation' type essays 100
dissertations: acknowledgements & abstracts 229–233; acknowledging strengths & limitations 225–227; appendices 233–235; approaches to data coding 197–199; choosing a suitable topic 140–151; completing a formal proposal 158–159; conclusion chapter 223–229; discussion chapter 220–223; ethical considerations 199–200; finding your professional niche 260–261; formatting 235–239; importance of effective signposting 176–177; introduction chapter 177–183; literature review chapter

183–192; managing your time 151–153; methodology chapter 192–201; ontology & epistemology 155–156, 196; possible research paradigms 154–155, 156–158; presenting at conferences 259; professional networking 256, 261, 265, 269; proofreading 239–241; publishing your dissertation 258–259; recommendations for future action 227–229; reflexivity 196, 200; results/findings chapter 211–220; rhetorical purpose of different chapters 174–175; signposting 176–177; structure & overall length 172–173; summarising in the conclusion chapter 223–225; testing a topic for validity 144–151; what to expect from your supervisor 161–164
doctoral study: CoRS (Confirmation of Research Status) 248; EdD 248–249; PhD 246–249; supervisors 247
double-dipping with assignments 53
drafting & editing 14

EdDs 246–249
ellipsis (as a linguistic device) 106
e-mail dos & don'ts 28
epistemology 155
essay writing 93–103
essential reading *vs.* optional reading 5
expectations on a masters 1–4
extensions on coursework deadlines 19
extenuating circumstances policy (EC) 19

field (lexico-grammatical features of a text) 104
finding a job in TESOL: cover letters 254; the creative job search 254–256; systematic record keeping 254–255, 257; the traditional job search 254–256; updating your CV 251–253; working in the higher education sector 257–258
finding your professional niche 260–261
further study after your masters 245–251

genre (as an approach to text analysis) 105–106
going back to work after your masters 251–258
group work 29

Harvard referencing style 70–71
hedging 81–83
historical approach to writing a literature review 187–188
how to address academic staff 28

integral citations 59

jobs in TESOL and Applied Linguistics: the creative job search 255; the traditional job search 254

learner diaries 110–112
lectures 40–43
lesson planning 128
lesson plans 131
lexical boost (as a linguistic device) 106
linguistic analysis tasks 103–109
linguistic devices 106
literature reviews 183–192

marking criteria 112
mention of statistics (as a linguistic device) 106
metaphors for lessons 129
methodology chapter in dissertations 192
mind-mapping 8–12
mixed methods research 157
MLA referencing style 70–71
mode (form a given text takes) 105
Moodle and other VLEs 40
move structure in academic writing 108–109, 116
multi-tasking & setting milestones 12–13

non-integral citations 59
note taking 41–43

observation cycle: post observation 127; pre observation 126; while observing 127
observation tools & mechanisms 123–126
ontology 155
oral presentations 30–40; dealing with questions after 38, 39; delivery of 37–38, 39; eye contact in 38; key phrases for 33–34; opening strategies 34–35; 'owning' the content of

38–39; planning of 32; structure of 30–33; using PowerPoint slides in 34–36

paraphrasing 54–57
participation in seminar discussions 29–30
pastoral support 18–19
patchwriting 55
peer-based learning 29
peer micro-teaching 133–134
personal tutors 18
PhDs 246–249
phonetic word play (as a linguistic device) 106
pitfalls to avoid in a TESOL career 261–263
plagiarism 51–54
positivism (as an ontological paradigm) 155
post-positivism (as an ontological paradigm) 155–156
PowerPoint slides in oral presentations 34–36
practical implications of theories 120–122
pragmatism (as an ontological paradigm) 155
presenting at conferences 259
prioritising what to read 5–8, 32
professional endorsements (as a linguistic device) 106
professional journals 267–268
professional TESOL organisations 269
project management 12–17
promising to solve a problem (as a linguistic device) 106
proofreading 239–241
pseudo-science (as a linguistic device) 106
publishing your dissertation 258–259
puns (as a linguistic device) 106

qualifications other than a doctorate 249–251
qualitative research methodology: coding data 197–199; matching results with research questions 212–213, 218–219; nature of 193–194; presenting qualitative results 215–218; relative weighting of results for credibility 219; use of the simple past tense 217; using quotations from interviews 215–218
quantitative research methodology: ANOVA (Analysis of Variance) 241; Chi-square Test 242; Cohen's Kappa 242; Cronbach alpha coefficient 241; Factor Analysis 242; Likert scale Questionnaires 242; MANOVA (Multivariate Analysis of Variance) 242; Nature of 193; Normal Distribution 242; Null Hypothesis 242; Presenting Quantitative Results 213–214; t-Tests 241
quotations 59–65

reading lists 4–7
reading strategies 5–12
recommendations for future research in dissertations 227–229
reference lists 67–69
references to time (as a linguistic device) 106
referencing software 68–69
reflective writing 109–112
reflexivity 200, 206
reporting verbs for citations 57–58
research paradigms 150, 154–158
results chapter in dissertations 211–219
rhetorical purpose 174–175
rhyme (as a linguistic device) 106
running commentary for observations 123–125

self-plagiarism 53
self-study action plan 13
self-study hours 3–4
seminars 29
signposting language 175
skimming & scanning 6–8
staff-student relationship 27–29
statistical significance in quantitative research 193
step-by-step approaches to essay writing 94–99
strategies for effective reading 4–8
student welfare 18–19
supervisors- what to expect 160–164, 179–170
supporting claims 85
support services 18–19
synthesizing 65–66, 85–90

teaching observation 123
teaching practice 131
team teaching/teaching your own class 134
tenor (relationship in a text between writers & readers) 105
textual analysis 103–109
theory *vs.* practice relationship 120–122
time management 12–14
the traditional job search 254
Trinity College Diploma in English Language Teaching 249–250

understanding assignment requirements 94–95
university support services 18–19, 22–23
use of commands (as a linguistic device) 106
use of first-person pronoun 81
using electronic journals 15–17

working in higher education 257–258
working smart 14–18
writing a dissertation proposal 140–151, 158–159

Milton Keynes UK
Ingram Content Group UK Ltd.
UKHW020032141223
434334UK00016B/118